A Survival Guide to Social Media and Web 2.0 Optimization:

Strategies, Tactics, and Tools for Succeeding in the Social Web

D1635858

A Survival Guide to Social Media and Web 2.0 Optimization:

Strategies, Tactics, and Tools for Succeeding in the Social Web

by Deltina Hay

Wiggy Press

DALTON PUBLISHING

Wiggy Press, a nonfiction line from:

Dalton Publishing
P.O. Box 242
Austin, Texas 78767
www.daltonpublishing.com

Edited by Ric Williams

Assisted editing and research by Neil Kahn

Cover design and interior images by Jason Hranicky

Interior design and typesetting by Deltina Hay and Jessica Hillstrom

Resource CD forms by Tamar Design+Marketing

ISBN: 978-0-9817443-8-4

Library of Congress Cataloging-in-Publication Data

Hay, Deltina.   UNIVERSITY OF CHICHESTER

  A survival guide to social media and Web 2.0 optimization : strategies, tactics, and tools for succeeding in the social web / by Deltina Hay.

     p. cm.

  Includes index.

  ISBN 978-0-9817443-8-4

  1. Web 2.0. 2. Web site development. 3. Online social networks. I. Title.

  TK5105.88817.H39 2009

  006.7'54--dc22

                            2009012117

For my Mother,

without whose support all would have been lost...

Acknowledgments

Thanks

Thanks to Dalton Publishing's authors and fans for use of images, videos, screen shots, galleries, and widgets. Specifically, Ric Williams, W. Joe Hoppe, Lyman Grant, Les McGehee, Robert Stikmanz, Joe O'Connell, Owen Egerton, Kimberlie Dykeman, Michael Gilmore, Christine and Ethan Rose, Spike Gillespie, Katherine Tanney, and Gary Kent.

Special thanks to Les McGehee, Cynthia Baker, and Kimberlie Dykeman for volunteering their social media strategies as examples, and to Robert Stikmanz for use of Nod's Way as the basis for the "Oracle of the Day" widget. Thanks to Jessica Hillstrom and Tamar Wallace for their contributions, and a special thanks to Jason Hranicky for his hard work and patience.

Thank you to the following companies for use of their social media newsrooms and news releases as examples:

© Fathom SEO 2009. All Rights Reserved. Screen shots used by permission.
© SHIFT Communications, LLC 2009. All rights reserved. Screen shots used by permission.
© Accolades Public Relations 2009. All rights reserved. Screen shots used by permission.
© Les McGehee 2009. All rights reserved. Screen shots used by permission.
© Kimberlie Dykeman 2009. Pure Soapbox is a registered trademark of Kimberlie Dykeman. Screen shots used by permission.
© Owen Egerton 2009. All rights reserved. Screen shots used by permission.

A very special thanks to Neil Kahn for her relentless pursuit of permissions, tireless research, excellent proofreading, and willingness to hold it all together when I needed to write.

And even though he now knows more about RSS feeds than he ever cared to, this is a better book thanks to my editor Ric Williams' dogged persistence to keep my writing understandable and in the present tense. I also thank him for his friendship and steadfast encouragement, despite my occasional whining.

Permissions Granted

The author would like to thank the following companies for permission to use their screen shots. The following are trademark holders of the listed services' logos, graphics, designs, page header, button icons, scripts, and other services. All rights are reserved and used by permission:

Trademark Notice

Notice of Liability

Table of Contents

Introduction

About This Book

It is no secret that the future of the Internet is the Social Web, and that the future is very much this very instant. Millions[1] of people and businesses are interacting and collaborating on social networking sites, media communities, social bookmarking sites, wikis, and micro-blogging sites, as well as sharing information via millions of RSS feeds and blogs. They are doing it right now, 24/7, and you and your business want to be a part of this extraordinarily powerful movement with as professional and efficient a presence as possible while optimizing your business potential and keeping your expenses to a minimum.

Success in today's Internet absolutely depends on your entire Web presence, not just on search engine optimization (SEO). Spreading your net as wide as possible by improving your presence in the Social Web helps you reach millions of potential clients or readers that you may not have reached otherwise. You cannot afford to bet that a customer will somehow stumble upon your Website on page 100 in a Google search. Learn and implement the Social Web tools described in this book and you will be surprised at how easy you can access millions of customers otherwise unavailable. And, yes, a residual benefit of using these tools is improved placement on that proverbial Google search.

So, what is this social media and Web 2.0 optimization that helps you maximize this Internet presence? It can be summed up with three general terms: interactivity, sharing, and collaboration. Focusing on these three general areas, both at the level of your own Website and in the areas of the Social Web most suited to your book or business—areas we will help you identify—will greatly enhance your chances for success in this open-ended world of Internet opportunity.

Happily, building a strong presence in the Social Web does not have to break the bank or your back. With careful planning and preparation, you

---

[1] http://tinyurl.com/6o4q5a, from web-strategist.com

can build an impressive presence that you can maintain with little effort. The trick is to know what makes sense for your particular business or product, and only incorporate the tools that fit those goals. By planning ahead, you can also implement tools that will enhance each other and ultimately work together to help improve your presence and reduce your workload.

Research has shown that users of the Social Web actually want and encourage businesses and professionals to interact with them on their turf.[2] Of course you have to keep in mind that succeeding in the Social Web requires an authentic message. If you are going out there as a business or are promoting a product, just be up-front about it. Always read a site's submission guidelines and/or terms of use before proceeding. Some sites have no problem with having their service used to promote business, others have strict policies against it. There is a place for everyone in this new Internet arena if you simply present yourself straight up.

There are many books out there that discuss the theory of the Social Web and how to market within it. This is not one of them. This is also not a book about blogging, nor is it a book about how to get a zillion friends on your favorite social networking site. Blogging and social networking are only a small part of an optimized Social Web presence.

As a social media pioneer, the author has seen many tools come and go over the past few years. Her goal is to help you build a solid foundation in the Social Web using the tools of Web 2.0 that have weathered the social media storm. Once that foundation is in place, you will be equipped to integrate or utilize whatever new tools emerge next on the social media horizon.

This book wants to show you *how* to use strategies and tactics and the tools of Web 2.0 to build a successful Web presence. This book offers you the nuts and bolts of the Social Web through hands-on, real-world examples. You will be pleasantly surprised at how easy most of it is!

So push up your sleeves and let's get Social...

---

[2]http://www.readwriteweb.com/archives/majority_of_social_media_users_want_businesses_attention.php

A Brief Primer Before You Continue

In this section we discuss a few concepts and terms that you should have a general idea about before you delve into the body of the book. Though most of these items are defined in their respective sections, they are concepts that are used throughout the entire book.

RSS Feeds

RSS stands for Really Simple Syndication. An RSS feed is a file containing information that allows you to syndicate (share) that information across the Internet. Think of a feed as a subscription to individual packets of information. Imagine that instead of getting your local paper delivered to your door each day, every story within the paper was delivered to your desktop. This is what happens when you subscribe to a news site's RSS feed.

Widgets and Badges

Widgets are snippets of HTML, JavaScript, or Flash code, usually displayed graphically, that can be used to syndicate content, for example RSS feeds, or to add interactive features that users can drop onto their own blogs or Websites. Widgets are often customizable by the user and typically offer ways for users to pull information from the widget's originating site.

Many widgets are no more than glorified links rendered by graphics, while others are mini applications that pull their functionality from other sites that visitors can use right on your Website. Some examples that you have probably already encountered are Google ads and Amazon products that are featured on Websites or blogs, that when you click on them, take you to the respective site or product.

Content Management System (CMS)

By definition, a CMS is an application that is used to create, edit, manage, and publish content in an organized way. Web applications like WordPress, Joomla!, and Drupal do this by storing information in a database, and using scripting languages like PHP to access the information and place it on a Website.

CMSs are the perfect way to create a Website that is social media and Web 2.0 optimized because they have built-in RSS feed and widget technology.

WordPress

Though WordPress began as a blogging platform, it has evolved into a very user-friendly CMS. We demonstrate the use of WordPress to power a Website throughout the book.

Placing Code

Much of the Social Web is about sharing information. Many times this means pulling information from outside sources onto your own Website or blog. This is typically accomplished by copying some kind of programming or scripting code like HTML, Javascript, or Flash from another site and "placing" (or copying) it on your own site.

We first discuss placing code when we show you how to pull other's RSS feeds onto your site in Chapter 3. Throughout the rest of the book, the concept is discussed as we show you how to promote your presence in the Social Web, and especially when we discuss widgets and badges.

If you are using a CMS to power your site, placing code is a function that is built into the CMS infrastructure, so the process is relatively painless.

If you are placing the code on a traditional Website, however, only you will know where and how to place the code within your own HTML. Regardless of how you created your Website, whether with Dreamweaver, Site Builder, or just within a text file, your end result (as long as you did not use a scripting language to build it) will consist of a series of HTML files. The code you copy from the widget source is placed directly inside your HTML code using whatever method you typically use to edit your HTML code.

If you have a developer who maintains your Website, it is probably best for you to copy the code yourself, send them the code, and tell them where you want the widget or other application to appear on your site.

Search Engine Optimization (SEO) Jargon

Metadata

As we mention in the "Interchangeable Terms" section on Page 21, key terms, tags, and keywords are used interchangeably throughout the book. Keywords or key terms are the terms that help search engine robots properly categorize your Website in the search engines. Think of them as the words or terms someone would enter in a Google search to find your site. In social applications and tools, "tags" are the equivalent of key terms.

It is also important that you know what we mean by "Meta Keywords" and "Metadata" in general. Generically, the term "metadata" means information about information. Metadata, as it is used in Websites then, is information about the information contained on a Website. This information helps search engine robots better categorize a Website. A Website's page rank in a search engine like Google is greatly affected by how well the site's metadata actually matches the information contained in the body of the Website.

The metadata of a Website is defined in the header of the Website's HTML. There are three main sections of metadata: Title, Description, and Keywords. The title should only be around 75 characters, while the description will be more like 160 characters. The meta keywords are separated by commas, and should not exceed 20 terms, though most search engines only look at the first 10. It is important to repeat a Websites keywords within its meta title and meta description as well.

IMPORTANT: Using consistent key terms throughout your entire traditional and Social Web presence is *essential* to your overall success, not only in the Social Web, but in how you and your Website are ranked in traditional search engines!

Landing Pages

A landing page is the page on a Website that a specific link returns to. So, if you place an ad or post a blog comment somewhere on the Internet and include a link within that information, the landing page for that link is where it sends the user to your site when they click on the link. It is common practice to create specific landing pages for tracking ads and other campaigns since page traffic is easily measured.

Who Should Read This Book

This is a book for the do-it-yourselfer: the resourceful business owner, the motivated author, the innovative publisher, the head of your company's IT or marketing department, as well as the student of marketing, media, PR, Web development, or Internet studies.

Anyone who wants to succeed in today's Internet can benefit from reading this book, even if you have already started building a Social Web presence.

This book is highly recommended for college or university courses covering the subjects of Social Media, Web 2.0, New Media, or Internet Marketing, and for those wishing to break into the field of social media.

How To Use This Book

If you want the full benefit of this book, start at the beginning. Read the "Creating Your Social Media Strategy" chapter and complete the worksheet for your own strategy. This will save you time overall, since planning your strategy will bring to light which social media tools will work best for your own business or product.

Then, straight on to the "Preparation" chapter. Following the guidelines in this chapter will save you much time in implementing your plan. Pretty much every chapter in the book will refer back to this chapter.

From here, you can use your strategy as a guide to the chapters on tools that will benefit your presence the most.

Conclude with the "Pulling It All Together" and "Measuring Your Success" chapters. The former will help you integrate many of the tools you choose to implement, and the latter will show you ways to see what part of your strategy is working best for you. The "Looking to the Future" chapter will help you look at what tools you should consider for your long-term social media plans.

Chapter Autonomy

This book is written so that each chapter can be a stand-alone guide to its topic. You can skip around all you wish, but it is recommended that you read the chapters "Creating Your Social Media Strategy" and "Preparation" first.

Resource CD

The resource CD contains linkable resources and suggestions for further reading organized by chapter. The CD also contains fillable forms and worksheets to be used in your entire Social Media Strategy. You will notice references to the sheets and forms throughout the book. Each chapter concludes with a section that outlines what can be found on the CD for that chapter.

Replacement CDs can be purchased from the publisher.

Appendices

There are four appendices, three of which ("Installing WordPress," "Building Your Own RSS Feed," and "Creating Your Own Widgets") were pulled from the regular flow of the book because of their complexity. They are all straightforward guides to their topics, but may be a bit advanced for most readers. The final appendix, "WordPress 2.7" was added to reflect last minute changes to this platform.

Conventions

Footnotes: Traditional footnote references are used for standard footnotes, and bracketed footnotes are used for references to URLs.

Navigation: Navigation on a site or within an application is depicted as "First Level Menu Item/Second Level Menu Item/Third Level Menu Item" and so forth.

Interchangeable Terms

Key Terms: The terms "Key Term," "Keyword," and "Tag" are used interchangeably throughout the text.

Widgets: The terms "Widget," "Badge," and "Gadget" are used interchangeably throughout the text.

WordPress: The terms "WordPress admin panel," "WordPress backend," and "WordPress dashboard" are used interchangeably throughout the text.

Online Support

The author has a companion social network and forum at Ning.com.[3] Please visit this site if you have any questions about the book or want to connect with other readers. The author also posts updated information about the book's content to this network.

Platforms Discussed In the Book

We discuss many different software and online platforms throughout this book. It is important for you to note that these platforms are constantly changing. However, we have tried to give you a general idea of the capabilities of each one, so that even if the look and feel of a platform changes, you will still have an understanding of its functionality.

Even though we may demonstrate only one platform for a given topic, please be aware that there are many other choices available. For instance, we discuss WordPress a lot as a blogging platform and content management system, but you could just as easily use Blogger, Typepad, Joomla!, or Drupal. Our demonstration methods are not meant to be preferential; they are meant to offer the reader the best overall approach to a successful experience in the Social Web.

---

[3] http://socialmediasurvivalguide.ning.com

1 Creating Your Social Media Strategy

There are three general areas to keep in mind when planning a strategy for optimizing your presence in the Social Web: interactivity, sharing, and collaboration. Interactivity can come in the form of writing blog posts, commenting on others' posts, or participating in social networking communities. Sharing can be as easy as uploading images and video clips onto media communities. Collaboration can be achieved by contributing to social bookmarking sites or wikis.

It is important to understand the difference between optimizing your presence in the Social Web versus optimizing your Website *for* the Social Web. Optimizing your presence in the Social Web does not necessitate having a Website. Many of the tools you want to use are hosted on other social Websites or platforms like social networking, social bookmarking, or crowd-sourcing sites. If you do have a Website in place, however, you want to include optimizing it for the Social Web in your strategy as well.

It is easy to get overwhelmed with all of the new social media and Web 2.0 tools and technologies that pop up on the Internet on an almost daily basis. But a carefully planned and executed strategy can alleviate your stress and ensure your successful transition into the new Social Web.

Important First Decisions Regarding Websites, Blogs, And RSS Feeds

The one bit of technology essential to your Social Web success is an RSS feed, discussed in more detail in Chapter 3, "RSS Feeds & Blogs," but, in short, you have two choices:

- Start a blog which has built-in RSS feed technology, or
- Create your own RSS feed using an XML file.

Creating a blog is by far the easiest solution to this, and you do not need to become a "blogger" to take advantage of the technology.

If you choose to create a blog to accommodate your RSS feed, you then need to decide whether you will create the blog external from your site (on WordPress.com, Blogger.com, or Typepad.com, for example) or host it on your own site.

Finally, if you choose to host the blog yourself, does it make sense to completely replace your existing Website (or build a new one) using WordPress as a Content Management System (CMS), or another CMS like Joomla! or Drupal? This latter choice is an optimal solution, since using a CMS as a platform for your Website means that you get a built-in RSS feed and the ability to integrate widgets and other Web 2.0 and social media tools with little effort (see Chapter 4, "Building a WordPress Powered Website").

If you are not in a position to rebuild your existing Website, or start a new one using WordPress, the recommended solution is to create a blog in a directory on your own server or hosting account. Free hosting services like WordPress.com, Blogger.com, and Typepad.com tend to restrict many plugins and other advantageous features you may want to implement. Many hosting sites offer one-click installations of WordPress toward this end (see Page 103).

Another option is to use one of the new services popping up on the Internet like Plumb Social.[1] These services help streamline your entire Social Web presence.

---

[1] http://www.plumbsocial.com

Here is a list of possible scenarios based on the options above:

- Keep your existing Website in place, and:
  › Create your own RSS feed
  › Create a blog external to your site
  › Host a blog in a directory on your site
  › Use a service like Plumb Social
- Rebuild your Website or create a new one using WordPress as a CMS, or another CMS

Mapping Your Strategy

The next step in a successful strategy is to decide which tools make sense for you or your business to implement. Just because a tool exists, doesn't mean it is right for your needs. Choose tools that best fit your *current content*, not content you *plan* to create later. This is key to creating a *manageable* strategy out of the gate—you can add to it later if you choose.

Here are some general areas to consider:

Social Networking (Facebook, MySpace, LinkedIn, etc.)

It is a good idea to have a healthy profile on one if not two of these social networking sites.

Micro Blogging (Twitter, Jaiku, etc.)

These sites have become as popular as blogging. we recommend a healthy presence in at least one of them.

Other Social Platforms (Tumblr, Squidoo, etc.)

If you have a lot of content, these platforms are a good addition to your strategic tool kit.

Social Bookmarking and Crowd-Sourcing (StumbleUpon, Digg, etc.)

Building a presence in several of these sites and contributing regularly is highly recommended for any strategy.

Blog Commenting

Becoming part of the conversation is a very important part in any social media strategy. As you are surfing the Web and/or searching for sites and blogs to share on social networking and crowd-sourcing sites, take the time to comment on others' blog entries.

Media Communities (Flickr, YouTube, etc.)

Sharing your multimedia content is an important part of any strategy, even if you only have a few images.

Social Calendars

Consider these if you host or attend a lot of events.

Podcasting

Podcasts are not difficult to create. They can be particularly effective if you have plenty of instructional material or you conduct interviews.

Vidcasting or Webcasting

These can be powerful viral tools for people or companies who have the resources to create and maintain them.

Widgets and Badges

Placing widgets and badges from other social sites on your Website or blog can help make your site more interactive.

Virtual Worlds

This is one technology that should be given considerable forethought. The learning curve is steep and consultants are expensive. However, for the right product, it could serve as a powerful marketing tool.

Social Media Newsrooms

This tool is ideal for authors, publishers, or other companies who garner a good amount of media coverage or produce regular news releases.

Custom Widgets or Applications

These are your own custom-built widgets or applications that can virally carry your brand into the Social Web.

Hosting your own Blogs, Social Network, Wiki, etc.

These tools are best suited for companies with a large customer base or who have many active advocates for their brand or service.

Sample Strategies

The following are social media strategies based on actual case studies. You can use the strategy worksheet on the resource CD to create your own. There is a lot of redundancy in these plans, so if you are looking for a strategy for a specific type of business, focus on the one that makes the most sense for you.

The five strategies are:

- Service Business/Consultant
- Author/Media Personality
- Entrepreneur/Performer
- Publisher/Product Business
- Public Relations Firm

Strategy One: Service Business/Consultant

Case Study: Social Media Power (SMP)[2]

Strategic Needs and Goals:

Social Media Power is a Web 2.0 development firm that specializes in providing quality resources for businesses, authors, and publishers.

The need for a good social media strategy for SMP is obvious. They need to utilize the applicable tools they readily recommend to clients and build a solid presence in the Social Web ahead of their competitors.

Since SMP is a service-oriented business, the goal of its social media strategy is to establish the company as a leading authority in their area of expertise: the application of social media and Web 2.0 tools and technologies. Since their business actually specializes in social media, their strategy tends to include a wide range of tools as examples.

---

[2] http://www.socialmediapower.com

Tactics:

Optimizing SMP's Website and RSS Feeds

SMP uses WordPress as a CMS (see Chapter 4, "Building a WordPress Powered Website"). Their site is entirely powered by WordPress, so their RSS feed is their blog. Their feed is submitted on FeedBurner and they can take advantage of FeedBurner's options such as offering their feed as an email newsletter to their readers (see Page 51). They use a customized WordPress theme that gives them flexibility in design and functionality, as well as the ability to easily drop in widgets and badges from other social sites. They also make it easy for visitors to share their site with others, and to comment on the content.

Blogging

Many of SMP's blog posts are instructional in nature so they tend to be quite long. They offset this by offering their "Social Media Tips of the Day," which also keeps the blog dynamic and lessens the workload for the contributors. SMP also generates reviews and top-ten lists, which can be quite popular if the content is well researched.

Social Networking

SMP maintains a MySpace page, a Facebook profile, and a Facebook page. It also has profiles in LinkedIn, Plaxo, and a few other professional networking sites. SMP is also a member of several niche groups within these communities.

Micro Blogging

SMP maintains an account with Twitter (see Page 162).

Other Social Platforms

SMP creates a "Lens" on Squidoo (see Chapter 11, "More Social Tools") for each major post or article they write.

Social Bookmarking, Crowd-Sourcing, and Blog Commenting

SMP has an account and contributes regularly to approximately 12 social bookmaking and crowd-sourcing sites. They try to bookmark 10 to 20 sites or blog posts per week, in addition to their own. SMP is also a member of several niche groups within some of these sites. As they are bookmarking sites and blog entries, SMP also stops to comment on blog entries they find interesting.

Media Communities

Since most of SMP's content is written, media communities are not tools they currently utilize to their full potential. They will work this into their strategy when they start producing podcasts and vidcasts, and/or photos from events or presentations.

Widgets and Badges

The widgets and badges that SMP places on their site vary from time to time. They include feed widgets, and widgets and badges that link directly to their other Social Web presences, so that others can connect to them on the respective sites.

Social Media Newsrooms

SMP uses a custom page in WordPress to create a social media newsroom (see Page 260) that integrates seamlessly with their site. Their newsroom also includes a section for published articles by the SMP team members. SMP uses the newsroom to announce new books, themes, and other products, in addition to general media coverage and news releases.

Custom Widgets or Applications

SMP has a Facebook application that is built using Widgetbox (see Page 235). They also create their own free WordPress themes that help get their name into the Social Web.

Hosting your own Blogs, Social Network, Wiki, etc.

SMP offers a service called "Plumb Social"[3] to its clients. They literally host and maintain their clients' blogs and integrate them with the clients' other social media tools.

---

[3] http://www.plumbsocial.com

Testimonial:

Social media is our business, so it is important that we stay abreast of new developments and tools. However, we are not too quick to implement every new tool that comes along—we prefer to test drive potential services before we add them to our official toolbox. We have also made our share of mistakes, and learned from them. This experience is what we hope will benefit our clients.

—The Social Media Power Team

Strategy Two: Author/Media Personality

Case Study: Kimberlie Dykeman/Pure Soapbox[4]

Strategic Needs and Goals:

Kimberlie Dykeman (KD) is an author, media personality, and motivational speaker. Her SOAPBOX® brand is a perfect fit for the Social Web, and the Web offers a great opportunity to market her book *Pure Soapbox...a cleansing jolt of perspective, motivation, and humor.*

KD's vignettes are perfect blog snippets, and she also produces video for a number of PR firms. As a visionary, KD foresees the need for getting these multimedia products out into the Social Web.

The goal of KD's strategy is not only to promote her brand and her book, but also to position herself as a tech-savvy multimedia personality.

Tactics:

Optimizing KD's Websites and RSS Feeds

Since KD's goal is to market her SOAPBOX® brand independent of herself, she made the decision to maintain a traditional Website (KimberlieDykeman.com), a WordPress powered site (PureSoapbox. com), and an external blog.[5]

Her traditional Website promotes her as a media personality, which is also what her external blog accomplishes. Her WordPress powered

---

[4] www.kimberliedykeman.com, http://www.puresoapbox.com,
[5] http://kimberliedykeman.com/blog

site, however, directly promotes her brand and her book, complete with a separate blog. KD does a fantastic job of integrating these sites and blogs, too. She feeds both her blogs into each other, and cross-promotes all of her sites with ease.

On PureSoapbox.com, KD also does a good job of making it easy for others to share or comment on her content. She also displays badges and widgets from other social sites where she has a presence such as Facebook and LinkedIn.

Blogging

KD blogs about her appearances and accomplishments on her external blog, while limiting her PureSoapbox.com entries to her SOAPBOX® brand vignettes. KD submits to sites that solicit guest bloggers. She spotlights one of her vignettes in each submission.

Social Networking

KD has a healthy presence in a number of social networking communities, including Facebook and MySpace. She also maintains a Facebook page for Pure Soapbox.

Micro Blogging

KD uses the LinkedIn, Plaxo, and Facebook notes venues for micro-blogging and networking.

Other Social Platforms

KD's SOAPBOX® blogs and on-camera updates also plug into Blogger, Gindie, and Naymz sites. A Squidoo Lens is in KD's immediate plan.

Media Communities

KD has accounts with Flickr and YouTube, and imports both to her sites via widgets and badges.

Social Calendars

KD uses Upcoming [6] to input her events, and offers a feed to them via a widget on her WordPress site.

---

[6] http://www.upcoming.org

Podcasting

KD plans to produce and distribute podcasts and vidcasts of her vignettes.

Vidcasting or Webcasting

KD is the executive producer and host of Shelflife.tv, an online interview series presented by Phenix and Phenix Literary Publicists. KD is also a producer and host for Web2Point0.tv, a developing online network featuring industry-specific interviews of thought-leaders. Also on this network she plans to produce and host a channel called "Kimberlie Dykeman's SOAPBOX® Spotlight," with a brand-specific interview series featuring interviews with industry leaders and visionaries.

Widgets and Badges

KD displays widgets from her social networking profiles and imports images from her media communities and social calendars using widgets and badges—especially on her social media newsroom.

Social Media Newsrooms

Since KD has quite a bit of media coverage, she has a social media newsroom[7] that is maintained as a courtesy of her publisher, Dalton Publishing.

Custom Widgets or Applications

KD maintains a "blidget" from Widgetbox that also serves as a Facebook and Bebo application.

Testimonial:

My SOAPBOX® brand is a multifaceted deliverable with multi-platform capabilities. Embracing the capabilities of Web 2.0 through social media and marketing initiatives was a challenge but it was the best first-step to take to garner unspecified attention to the upcoming book.

Now that I am published, the sites, blogs, etc. all work in tandem with traditional PR for the book, which I have initiated through Phenix & Phenix Literary Publicists. Top that with the viral, growing reach of the

---

[7] http://www.puresoapboxnewsroom.com

other online channels and networks, and the names Kimberlie Dykeman, Pure Soapbox, and SOAPBOX® are in line to garner greater visibility, credibility boosts, and broader revenue opportunities. These efforts are proving their value daily across the board!

—*Kimberlie Dykeman*

Strategy Three: Entrepreneur/Performer

Case Study: Les McGehee[8]

Strategic Needs and Goals:

Les McGehee (LM) is known for his award-winning interactive comedy shows and memorable training and speaking events—his clients come from all industries. He also has a successful book on improvisation entitled *Les McGehee Plays Well With Others.*

LM has one of those professions that is just too difficult to explain in an elevator speech. As a result, he immediately saw the need to get his message out by utilizing the tools of the Social Web.

In addition to promoting his speaking and comedy events, LM's strategic goals are to get the word out about his books and upcoming events. One form of media that does this well for him is video.

LM also has two ComedySportz franchises, one in Austin and one in San Antonio. He chose to use Plumb Social to service all of his social media needs for those franchises.[9]

Tactics:

Optimizing LM's Website and RSS Feeds

LM uses WordPress as a CMS. His site is powered by WordPress, hence his blog serves as his RSS feed. LM uses a customized WordPress theme that gives him flexibility in design and functionality, as well as the ability to drop in widgets and badges from other social sites easily.

---

[8] http://www.lesmcgehee.com
[9] http://csz.plumbsocial.com/

Blogging

LM does not have the time to post blog entries as often as he would like, so he has found an alternative to keeping his site's content dynamic: He populates his home page with the newsletter that he sends out to his mailing list periodically. Though this is not an optimal solution, it at least keeps his site from sitting stagnant for too long at a time. When he does post entries, however, they are rich in content, and have a lot of staying power, since he blogs about interesting topics to his niche market of improvisation.

Social Networking

LM has a healthy presence in a number of social networking communities, including Facebook and MySpace. He also has profiles in LinkedIn and several improv community social networks.

Other Social Platforms

A Squidoo Lens on improvisation is in LM's future plans.

Media Communities (Flickr, YouTube, etc.)

LM has accounts with Flickr and YouTube, and imports images and video onto his site using widgets and badges. He also uses Splashcast, and there are downloadable flash clips on the site, too.

Social Calendars

LM uses Upcoming to input his events, and offers a feed to them via a widget on his site.

Vidcasting or Webcasting

LM maintains a Webcast on Splashcast[10] as video is the most effective method for him to get his message out.

Widgets and Badges

LM imports images from his media communities and social calendars, and streams video from his Webcast using widgets and badges.

---

[10] http://www.splashcast.net

Social Media Newsrooms

Since LM has a fair amount of media coverage, he also maintains a social media newsroom.[11]

Testimonial:

I have found that having a site that is social media savvy is extremely valuable to my operations. I newsletter; people visit the site; they link elsewhere or explore my media.

Also, the social media newsroom is a must. For my bookings and promotional needs it is very helpful. Clients find what they need and I spend less time trying to help them.

I make my living as a comedian, author, speaker, actor, educator, trainer, producer, and musician. It is tough to describe what I offer because clients enjoy using my skills in so many different ways. Because of that, I find that the media and interactivity of my site really help people to "get it."

—*Les McGehee*

Strategy Four: Publisher/Product Business

Case Study: Dalton Publishing[12]

Strategic Needs and Goals:

Dalton Publishing (DP) is an independent press located in Austin, Texas. Their titles range from fiction to poetry to non-fiction.

DP saw the need for a strong presence in the Social Web for both them and their authors as soon as they heard of blogging. Blogging is a natural fit for writers, and the Social Web is also an ideal way to get the word out about books.

DP's primary goal is to sell books. However, the end to that goal can involve many different tactics. Hence the goal of their social media strategy is to get the word out about their authors and their books, with the intention of generating sales. DP is also the prototype for Plumb Social.[13]

---

[11] http://www.lesmcgehee.com/newsroom
[12] http://www.daltonpublishing.com
[13] http://testsite.plumbsocial.com

Tactics:

Optimizing DP's Website and RSS Feeds

DP's WordPress powered site uses a highly customizable theme from iThemes.[14] They wanted the convenience of using WordPress as a CMS, but did not want the actual blog to be the focus of the site. The site is organized like a traditional site, complete with bookstore and individual media pages for each book, but since it is powered by WordPress, it is very easy for them to integrate "social" badges and widgets throughout the entire site, especially in the sidebars and the footer.

Each title's media page offers print-ready images and media materials, a multimedia section, purchase information, and links to the author's social media newsroom and various social networking sites.

There are a number of features DP plans to implement soon, including a page that feeds all of their authors' blogs onto one page of the site, and a social media resource section.

DP feeds its blog posts as RSS feeds into its social networking profiles and its Plumb Social account as well.

Blogging

Most of DP's posts tend to be announcements about author accomplishments or events. Their presence in the Social Web is mostly attained outside of their Website or blog.

Social Networking

DP maintains a healthy presence in both MySpace and Facebook. They utilize these outlets to send announcements about events and author kudos. They also maintain a presence in literary social networks like GoodReads and LibraryThing.

Social Bookmarking and Crowd-Sourcing

DP has an account and contributes regularly to several social bookmaking and crowd-sourcing sites.

---

[14] http://www.ithemes.com/

Media Communities

DP uploads all of its event photos, author photos, book covers, etc. to Flickr. They are careful to name their files descriptively and give good descriptions and use consistent, searchable tags. Though they do not post their own video clips on YouTube, they do add their authors' videos to their playlist and create galleries by importing the clips onto their Plumb Social site.

Widgets and Badges

DP uses widgets and badges on their site to highlight their presence in the Social Web and to show off their Flickr photos.

Social Media Newsrooms

DP creates and maintains social media newsrooms for each of its authors who tend to acquire a good amount of media coverage.

Custom Widgets or Applications

DP has a custom, viral widget for one of its products: an ancient oracle called *Nod's Way*.

Hosting your own Blogs, Social Network, Wiki, etc.

DP maintains a social network called the Dalton Gangway for its authors and their fans at Ning.com.[15] The network is meant for authors to share their marketing successes as well as a place where readers can learn more about their favorite DP authors.

Testimonial:

Social media benefits our book publishing business in many ways. Each of our authors gets added exposure to potential readers through their blogs and social media newsrooms, and the company has a powerful venue from which to attract readers and create buzz through social networking and blogging sites. We have a tremendous amount of multimedia that can get a lot of mileage on the Social Web and we take full advantage of that opportunity. Our marketing and PR efforts are almost exclusively targeted toward the Internet as a direct result of social media.

—*The Dalton Publishing Team*

[15] http://daltonpublishing.ning.com/

Strategy Five: Public Relations Firm

Case Study: Accolades Public Relations[16]

Strategic Needs and Goals:

Accolades Public Relations (APR) is a results-oriented communications firm committed to progressive strategies in public relations and marketing.

APR prides itself in being a PR firm with vision. Its principals saw the future of PR spreading to the Internet and the Social Web, and also saw the need to be an integral part of it.

As a PR firm, APR's strategic goals in social media lie in their need to market themselves as well as their clients. To that end their goals are to position themselves as a strong force in "PR 2.0" and to feature their clients through their social media newsroom.

Tactics:

Optimizing APR's Website and RSS Feeds

APR uses WordPress as a CMS while maintaining the look and feel of a traditional Website. They burn their RSS feeds to FeedBurner and offer several options in the form of categories (PR news, Client news, Entire feed, etc.). This can work well for companies who have many posts a week that cover a number of different topics.

APR's site is nicely optimized. They make it quite easy for visitors to bookmark their site; they list their most recent posts and links to their social networking profiles in the sidebar; and they offer tag clouds to their content.

Blogging

APR does not blog as regularly as they would like, but they offer dynamic content in their social media newsroom. When they do blog, though, their posts address issues within their industry, especially as it applies to social media and PR.

---

[16] http://www.accoladespublicrelations.com

Social Networking

APR maintains healthy profiles and pages in Facebook and MySpace, as well as LinkedIn and Twitter. They feed their RSS feed (via their blog posts) into both their MySpace page and their Facebook page.

Social Bookmarking and Crowd-Sourcing

APR has an account and contributes regularly to several social bookmaking and crowd-sourcing sites.

Media Communities

APR has accounts in Flickr and YouTube. They integrate the firm's photos and their clients' images and videos into their Website as well as their social media newsroom.

Widgets and Badges

The widgets and badges on the APR site's sidebar reflect their presence in the Social Web.

Social Media Newsrooms

APR's social media newsroom[17] accomplishes two things: It highlights APR's presence in the Social Web and it serves as a way for them to feature the media coverage they get for their clients.

Testimonial:

Possessing a social media presence has offered crucial positioning for our PR firm. We have learned firsthand how to connect with visitors to our Website in more interactive and conversational ways. Our WordPress site allows us to quickly change the content, to offer blog commentary, and to demonstrate our capabilities through the news we garner for our clients.

I have had many clients comment on the fact that they selected our firm because our site revealed our understanding of new media technologies and strategies. The experiences of optimizing our site and cultivating

---

[17] http://www.accoladespublicrelations.com/newsroom

Web relationships have deepened our knowledge of the power of PR 2.0. We are better equipped now to envision and execute social media campaigns for our clients. The Web is your oyster—if you understand how to use open source technologies.

—Cynthia Baker, President, Accolades Public Relations

This Chapter On The Resource CD

- Further Reading
- Linkable Resources
- Fillable Forms:
  › Social Web Strategy Worksheet

2 Preparation

Once your strategy is in place, use it to prepare the content you will need for implementation. Try to resist the urge to just "wing it." Proper preparation of your descriptions, biographies, and other blurbs will greatly increase your exposure in the Social Web.

There is a fillable preparation worksheet on the resource CD that covers the following information as well.

Key Terms Or "Tags"

You are probably familiar with key terms or "keywords" since they are used in search engine optimization. Keywords are the terms that help search engine robots properly categorize your Website in the search engines. Think of them as the words or terms someone would enter in a Google search to find your site.

In social applications and tools, "tags" are the equivalent of key terms. You want to generate a good list of one, two, and three-word tags that will help define your presence in the Social Web. You will use these tags often as you implement your strategy.

Try to make a list of at least 20 tags. Choose tags that are not too generic, the same way you would choose good key terms. For instance, the tag "fiction" is too generic. Using tags like "young adult fiction" or "ontological fiction" will get you better results. Be sure and include the name of your business, book titles, authors, and business principals in your tag list as well.

There are a number of tools for finding good keywords.[1] Refer to the resource CD for more options.

Important First Decisions Regarding Your Profiles

Before proceeding, you need to decide two things:

1. What "entity" will you be representing in the Social Web? If you are an author, this will be your book; if you are a business owner, this will be your business. If you are a publisher or an author who intends on writing more than one book, you may want to think this through. For instance, if you are a publisher, you may decide to create a presence for your press as well as for each of your titles. Whereas if you are an author with several books, you may want to make your name/pseudonym or the name of your book series your entity as opposed to just the name of one of your books.

2. Which person within your organization will be representing you in the Social Web? You cannot always use your business or book name as the account holder of social sites. You will need to populate many of the profiles for an actual person. If you are an author, this is a given; but if you are a business, you will want to choose someone within your organization who has the time to contribute to these sites on occasion. This person should also feel comfortable disclosing a certain amount of personal information about themselves.

Once you have decided on your entity and your representative, gather the following information. Be sure to use one or more of your best tags in every description and biography.

---

[1] http://www.google.com/sktool/#

Information for Entity:

- Name of entity
- Tag line
- Short description
  - › 50 to 60 words
  - › Use at least two of your best tags
- Long description
  - › 175 to 200 words
  - › Use at least three of your best tags
- Website URL
- Year entity was founded
- Mission statement
- Product list (if applicable)
- Gender and birth date (These fields are required to register in some social sites, and since the age of your book or business would not make sense, use something else that has meaning for you.)
- Logo or book cover art

Information for Representative:

- Name of representative
- Brief biography
  - › 100 words
  - › Use two of your best tags
- Gender
- Birth date (This does not need to be public.)
- The following information is optional in most sites, however, it will make your representative more likely to find contacts in social networking sites:
  - › Hometown
  - › Activities
  - › Interests
    - Music
    - TV

- Movies
- Books
  › Favorite quotes
  › Favorite people/heroes
  › Education
    - College/university
    - Class year
    - Concentration
  › Work
    - Employer
    - Position
    - Description
    - City/town
- Photo to use for social networking profiles

Your Existing Social Presence

Compose a list, along with user names and links to your profile pages, of the places where you already have a presence in the Social Web.

Information For Social Calendars

Prepare a list of upcoming events to post to social calendars that includes:

- A short name
- A description (that includes tags)
- Date
- Time
- Venue
- Contact name and email
- A list of tags

Optimizing File Names

It is important that you rename multimedia files with descriptive names before you upload them to media communities like Flickr or YouTube. The name of a multimedia file can often get the file better exposure than its title or description. With that in mind, try to rename files using at least one of your best tags.

Preparing Your Multimedia Items

- Gather all:
  - › Images you plan to share in media communities like Flickr
  - › Video clips you plan to share in media communities like YouTube
  - › Audio clips that can be used as podcasts
- For each image or clip above:
  - › Create a short list of tags
  - › Rename the file using at least one tag
  - › Create a short title and description using at least two tags

Gathering Content For Blog Posts

- Gather information you may already have at your disposal to use as blog posts, including:
  - › Excerpts from your existing Website
  - › White papers you may have written
  - › Articles you may have published
  - › Book excerpts
- For each bit of information that will become a blog post:
  - › Prepare a list of tags
  - › Prepare a list of links that will go into the body of the post
  - › Prepare a short title using at least two tags
  - › Prepare a short description using as many tags as you can

This Chapter On The Resource CD

- Linkable Resources
- Fillable Forms:
    › Preparation Worksheet

3 RSS Feeds & Blogs

RSS Feeds

RSS stands for Really Simple Syndication. An RSS feed is a way of syndicating (sharing) information across the Internet. Think of a feed as a subscription. Imagine that instead of getting your local paper delivered to your door each day, every story within the paper was delivered to your desktop. This is what happens when you subscribe to a news site's RSS feed. RSS has become so popular and is so easy to implement that most Websites have a feed of some sort available to its visitors.

Generally, the process works as follows:

- Content (like news stories, blog entries, or press releases) in the form of a properly prepared file is generated from a Website as an RSS feed.
- The "feed" is made available for subscription to visitors who have access to a "feed reader."
- The subscriber can read each story that is added to the Website's feed without ever having to return to the original site.

- A subscriber can have as many subscriptions as they like. Each time they open their feed reader they will be informed of new stories that are available for each of their subscriptions.

Web 2.0 is about sharing and interactivity. Having an RSS feed that offers a way for visitors to easily access your content accomplishes both of these goals.

The Feed Reader

In order to subscribe to an RSS feed, you need access to a feed reader or "aggregator" as they are also called. There are a number of Web-based feed readers available, as well as readers you can install on your desktop.

Figure 3.1 shows Google Reader,[1] a Web-based feed reader. From here you can subscribe to feeds, read entries from your current feed subscriptions, search available feeds, and more.

Figure 3.1. Google Feed Reader

Figure 3.1 also shows how to add a new subscription by entering the feed's URL if you know it. Figure 3.2 shows the items from one of the feeds this user is subscribed to.

The next section discusses how you can subscribe to a feed using your preferred feed reader from any Website that has an RSS feed in place, and how to offer your own feed for subscription. Refer to the resource CD for a list of popular feed readers.

---

[1] http://www.google.com/reader

Figure 3.2. Feed Subscription in Google Reader

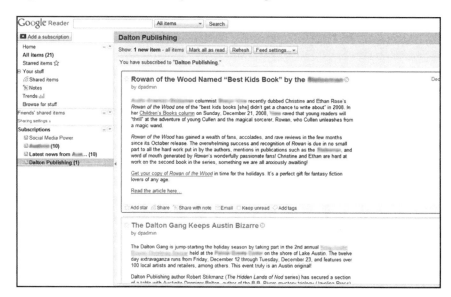

Desktop feed readers are convenient if you do not always have access to the Internet. FeedReader3[2] and RssReader[3] are two good ones.

The Feed

An RSS feed is an XML file that is formatted so that any feed reader can decipher and organize the contents of the file. The result is a file containing many stories (called items) that is kept up to date by the feed's author. Read more about how this is done in Appendix B, "Creating Your Own RSS Feed."

A blog *is* an RSS feed. Since blogging platforms have built-in RSS feed technology, each blog post becomes an item of the blog's RSS feed. This is very convenient if you do not need to have too much control over the functionality of your RSS feed.

---

[2] http://www.feedreader.com
[3] http://www.rssreader.com

Figure 3.3 shows the blog for the site, Social Media Power.[4] Figure 3.4 shows the same blog as it appears as a subscription in Google Reader.

You can subscribe to Social Media Power's RSS feed in a few different ways. One way is to look for the RSS icon. In Figure 3.3, the icon is just to the right of the "Social Media Power" title at the top of the page (the square icon with the dot and two curved lines). Clicking on this icon, you get the screen in Figure 3.5. From here, you can subscribe to this feed using any number of feed readers.

Figure 3.3. Social Media Power's Blog

Figure 3.4. Social Media Power's Blog Feed in Google Reader

---

[4] http://www.socialmediapower.com

Figure 3.5. Subscribing to a Feed via FeedBurner

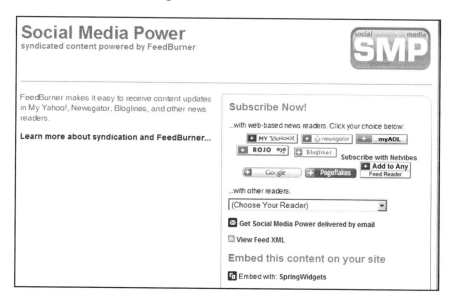

You can also enter your email address (to the right of the RSS icon) and receive this site's latest feeds in an email once a week (See Figure 3.6).

Figure 3.6. Subscribing to a Feed via Email

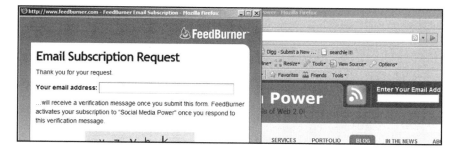

The other place to subscribe to the site's feed is to click on the button that says "Subscribe" on the right side of the page in Figure 3.3 (notice it also displays a small RSS icon). Figure 3.7 shows the screen that results when that button is clicked.

From here, you can choose to subscribe to this site's feed using any number of feed readers. This functionality is made possible by a feed widget called AddtoAny (see Page 240).

Figure 3.7. Subscribing to a Feed via AddtoAny

Blogging platforms are not the only applications that have built-in RSS technology. Content Management Systems (CMS) like Drupal[5] and Joomla![6] also have this feature, as do many other commercial Web publishing applications.

Figure 3.8 shows the RSS feeds offered by *The Austin Chronicle*.[7] Note that they have several feeds available. This is a common practice for larger news sites since not all their readers are interested in the same sections of the publication.

Figure 3.8. The *Austin Chronicle's* RSS Feeds

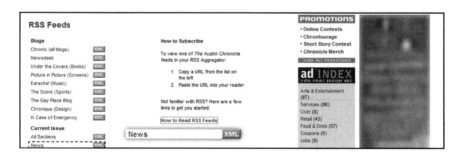

---

[5] http://www.drupal.org

[6] http://www.joomla.org

[7] http://www.austinchronicle.com

To subscribe to one of these feeds, you can click on the XML button to the right of the feed. Depending on your browser, this results in a page like Figure 3.9.

Figure 3.9. Subscribing to the *Austin Chronicle* Feed

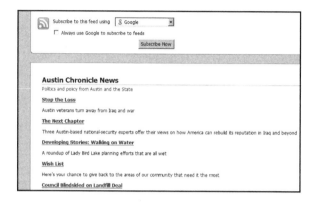

Choosing Google Reader as your reader of choice results in Figure 3.10. Clicking on "Add to Google Reader" adds the feed to your Google Reader account. Figure 3.11 shows how the feed is displayed in Google Reader.

Figures 3.10 & 3.11. *Austin Chronicle* Feed in Google Reader

As you can see, different Websites may offer their feeds differently, but the ultimate result is the same.

Displaying Feeds On A Website

You don't need a feed reader to access RSS feeds, only to subscribe to them. Many Websites display feeds from other sites that allow you to click through to the original story. Figure 3.12 shows the home page of Plumb Social,[8] a sister site to Social Media Power. In the right sidebar of this site is an area that displays the latest stories from Social Media Power's RSS feed. Clicking on one of the story titles brings you directly to the full story on Social Media Power's site.

Figure 3.12. Displaying Feeds on a Website

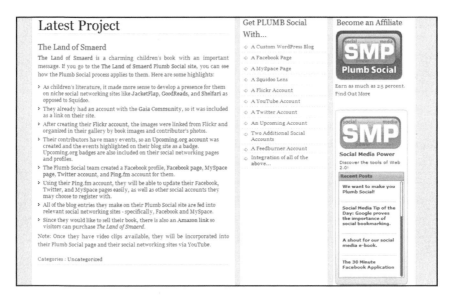

On a Blog or CMS

Blogging and CMS platforms also have built-in functionality for displaying RSS feeds. Figure 3.13 shows the built-in RSS plugin in the WordPress backend. To add an RSS feed to your sidebar, you enter the

[8] http://www.plumbsocial.com

feed's URL, a title for the feed, and select some other display settings, and you are set. Read more about plugins and WordPress in Chapter 4, "Building a WordPress Powered Website." Each CMS platform has its own version of this plugin that allows you to add RSS feeds to your site easily.

Figure 3.13. Adding an RSS Feed to a CMS

On a Traditional Website

Even if your Website is not powered by WordPress or another CMS, there are still ways of offering feeds on your site. You can use a service like Google AJAX API[9] to generate code to place on your Website, or ask your Webmaster to do it for you.

Figure 3.14 shows the Dynamic Feed Control Wizard for Google AJAX API. This wizard can help you create custom feeds that you can display on your site. You can display a single feed or several feeds in their "Vertical Stacked" format. You can enter the URL of a feed you already know or enter key terms that generate a series of feeds based on those terms.

Once you have your feed just the way you want it, click the "Generate Code" button and copy the generated code.

---

[9] http://code.google.com/apis/ajaxfeeds/

Figure 3.14. Using Google Feed Control Wizard

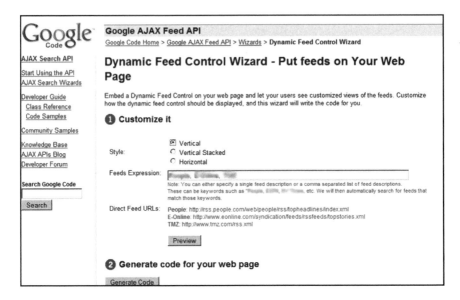

Figure 3.15 shows part of the generated code for the Social Media Power feed. You can then paste the code within the HTML of your Website. See Chapter 9, "Widgets & Badges," for more instruction on placing code on a Website.

Figure 3.15. Generated Code From Feed Control Wizard

Copy and paste the following where you want your dynamic feed control to appear. Do not place it within the `<head>`
... `</head>` section of your page unless you plan on relocating the `<div id="feed-control"></div>`
elements out of this chunk of code.

```
<!-- ++Begin Dynamic Feed Wizard Generated Code++ -->
  <!--
  // Created with a Google AJAX Search and Feed Wizard
  // http://code.google.com/apis/ajaxsearch/wizards.html
  -->

  <!--
  // The Following div element will end up holding the actual feed control.
  // You can place this anywhere on your page.
  -->
  <div id="feed-control">
```

Using Feed Widgets

The Social Media Power feed that is displayed on the Plumb Social Website in Figure 3.11 on Page 54 was created using a feed widget from Widgetbox.[10] There are a number of nice widgets like this for offering or displaying your feeds. See Chapter 9, "Widgets and Badges" for more information.

Options For Creating An RSS Feed

Creating Your RSS Feed From an XML File

As mentioned above, an RSS feed is nothing more than an XML (extended markup language) file that can be read by feed readers. Appendix B demonstrates how to build your own RSS feed using XML. It is recommended that you take a look at this appendix even if you do not plan on building an RSS feed. It will help you gain a better understanding of how RSS feeds work.

Using Software to Create Your RSS Feed

There is software available to help you build RSS feeds with little effort. However, it is recommended that you are familiar with the structure of an RSS file and the options available for building one before using the software. Appendix B can help you gain this understanding.

Figure 3.16 shows one of the screens used to create an RSS feed using FeedForAll.[11] Refer to Appendix B for clarification on the options listed in the figures, specifically: Title, Description, URL, and Pub Date.

The end product of this process is an XML file that you upload to your site and make available for others to subscribe to. Figure 3.17 shows the resulting file, and Figure 3.18 shows how the feed will look to the subscribers.

---

[10] http://widgetbox.com
[11] http://www.feedforall.com

Figure 3.16. Creating an RSS Feed with FeedForAll

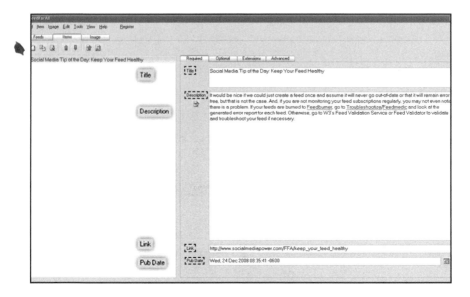

Figure 3.18. Resulting FeedForAll Feed

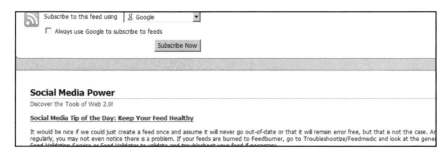

Armed with a basic understanding of the information in Appendix B, you can build a feed like this in as little as an hour. Once the feed is in place, you will only need to add new items or stories as they become available. You can add as many stories as you need at one time and postdate the publication dates as well.

There are also a number of services available that can help you create your feed and host it for you. One of these is MoreOver RSS Feed Builder.[12]

---

[12]http://w.moreover.com/public/products/feed_builder.html

Figure 3.17. XML File Created by FeedForAll

```
<?xml version="1.0" encoding="UTF-8"?>
<rss
     xmlns:content="http://purl.org/rss/1.0/modules/content/"
     xmlns:dc="http://purl.org/dc/elements/1.1/"
     xmlns:sy="http://purl.org/rss/1.0/modules/syndication/"
     version="2.0">
     <channel>
          <title>Social Media Power</title>
          <description>Discover the Tools of Web 2.0!</description>
          <link>http://www.socialmediapower.com/FFA</link>
          <docs>http://blogs.law.harvard.edu/tech/rss</docs>
          <lastBuildDate>Wed, 24 Dec 2008 10:43:35 -0600</lastBuildDate>
          <pubDate>Wed, 24 Dec 2008 08:47:42 -0600</pubDate>
          <generator>FeedForAll v2.0 (2.0.2.9) unlicensed version
http://www.feedforall.com</generator>
          <image>
               <url>http://www.socialmediapower.com/images/SMPWeb.jpg
</url>
               <title>Social Media Power</title>
               <link>http://www.socialmediapower.com/FFA</link>
               <description>Social Media Power Logo</description>
          </image>
          <item>
               <title>Social Media Tip of the Day: Keep Your Feed Healthy
</title>
               <description>It would be nice if we could just create a
feed once and assume it will never go out-of-date or that it will
remain error free, but that is not the case. And, if you are not
monitoring your feed subscriptions regularly, you may not even notice
there is a problem. If your feeds are burned to Feedburner, go to
Troubleshootize/Feedmedic and look at the generated error report for
each feed. Otherwise, go to W3€™s Feed Validation Service or Feed
Validator to validate and troubleshoot your feed if necessary.
</description>
               <link>
http://www.socialmediapower.com/FFA/keep_your_feed_healthy</link>
               <guid isPermaLink="false">B9709467-A518-4BF1-ABC3-
FF033D9BAA0C</guid>
               <pubDate>Wed, 24 Dec 2008 08:35:41 -0600</pubDate>
          </item>
     </channel>
</rss>
```
or Help, press F1

Using a Blog as Your RSS Feed

Starting a blog is probably the easiest way to create an RSS feed. Blogging platforms like WordPress have built-in RSS technology so that each blog entry becomes an "item" of the feed, complete with titles, descriptions, links, and categories that you add to each blog entry. Continue on to the "Blogs" section of this chapter for more information.

Planning Your Feed

How will you create your feed?

- Create your own XML file
- Use software or a service to create your feed
- Use a CMS to serve as your feed
- Start a blog to serve as your feed

How many feeds will you have?

If you have a lot of content, you may want to create several feeds: one for news, one for press releases, one for events, and so forth. If you have a news site, you may even break your feeds up by category like the *Austin Chronicle* feed in Figure 3.8 on Page 52.

As another example, Dalton Publishing creates social media newsrooms for each of its authors (see Chapter 10, "Social Media Newsrooms"). The newsrooms include sections for new releases, media coverage, book reviews, and events. Figure 3.19 shows how these newsrooms break out the RSS feeds accordingly.

Figure 3.19. Feeds on a Social Media Newsroom

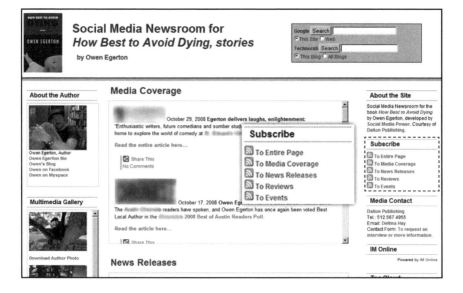

This is convenient not only for the press or others interested in subscribing to specific information about this author, but for the author as well. Authors can offer links to their latest media coverage, events, etc. by featuring the respective feed on their own Website or blog (see Figure 3.20).

Figure 3.20. Social Media Newsroom Feed on a Website

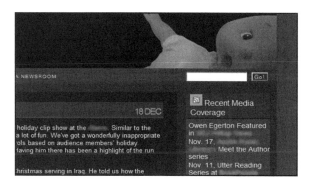

Titles, Descriptions, Categories, and Links

You have a title and description for your main feed or "channel" (see Appendix B), as well as titles and descriptions for each individual feed item. Plan these titles and descriptions so they use some of your best key terms every time (see Chapter 2, "Preparation").

Your item descriptions may be the only thing a potential reader sees before they make a decision to read the full story. Make sure these descriptions do a good job of hooking the reader while still accurately describing each story.

Assigning relevant and meaningful categories to each feed item is important for your feed to get properly listed in the feed directories. Compose a category list of your best key terms, and draw mostly from this list.

Each of your feed items should have a unique link that brings the reader directly to the full story.

Content for Your Feed

It is important to keep your feed items fresh and plentiful. Even if you don't have a lot of content, good planning can make it go further.

- Gather any existing content you have available. This may include:
  › Print articles
  › E-zine articles
  › Newsletter stories
  › Press releases
  › Media coverage
  › Upcoming events
  › White papers
  › Informative sections of your Website
  › Book trailers
  › Book excerpts
  › Podcasts
  › Video clips
- Make a list of external links. These may include:
  › Industry blogs you are reading
  › Articles of interest to your industry
  › Websites of interest
  › News sites
  › Other RSS feeds
- Make a list of people in your industry who may be willing to contribute to your feed.
- Make a list of possible topics. These may include:
  › Article or story topics
  › Interviews
  › Reviews of books, tools, or Websites relevant to your industry
  › Top 10 lists
  › Tips

Once your content is gathered and your lists complete, start a calendar of entries for your feed. Mix up selections from the general areas mentioned above.

Existing Content: Try and get as much mileage out of your existing content as you can. Some of your existing articles, white papers, or other content can probably be broken down into many smaller entries.

External Links: Use these links for story ideas, sites to review, or blogs you can start a dialogue with.

Other People: Invite industry leaders to contribute to your feed.

Possible Topics: Writing top 10 lists and tips is a good way of quickly adding content to your feed to keep it fresh. Mix them up with beefy, informative articles, though.

Use a sheet like the one in Figure 3.21 to prepare your feed entries. See the resource CD for a fillable worksheet like Figure 3.21 as well as a worksheet for planning your entire RSS feed.

Figure 3.21. RSS Feed Entries Worksheet

Feed Name: Social Media Power				
Pub Date	**Title**	**Description**	**Link**	**Categories**
08/28/08	The 30 Minute Facebook Application	Demonstrate a way for anyone with an RSS feed to painlessly build a Facebook application in only 30 minutes.	http://www.socialmediapower.com/2008/08/28/the-30-minute-facebook-application/	Facebook, Facebook Applications, Social Media, Web 2.0, RSS feeds, Bebo
09/01/08	Social Media Tip of the Day: Keep Your Feed Healthy	Social Media Power's tips on keeping your RSS feed fresh, indexed, and error free.	http://www.socialmediapower.com/2008/08/20/social-media-tip-of-the-day-keep-your-feed-healthy/	RSS feeds, Social Media, Web 2.0, Feedburner, Feed Validator

Optimizing and Promoting Your Feed

Read the section "Optimizing and Promoting Your Blog and RSS Feed" at the end of this chapter (see Page 72).

Blogs

In its simplest form, a *blog* is a tool for posting information chronologically and allowing others to comment. Blog posts can be organized into categories and indexed using tags that are read by blog indexes (much the same way as key terms are read by search engines). Users then use tags to search blog indexes on subjects that interest them.

But remember from the previous section that a blog is also an RSS feed. It is because of this that you should not buy into the stigma that is often associated with blogging. For our purposes, we focus on how blogging serves a vital role in accomplishing social media and Web 2.0 optimization, and how you can use WordPress to maximize the exposure of your blog, not only in blogging and RSS feed indexes, but in search engines as well.

If you need more information on how to blog in general, refer to the "Linkable Resources" and "Further Reading" sections for this chapter on the resource CD.

The Thread That Binds Your Social Web Presence

As we have said, social media and Web 2.0 optimization can be broken down into three general areas: interactivity, sharing, and collaboration. Adding a blog to your Web presence covers each of these areas. You are freely sharing information, encouraging interactivity through visitor comments, and offering an atmosphere of collaboration for all of your visitors.

Many of the sites and tools that you implement in your social media strategy allows you to integrate blogs and RSS feeds directly into them. For instance, both Facebook and MySpace have applications that allow you to pipe RSS feeds or blog entries directly onto your page or profile (see Chapter 6 and Chapter 12, "Social Networking & Micro-Blogging" and "Pulling It All Together," for more information).

Having an informative and engaging blog or RSS feed therefore gives you an edge over many of your competitors in more places than just on your Website or in the blogosphere.

Know Your Audience, Know Your Blog

A blog, like an RSS feed, can serve many purposes. Knowing the audience you want to target is the best starting place to determine your blog's purpose. Like any good media provider, knowing what your audience wants to read is imperative to your success.

As an example, the blog at Social Media Power[13] is dedicated to providing a resource for those interested in social media and Web 2.0 optimization. If I suddenly started blogging about Wolfgang, my eccentric problem cat, I would likely lose some readers. Instead, we keep our posts consistently on topic: writing informative articles, tips, and reviews on the topics of social media and Web 2.0.

The blog for Dalton Publishing,[14] however, caters to a different audience. They are writing for their current and prospective authors, their distributor, their authors' readers, and others in the industry. Therefore, their blog tends to be more of a hodge podge of information: upcoming events, media coverage, announcements, kudos, etc.

So it isn't that your blog shouldn't have different types of posts, just that you should keep your audience in mind when posting.

Types of blogs you might consider:

- A corporate RSS feed covering company news, articles, press releases, and the like.
- An educational or how-to blog offering articles and resources on a particular topic.
- An industry blog offering news, interviews, and resources within a particular industry.
- A blog about a particular product, author, or book.
- A straight news or entertainment feed.
- A traditional blog that is more conversational and casual than a news feed or corporate blog.

If you have content that falls into several distinct categories like events, news, press releases, or reviews, you can use categories to define several feeds within the same blog. Offer your readers the option of subscribing to specific parts of a feed rather than the entire feed. See "Optimizing and Promoting Your Blog and RSS Feed" on Page 72 for more information.

---

[13] http://www.socialmediapower.com/blog
[14] http://www.daltonpublishing.com/blog

Options for Starting Your Blog

Starting a Free Blog

You can start a free (or near free) blog at WordPress.com, Typepad.com, or Blogger.com. These blogs have limited capabilities, but you can upgrade to premium services that will open up more options.

Starting a Blog on Your Website

Many hosts have one-click installs of WordPress or other blogging platforms. Check with your hosting company to see if they have this option available. If not, you can install WordPress in a folder on your Website. Refer to Appendix A, "Installing WordPress," but follow the instructions for installing WordPress in a folder on your site, not in the root directory of your site.

Using WordPress to Power Your Website

You can use WordPress to power your entire Website and have your blog built in to your site. Refer to Chapter 4, "Building a WordPress Powered Website." Or, instead of replacing your main Website with a WordPress powered site, you can build a "Blog Site" or "Social Media Portal" with WordPress that has its own domain name and hosting account (if necessary). This site can be dedicated to hosting your blog and highlighting all of your areas of interest in the Social Web. An example of this is the service called Plumb Social.[15]

Main Elements of a WordPress Blog Post

Figure 3.22 shows the most basic elements of a blog entry in WordPress:

Title: The title is how your blog appears to others in your blog listings as well as the first thing subscribers see about a post when receiving your RSS feed or when they see your post in a directory.

Permalink: This is the permanent link to this blog entry. In WordPress settings, you can define the default style for permalinks. You can also override the default permalink for any blog entry. In our example, the

---

[15] http://www.plumbsocial.com

Figure 3.22. Elements of a Blog Post, Top

default permalink structure is nameofblog.com/year/month/day/title. If we choose, we can change the title portion of the permalink to make it shorter or have no dashes. Permalink structure is important. Read more about permalinks in "Optimizing and Promoting Your Blog and RSS Feed" on Page 72.

Post: This is where the body of your blog entry is composed. Above this box are functions for you to format your blog entry, including text styles, bulleted lists, block quotes, inserting images and other media, and much more. Check this chapter's section on the resource CD for links about using WordPress.

Links: Figure 3.23 shows how to insert a link into a post by highlighting text and clicking on the closed chain link. How you do this is important. Read more about links within your posts on Page 73.

Figure 3.23. Creating Links in Blog Posts

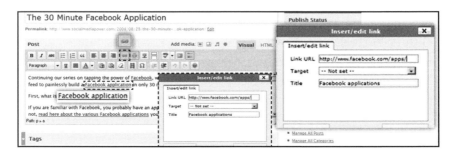

Categories: Categories help you group your posts by similar topics. They also have a hierarchy, so you can have parent and child (or sub) categories. When a visitor clicks on a category while viewing your blog, they will be able to view each post that is assigned to that category. Choice of categories is also important to blog optimization "Optimizing and Promoting Your Blog and RSS Feed" on Page 73.

Tags: Tags are similar to categories in that they help group blog posts by similar topics, but tags have other uses as well. Tags are used by many plugins, including tag cloud plugins, that give users a visual representation of your blog posts. Tags do not have a hierarchical structure like categories. Tags are also used by RSS feed and blog directories as key terms, so you want to use these wisely. See "Optimizing and Promoting Your Blog and RSS Feed" on Page 73.

Categories vs. Tags: Tags are used more than categories to classify individual posts in blog and RSS indexes. A good rule of thumb is to use categories to organize your posts for easy navigation on your site, but to use tags as key terms that will help others find your posts off your site. This keeps you from having too many categories, yet as many tags as necessary to get good placement in the directories.

Excerpts: Excerpts are used to summarize your post, and to use as a good "hook" to get readers interested in your entire post when they stumble upon it in a blog directory. WordPress defaults to the first 55 words of the original post if you leave the excerpt blank, so if your lead is good in the original post, you may want to leave this alone. Excerpts are also used in trackbacks, explained below.

Trackbacks: A trackback is a method of notification between Websites. They are a way for you to comment on someone else's blog from your own site, and have your entry show up on their site as a comment or as a notification on their WordPress dashboard. So, if you want to comment on someone else's blog post, but you want your readers to see your comment, you can post a blog entry, cite the blog you are commenting on, and send a "trackback" to the blog you are citing. Your post will then show up as a comment on the "trackbacked" blog post. The comment will show up as the excerpt of your post with a link back to your entire post. Figure 3.24 shows where this is done.

This section demonstrates the most basic elements of a blog post. If you are not an experienced blogger, please reference the resource CD to learn more.

Figure 3.24. Elements of a Blog Post, Bottom

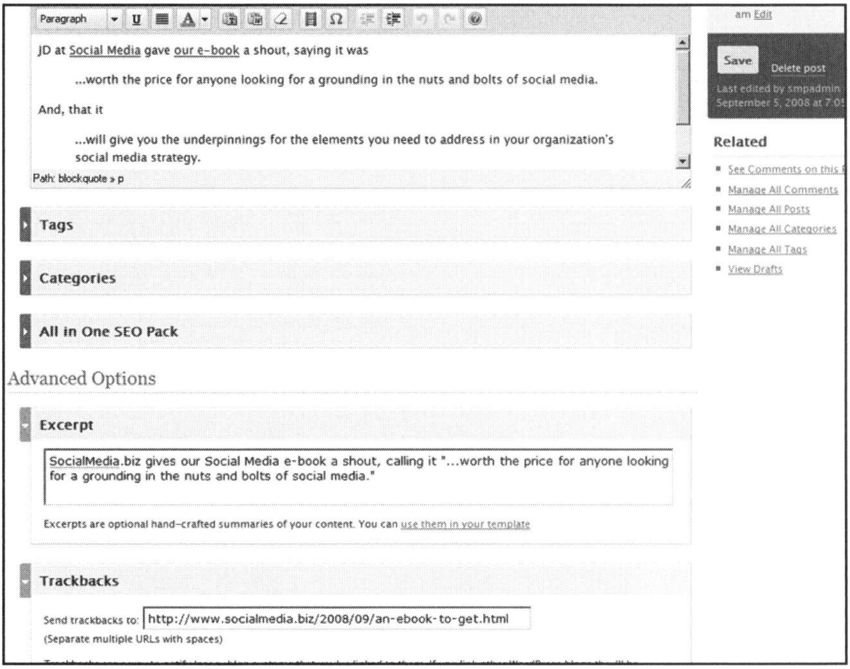

Planning Your Blog

Content

Read "Content for Your Feed" on Page 62 above. The same principles apply to gathering and preparing content for your blog.

Categories and Tags

Categories and tags are important elements of your plan, since they are what help others find your blog in the feed indexes and blog directories.

Choose your categories from the top level key terms you prepared in the Chapter 2, "Preparation." Recall that you use categories to organize your posts, so make these quite broad.

Use all of your key terms as tags, even the ones you chose for categories. The nice thing about tags is that you can have a lot of them without adding too much clutter to your site (unlike with categories).

Frequency and Delegation

Planning your blog entries ahead of time can help keep your blog populated with fresh content. Using a posting calendar like the one in Figure 3.25 can help this process. You can also use it for delegating the

Figure 3.25. Blog Entry Worksheet

Blog Name: Social Media Power

Pub Date	Title	Excerpt	Post (link text is underlined, followed by link to use)	Categories	Tags
08/28/08	The 30 Minute Facebook Application	Demonstrates a way for anyone with an RSS feed to painlessly build a Facebook application in only 30 minutes.	Continuing our series on tapping the power of Facebook (http://www.facebook.com), we will demonstrate a way for anyone with an RSS feed to painlessly build a Facebook application (http://www.facebook.com/apps/) in only 30 minutes...	Facebook, Facebook Applications, Social Media, Web 2.0, RSS feeds, Bebo	Bebo, blidget, blog, building a facebook application, Facebook, facebook applications, facebook page, RSS feed, Social Media, Social Media Optimization, social networking, social Web, widgetbox
09/01/08	Social Media Tip of the Day: Keep Your Feed Healthy	Social Media Power's tips on keeping your RSS feed fresh, indexed, and error free.	It would be nice if we could just create a feed once and assume it will never go out-of-date or that it will remain error free, but that is not the case. And, if you are not monitoring your feed subscriptions regularly, you may not even notice there is a problem. If your feeds are burned to Feedburner (http://www.feedburner.com), go to Troubleshootize/Feedmedic and look at the generated error report for each feed. Otherwise, go to W3's Feed Validation Service (http://validator.w3.org/feed/) or Feed Validator (http://feedvalidator.org/) to validate and troubleshoot your feed if necessary.	RSS feeds, Social Media, Web 2.0, Feedburner, Feed Validator	Feed Validation Service, Feed Validator, FeedBurner, healthy rss feeds, RSS Feeds, Social Media, Social Media Optimization, Web 2.0

Trackbacks	SEO Title	SEO Description	SEO Keywords		
http://docs.widgetbox.com/developers/blidget/	How to build a Facebook application in around 30 minutes.	This post will show you how to create a simple RSS feed application for Facebook and Bebo using widgetbox.com.	social media, facebook, facebook applications, building facebook applications, widgetbox, widgets, blidgets		
none	Social Media Tip of the Day: Keep Your Feed Healthy	Keep your RSS feed healthy using Feedburner and feed validators. Part of Social Media Power's tips and tools for Web 2.0 optimization.	social media, rss feed, feedburner, healthy rss feed, error-free rss feeds, social media optimization		

actual posting to others. You can even enter your posts ahead of time and postdate the publication dates. This form is available on the resource CD.

Comments and Commenting

Comments on Your Posts

Allowing others to comment on your blog posts is what makes blogging a vital part of Web 2.0 optimization. However, this does not mean that you should allow anyone and everyone to say whatever they please or to spam you with comments. Always set the most stringent settings on your blog discussion settings in WordPress and be particular on which comments you approve.

From your WordPress admin panel, go to Settings/Discussion to change these settings (see Figure 3.26). Checking all of these boxes ensures that all comments on your blog need to be approved by you before they appear on your site. This means you will be contacted via email each time a comment is posted, and will need to approve all new comments, but that is a small price to pay to make sure your blog maintains its integrity.

Figure 3.26. Controlling Comments on a Blog

Default article settings	☑ Attempt to notify any blogs linked to from the article (slows down posting.)
	☑ Allow link notifications from other blogs (pingbacks and trackbacks.)
	☑ Allow people to post comments on the article
	(These settings may be overridden for individual articles.)
E-mail me whenever	☑ Anyone posts a comment
	☑ A comment is held for moderation
Before a comment appears	☑ An administrator must always approve the comment
	☑ Comment author must fill out name and e-mail
	☑ Comment author must have a previously approved comment

Commenting on Other Blogs

Becoming part of the conversation is important to building a healthy Social Web presence. However, do not comment for the sake of commenting—that is considered spam.

The following strategy can save you time and help to optimize your efforts:

- Click through to the bloggers who leave good comments on your blog posts. If there is something on their site that interests you, leave a comment.
- Try to use trackbacks to comment on others' blog posts when appropriate.
- Search Technorati[16] and Google Blog Search[17] for a handful of blogs that you feel you could comment on regularly and subscribe to them in a reader. This keeps you abreast of any posts you might want to comment on.
- Periodically search blog directories using your best key terms to find blog posts to comment on.
- Always use your real name, a valid email address, and your complete URL (a complete URL includes "http://www." at the beginning) when posting a comment, even if they are not required.

Optimizing And Promoting Your Blog And RSS Feed

Your RSS feed or blog will do you little good if nobody knows about it or cannot subscribe to it. This section highlights ways for you to optimize and promote your feed. Most of these tips are for both blogs and RSS feeds, but some of them only apply to blogs. It is made clear if something only applies to blogs.

Your Feed or Blog Content

Edit Your Content

Edit and proofread your feed or blog entries for accuracy every time you post. If you or your staff do not have the time or skills to do so, consider hiring a professional editor. If you write your posts ahead of time as

[16] http://technorati.com/
[17] http://blogsearch.google.com/

suggested in the previous section, you can save money since editors usually have a minimum charge and can get a lot done in one session.

Titles

Always use at least one or two of your best key terms in your blog or feed titles. This gives you better placement in the directories as well as better search engine placement.

Categories and Tags (tags only apply to blogs)

When posting blog entries, you should assign categories and tags to them *every* time. Most blog indexing sites use categories and tags to index blog entries. Draw from your top level key terms for categories and all of your key terms for tags.

Links

Link to as many other blogs or Websites from within each of your posts as you can and trackback to them whenever possible (see the "Blogs" section on Page 63).

When creating links within a post, use key terms as the link text. Figure 3.27 shows an example of this. Each link in this post uses key terms as the link text. So, "Facebook" links to Facebook.com, "Facebook application" links to the Facebook application page, Facebook.com/apps, and so forth.

Figure 3.27. Text Links in Blog Posts

The 30 Minute Facebook Application

○ Posted by **smpadmin** August 28, 2008

Continuing our series on tapping the power of Facebook, we will demonstrate a way for anyone with an RSS feed to painlessly build a Facebook application in only 30 minutes.

First, what is a Facebook application?

If you are familiar with Facebook, you probably have an application or two on your page or profile already. If not, read here about the various Facebook applications you can utilize. Yes, some of them are silly things that you will never use, but many of them can really help enhance your business Facebook presence. Thousands of people search this application directory every day, so having your own application on Facebook gives you much more exposure within the social community.

Now, creating your application:

To create your 30-minute Facebook application, you will first create a widget of your RSS feed, then turn that widget into an application on Facebook.

Each link in the post also contains a key term that is used as a tag and/or category for the post. This tactic gives each of your posts more relevance in directories and search engines.

Signatures

Attaching a signature at the end of each of your posts can encourage visitors to subscribe to your feed and aid in promoting your other sites or products. Figure 3.28 shows the signature at the end of one of the Social Media Power posts. This is also a good place for a copyright statement if you need one. Notice that there are three pound signs before this signature. It is best to keep your signature clearly separate from the post content.

Figure 3.28. Blog Post Signature

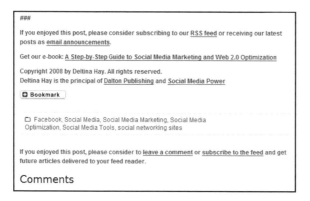

Search Engine Optimization (SEO)

SEO For Your Blog (only applies to blogs)

Since WordPress produces PHP as opposed to HTML, posts and pages do not necessarily have the metadata in their source that is required for search engine robots (read more about metadata on Page 17). However, there are ways around this problem. A good SEO plugin for WordPress is The All in One SEO Pack.[18] This plugin lets you assign proper metadata to each of your posts and WordPress pages so that they get good placement

---

[18] http://wordpress.org/extend/plugins/all-in-one-seo-pack/

in search engines. You input the metadata from the same interface that you enter the post. The title, description, and keywords entered here become the metadata for that post. See Figure 3.29.

This plugin also helps you assign metadata for your site as whole.

Figure 3.29. SEO All In One Pack Plugin in Action

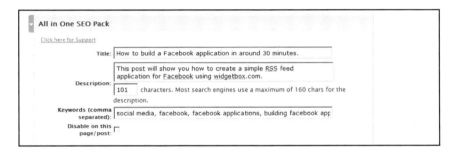

Permalinks (only applies to blogs)

As discussed in the previous section, permalinks are the direct link to each of your blog entries. You want to use a permalink structure that does not use any special characters (these are often called "pretty" permalinks). Since WordPress is written using PHP, the default permalinks look something like this: http://yoursite.com/?p=6. Search engines often ignore links that contain characters like the ones in "?p=6." Choose a permalink structure that does not use them. To change the structure, go to the backend of WordPress; go to Settings/Permalinks. Figure 3.30 shows the common permalink settings. To make your permalinks "pretty," choose any of these options except the default.

Figure 3.30. Defining Permalinks in WordPress

Common settings	
⊂ Default	http://www.socialmediapower.com/?p=123
⊙ Day and name	http://www.socialmediapower.com/2008/12/30/sample-post/
⊂ Month and name	http://www.socialmediapower.com/2008/12/sample-post/
⊂ Numeric	http://www.socialmediapower.com/archives/123

External Links or "Link Baiting"

This is actually an SEO tip you can use for any Website. Use meta keywords in any link text that points back to your Website. These are the meta keywords that are in your site's header (see Page 17 of the Introduction), not just arbitrary key terms. Whenever you can use text as links back to your site, use these terms to do so. As an example, we use the following blurb at the end of each article we submit to e-zines and the like for Social Media Power:

Deltina Hay is the principal of Social Media Power, a Web 2.0 development firm in Austin. Ms. Hay's graduate education in computer science, applied mathematics, and psychology led her naturally to social media consulting. Find out more about using social media and Web 2.0 tools from her new straight forward, easy-to-follow e-book on social media marketing and Web 2.0.

The term "social media" links to SocialMediaPower.com and "social media marketing" links to the e-book page on that site. We are also careful not to clutter these bios with links—two is a good limit. Search engine robots consider external links that are similar to meta keywords very relevant and will increase your page rank accordingly.

FeedBurner

FeedBurner[19] is a free service offered by Google that helps you manage your feed subscriptions, submit your feed to directories, promote your feed, troubleshoot your feed, and advertise your feed.

Burning Your Feed

By "burning" your feed to FeedBurner, all you are doing is creating an alternate URL for your feed that looks something like: "http://feeds. feedburner.com/YourBlogName." Doing this allows you to use the services that FeedBurner offers. This does not, however, negate your original feed URL—you can use either one of these URLs to represent your feed. It is best to use the FeedBurner URL as much as possible, though, since FeedBurner will only record stats for subscriptions to the URL they create for you.

---

[19] http://www.feedburner.google.com

To burn your feed, first get an account with Google (preferably an Adsense account), then while logged in to your Google account, go to the FeedBurner site. Figure 3.31 shows the FeedBurner screen where you can then enter your feed URL to burn. If you are using a WordPress blog for your feed, then your feed URL is "http://www.yourblogURL.com/feed." The next screen lets you change the name of your feed URL (see Figure 3.32). Once your feed is activated, you can start using the FeedBurner services.

Figures 3.31 & 3.32. Burning a Feed to FeedBurner

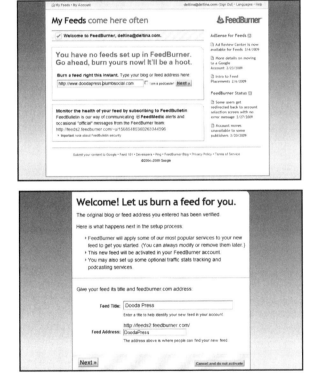

Analyze Menu

Figure 3.33 shows the FeedBurner Analyze screen. From here you can see statistics on all of the subscriptions to your feed or blog broken down by feed reader and type of subscription.

Figure 3.33. FeedBurner Analyze Menu

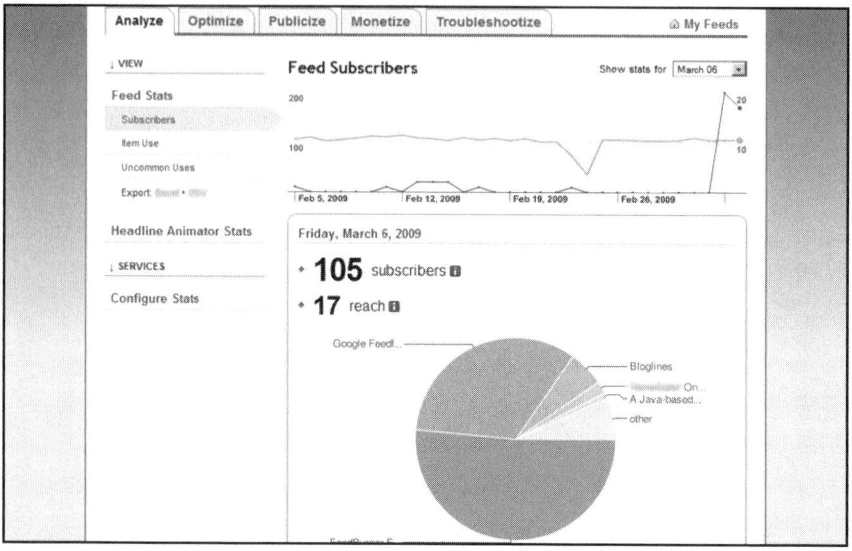

Optimize Menu

From the Optimize menu (see Figure 3.34) activate the following services: "Browser Friendly," "Smart Feed," and "FeedFlare." These services help get your feed maximum exposure in the Social Web and make subscribing to your feed much easier for your visitors.

Activate "Link Splicer" if you have a lot of links saved to a social bookmarking site like Delicious.com.

Add your logo to your feed with "Feed Image Burner."

Activate the "Event Feed" if you have an Upcoming.org account, or use Google Calendar to keep track of upcoming events.

Publicize Menu

"Headline Animators" are nice for advertising your feed as a banner on other sites and in emails. You can create any number of banners or email signatures.

Use "BuzzBoost" to show your feed on other sites—you can even combine more than one feed using this feature. This works great for cross-promoting your feeds if you have multiple feeds and/or blogs.

Figure 3.34. FeedBurner Optimize Menu

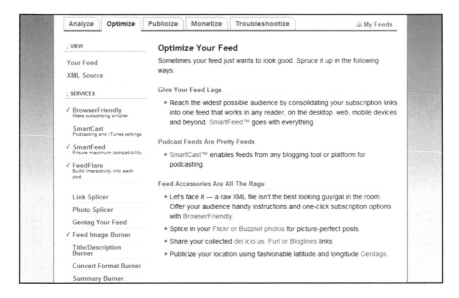

Using "Email Subscriptions," you can design custom emails of your feed entries along with a form to place on your site so that users can subscribe. Figure 3.35 shows how FeedBurner generates code for you to copy and

Figure 3.35. Creating a FeedBurner Email Widget

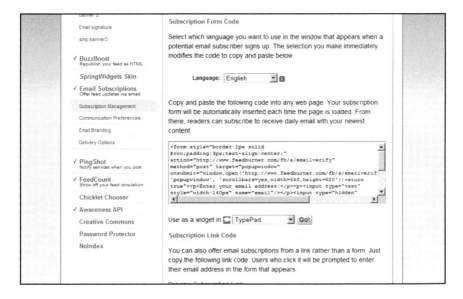

paste onto your blog or Website so that visitors can easily subscribe to your feed via email. Figure 3.36 shows this code in action.

Figure 3.36. FeedBurner Email Widget on Website

"PingShot" should be one of the first things you do once you burn your feed. FeedBurner will automatically ping (notify) some of the most important feed services each time you update your feed. See "About Pinging" in the "Directories" section below.

Once you have a substantial number of feed subscriptions, use "FeedCount" to add a feed count chicklet to show it off.

"Chicklet Chooser" offers some nice feed subscription icons to place on your blog or Website. You should do this as soon as you burn your feed, so you make your feed available to your site visitors right away. Figures 3.37 and 3.38 show the different options for your "chicklet." Once you choose your chicklet, you can copy the generated code and place it on your blog or Website.

Figure 3.37. FeedBurner Chicklet Chooser, Top

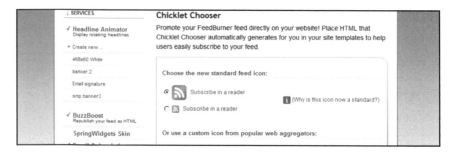

Figure 3.38. FeedBurner Chicklet Chooser, Bottom

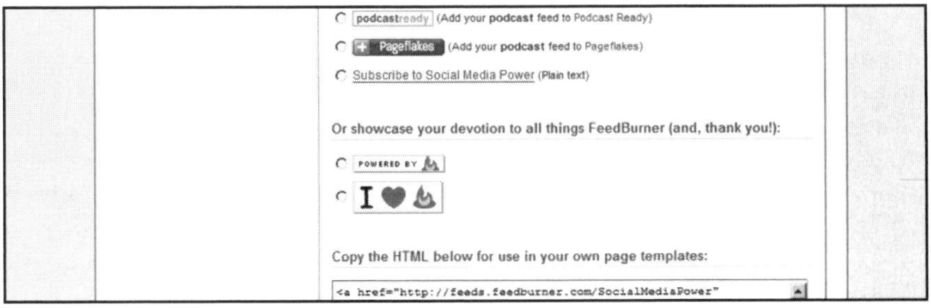

Burning More Than One Feed

You can burn as many feeds as you like on FeedBurner. In previous sections we discussed breaking your feeds up by topic or category. If you are using WordPress, you can burn more than one feed based on categories. Each blog category in WordPress has its own feed URL, based on the following structure: "http://www.YourBlogURL.com/wp-rss2.php?cat=6" where "6" is the category ID in WordPress. So, using the category ID, you can burn a feed of only the posts that are assigned that category.

To find the category ID in WordPress, go to the admin panel of WordPress, and then to Manage/Categories. Click on a category and you see the category ID in the address bar of your browser. Figure 3.39 demonstrates. Once the category "Authors" is clicked on, the URL in the address bar shows: "http://...categories.php?action=edit&cat_ID=8." So the ID for that category is 8.

RSS Feed and Blog Directories

These sites are called many things: Blog directories, RSS feed indexes, Blog and RSS feed search engines, etc., but they all have the same thing in common: They are all places you want your blog or RSS feed to show up if someone searches with your chosen key terms.

Figure 3.39. Finding a WordPress Category ID

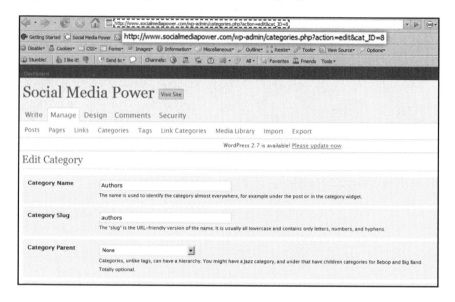

To avoid confusion, they will be referred to only as "directories" from here on. You can assume a directory is for both blogs and RSS feeds unless specified otherwise.

About Pinging

One of the things that makes blogs and RSS feeds so accessible is their pinging system. Pinging means that when you post an entry to your blog or RSS feed, certain directories and aggregators are automatically notified or "pinged" that your blog has a new entry. This keeps the directories up-to-date and eliminates the need for you to ping them yourself.

WordPress notifies Ping-O-Matic[20] each time there is a new post to your blog. You can use the service to ping your blog manually, too. Figure 3.40 shows the directories that Ping-O-Matic notifies.

If you have burned your feed to FeedBurner and activated "PingShot" (see Page 83) each service shown in Figure 3.41 will be notified each time you have a new feed or blog entry.

This does not mean, however, that you do not need to manually add your blogs and feeds to these directories. The pinging system only notifies a

[20] http://pingomatic.com/

Figure 3.40. Ping-O-Matic Pinging Service

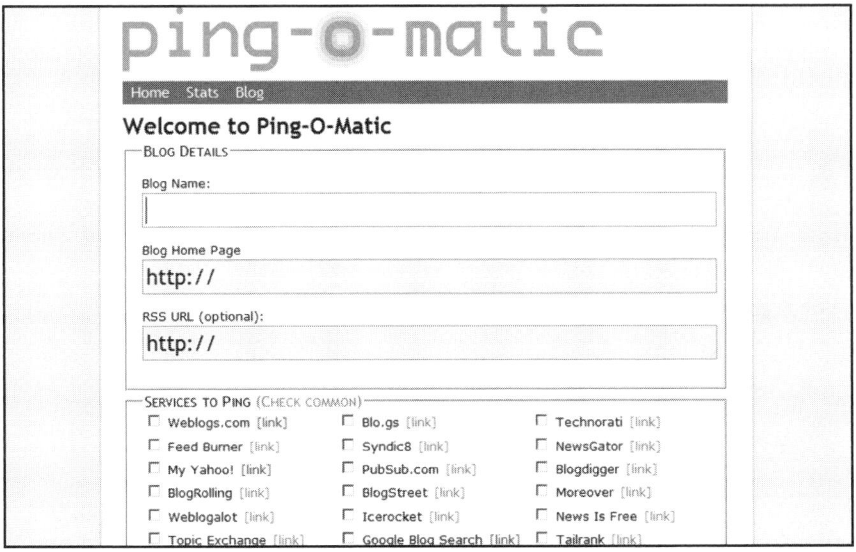

Figure 3.41. FeedBurner's PingShot Service

directory that your blog has a new entry; it does not list your blog for you in the directory. Besides, you want to do this manually so that you can put in place good tags and descriptions using your best key terms.

Submitting to Directories

When submitting your blog or feed to directories, complete the submission forms thoroughly. Use a cheat sheet like the one in Figure 3.42 so you have the necessary information on hand to copy and paste when submitting, as well as a sheet like Figure 3.43 to keep track of your submissions. These forms are also available on the resource CD.

Figure 3.42. Blog Directory Cheat Sheet

RSS Feed/Blog Information Sheet
For Submitting to Directories

Feed Name: Social Media Power

Feed URL: http://feeds.feedburner.com/SocialMediaPower

Feed Description: Tips and tools for social media marketing, Web 2.0 optimization, building WordPress sites, social networking, social bookmarking, crowd sourcing, and social media newsrooms, including social media ebooks and wordpress themes.

Feed Image URL: http://www.socialmediapower.com/images/smpWeb.jpg

Feed Tags/Categories: social media, social media marketing, web 2.0, social media ebooks, wordpress sites, social networking, social bookmarking, wordpress themes, social media newsrooms

Figure 3.43. Blog Directory Submission Tracking Form

RSS Feed and Blog Directory Submissions for: Social Media Power

Date	Site or Service Name	Site URL	Type of Service	Notes	Upkeep
01/02/09	Google Reader	http://www.google.com/reader	Reader	Opened an account and added feed to personal page.	None
01/02/09	Technorati	http://www.technorati.com	Blog Directory	Claimed blog and completed profile. Added description and tags.	Return and check that blog is being updated regularly and how others are saving, tagging, and commenting on posts.
01/02/09	RSS Network	http://www.rss-network.com/submitrss.php	RSS feed index	Needed to choose category and sub-category. Chose Internet Feeds/Marketing	None

An Example

Technorati is probably the most popular blog directory. In order to "claim" your blog, you need to get an account. Once you have an account, you can claim all of your blogs. Figure 3.44 shows how to create a good description and tags. Again, use your best key terms both as tags and in your blog's description.

Always read a directory's submission guidelines before submitting. Some directories are strictly news-based or have themes or regional appeal that may not be a good fit for your blog or feed.

Finding Directories

There are many feed and blog directories out there. Some of them are more important than others, but it is never a bad idea to get your blog initially listed in all of the directories that are good fits.

Figure 3.44. Claiming a Blog in Technorati

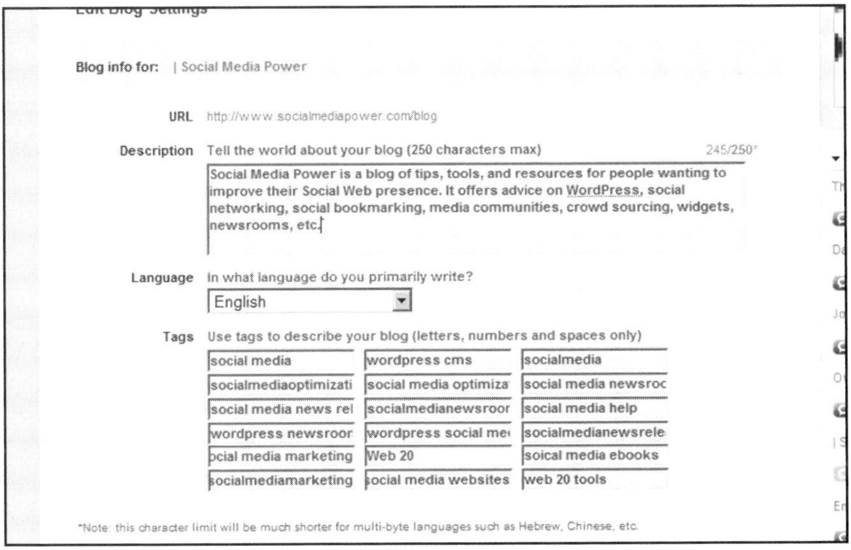

Here are two places to start:

- For RSS feeds: http://www.rss-specifications.com/rss-submission.htm
- For blogs: http://www.blog-connection.com/submit-blogs.htm

Refer to the resource CD for an extensive list of directories.

If you want to know the most important directories, check what Ping-O-Matic or FeedBurner submit to. See Figures 3.40 and 3.41 on Page 83.

Submission Services and Software

To save time, and perhaps get more exposure, you can use submission software like RSS Submit from Dummy Software,[21] or a submission service like FeedShot.[22]

---

[21] http://dummysoftware.com
[22] http://www.feedshot.com/

Other Ways to Promote Your Blog or Feed

Add Your Feed to Feed Readers

The best way to get your feed listed in the top feed readers is to get an account with them and subscribe to your own feed. See "The Feed Reader" section on Page 48. Be sure to get accounts with NetVibes,[23] PageFlakes,[24] Google Reader,[25] iGoogle,[26] My.Yahoo,[27] and My.MSN.[28]

Social Networking and Other Social Sites

In Chapter 12, "Pulling It All Together," we discuss integrating as many of your social tools as possible. For instance, you can pipe your feeds or blogs directly into your MySpace page, Facebook page, Squidoo Lens, etc.

Whenever you implement a new social tool or get an account with a social networking site, check to see if adding one or more feeds or blogs to your account is an option.

Feed Widgets

Figure 3.45 shows part of Social Media Power's front page. From here visitors can subscribe to their feed using the "Subscribe" button, which is an "AddtoAny" feed widget placed on their site (see Page 52). Visitors can also subscribe to the Social Media Power feed by clicking on the Widgetbox[29] widget that says, "Get my blog as a widget from Widgetbox." Clicking on this box reveals a stylized feed that can be customized by the user. Read more about feed widgets in Chapter 9, "Widgets & Badges."

---

[23] http://www.netvibes.com/

[24] http://www.pageflakes.com/

[25] www.google.com/reader

[26] http://www.google.com/ig

[27] my.yahoo.com

[28] http://msn.com

[29] http://www.widgetbox.com

Figure 3.45. Feed Widgets on SocialMediaPower.com

Social Bookmarking (only applies to blogs)

Figure 3.46 shows a couple of ways for visitors to save Social Media Power's blog to social bookmarking sites. They can bookmark the entire Social Media Power site to the social bookmarking site of their choice

Figure 3.46. Sharing Sites Using Social Bookmarking Widgets

by clicking on the "Share/Save" button in the right sidebar, or they can bookmark individual posts by clicking on the "Bookmark" button that is placed at the end of each post. These buttons are "AddtoAny" widgets and WordPress plugins (see Figure 3.47). Read more about these in Chapter 9, "Widgets and Badges."

Figure 3.47. Sharing Posts Using Social Bookmarking Widgets

Keeping Your Feed Healthy

It would be nice if you could create a feed once and assume it will never go out-of-date or that it will remain error free, but that is not the case. And, if you are not monitoring your feed subscriptions regularly, you may not even notice there is a problem.

If your feeds are burned to FeedBurner, go to the "Troubleshootize" menu to troubleshoot any problems with your feed. Running the "Feed Medic" utility (see Figure 3.48) on each of your feeds periodically can help avoid problems.

Figure 3.48. FeedBurner's Feed Medic

You can also go to W3's Feed Validation Service[30] to validate and troubleshoot your feed if necessary.

---

[30] http://validator.w3.org/feed/

An Optimization Plan for Your Blog or RSS Feed

- Your Content
    - › Edit your content
    - › Optimize titles, categories, tags, and links
- Attach signatures to your posts
- Search Engine Optimization (SEO)
    - › Implement The All In One SEO pack in WordPress
    - › Use pretty permalinks
    - › Optimize external links to your site
- FeedBurner
    - › Burn your feed or blog
    - › Activate services
        - Browser Friendly
        - Smart Feed
        - FeedFlare
        - Feed Image Burner
        - Email Subscriptions
        - PingShot
        - Chicklet Chooser
- Directories
    - › Submit feed or blogs to directories
    - › Use FeedBurner's PingShot
    - › Use feed submission software or service
- Other Ways to Optimize
    - › Submit to feed readers
    - › Advertise your feed
    - › Add to the rest of your social presence
    - › Use feed widgets
    - › Place social bookmarking buttons

This plan is recreated as a form on the resource CD.

This Chapter On The Resource CD

- Further Reading
- Linkable Resources
- Fillable Forms:
  › Planning Your RSS Feed Worksheet
  › RSS Feed Entries Worksheet
  › Planning Your Blog Worksheet
  › Blog Entries Worksheet
  › Blog Directory Cheat Sheet
  › Blog Directory Submission Tracking Form
  › Blog/RSS Feed Optimization Plan

4 Building a WordPress Powered Website

Using WordPress As A CMS

If you are in a place where you can rebuild your Website or start a new one, it is recommended that you use a content management system like WordPress to build it. RSS feed and widget technology is already built into the WordPress platform, so social media and Web 2.0 optimization can be achieved easily and naturally.

This chapter will only cover *some* of the features WordPress has to offer. We will only cover the essentials you need to create and maintain your site. You will find, however, a plethora of information in the WordPress documentation,[1] as well as on the WordPress forums.[2] There are many people on these forums who are more than happy to help you out.

The examples used in this chapter are based on WordPress versions 2.5.1 and 2.6. See Appendix D, "WordPress 2.7," to see the changes that have taken place in the latest version of WordPress.

---

[1]http://wordpress.org/
[2]http://wordpress.org/support/

What Does it Mean to Use WordPress as a CMS?

By definition, a CMS is an application that is used to create, edit, manage, and publish content in an organized way. Web applications like WordPress, Joomla!,[3] and Drupal[4] do this by storing information in a database, and using scripting languages like PHP to access the information and place it on a Website.

Using a common scripting language like PHP makes it easy for developers to create add-ons or "plugins" for anybody to upload and use with a particular CMS. Plugins are applications that perform a specialized function that the original CMS may be lacking. Some examples of plugins include search engine optimization applications, contact forms, survey applications, and image galleries.

CMS applications also use cascading style sheets (CSS) to make it easy for users to change the look and feel of their site, and for developers to contribute templates or themes that others can use to customize their sites. Theme developers also use PHP to control the overall functionality of a CMS.

WordPress is one of the easiest content management systems to learn and there are countless plugins and themes to choose from. The remainder of this chapter will be dedicated to showing you how to build a Website using WordPress, so many of these definitions will become more clear as we progress.

On Open Source Etiquette

The CMS applications I mention in this section are all open source applications. What that means to you is that the applications are free, as are most of the plugins and themes developed for them. To a developer, it means that there is a vast community of people working together to create a quality application they can be proud of.

The developers have put a lot of time into these projects. Please show them respect by:

---

[3]http://www.joomla.org/
[4]http://www.drupal.org/

- Making donations to the open source developers whose plugins you use regularly
- Never deleting the credits from the footer of a theme or a plugin

When using the support forums of an open source application:

- Always search the forums thoroughly for an answer to your question before posting.
- Give back if you can: Check the recent posts for questions from newcomers you might be able to answer.

Diversity Of WordPress Sites

Many people shy away from using a CMS because they fear their site will look too "templated." The figures throughout this chapter show a variety of sites that were all built using the WordPress platform. These sites seem to have little in common, but, as we will see in the next section, every site is composed of the same general content areas that are easily customized.

These sites began with an existing WordPress theme that was customized to fit their needs. Customizing a theme is not a difficult task, especially if all you want to change are colors and images. There are even themes that come with built-in options to change colors, header images, fonts, and other features.

Figure 4.1. EmpoweredbyWordPress.com

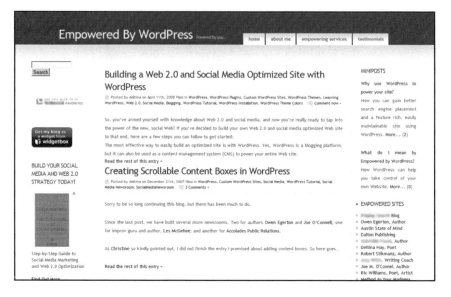

Figure 4.2. PureSoapbox.com, Part One

Figure 4.3. RicWilliams.com

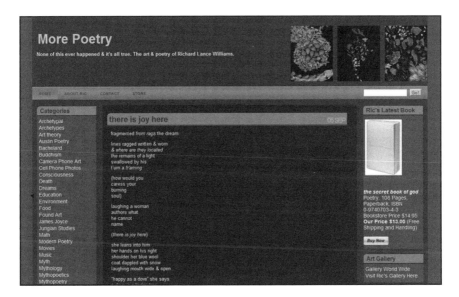

Figure 4.4. PlumbSocial.com

Figure 4.5. LesMcgehee.com

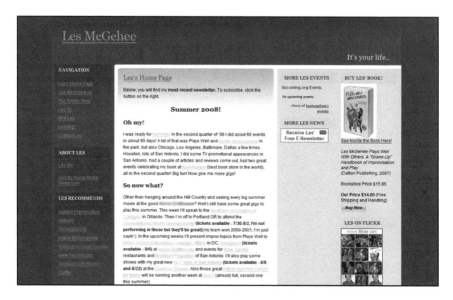

Figure 4.7. DaltonPublishing.com

Figure 4.6. SocialMediaPower.com

Figure 4.8. PureSoapbox.com, Part Two

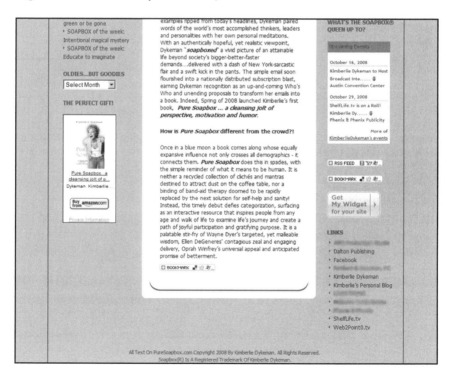

The Anatomy Of A WordPress Site

Before we go into specifics, let's look at the main elements of a WordPress site. Each of the examples in this chapter has these general areas, just represented a little differently. Refer to the images on the previous pages.

The Header

The header area is where the main header image is located, along with the title and tag line of the blog site. It is also where the navigation menu is typically located, if the theme has one.

The header can be as simple as the blog title and description like Figure 4.1, composed of a custom header image like Figure 4.2, or a combination of both as in Figures 4.3 and 4.4.

The header is usually the first element you want to customize to suit your own needs. For instance, you could easily replace the entire header with your own image and/or logo of the same dimensions. This is explained in greater detail when we discuss choosing themes and customizing.

Navigation Menu

The navigation menu is usually part of the header of the site, but is optional. Figure 4.5 shows a site without main navigation in the header. In this case the navigation is part of the sidebar elements.

The Main Body Area

This is the area where the actual blog entries reside. WordPress refers to this as the "content area." You can easily customize the content area by changing how many blog entries display on a page or whether you want to cut the entries short with a "read more" option, and many other ways.

Beginning with version 2.1 of WordPress, you have the option of having either a static home page as your front page, or your blog entries as the front page. If you choose a static home page, your blog will become another page that you would add to your navigation menu as opposed to the home page. Figures 4.1 and 4.3 on Page 94 show a site with blog entries on the front page. Figures 4.6 and 4.7 show a static home page.

The content area is usually located in the middle of the site as in Figures 4.1 and 4.2 on Page 94. They also could be off to the side or on the top as in Figures 4.4 (Page 95), 4.6, and 4.7

The Sidebars

The columns on either side of the content area (or below in some cases) are called "sidebars." They hold many of the other elements of your site, such as links, categories, search tools, recent blog entries, archived entries, photos, video streams, RSS feeds, widgets, badges, advertisements, etc. Sidebars are also where you implement many of the plugins you add to the site.

Typically, sidebars are on either side of the content area as seen in Figures 4.1 and 4.2 on Page 94. Many themes get more creative with their placement. Figure 4.5 on Page 96 has three sidebars: one on the left of the content area and two to the right. In Figure 4.6 on Page 97, there is one wide sidebar on the top of the left area of the site and two smaller sidebars underneath the wider one. Figure 4.7 on Page 96 shows three sidebars under the content area.

The Footer

This is the area of the site where credit is given. Do not remove the credit to WordPress or to the theme designer from the footer of a WordPress site. There are a lot of people who have donated their time to this free, open source project, and it is never good form not to give them due credit. You should place your own copyright statement in the footer as well. Figure 4.8 on Page 97 shows a footer area.

Sidebar Widgets

Sidebar widgets are the different elements or modules you can place on your sidebars. You can have as many of these widgets as you like and can arrange them however you choose.

Each widget performs a specific function. For example, in Figure 4.5 (Page 96) on the left sidebar of the site, the widgets are:

- "Navigation" which lists all of the pages on the site.
- "About Les" and "Les Recommends" which are lists of external links.

On the right sidebars the widgets are:

- "More Les Events" - a widget from the social calendar Upcoming.org that lists his upcoming events.
- "More Les News" - a widget from the newsletter generator Constant Contact that allows users to subscribe to his newsletter.
- "Buy Les's Book" - a widget that can be used to purchase his book using his Paypal account.
- "Les on Flickr" - a Flickr widget that displays his photos in a little flash "badge."

WordPress comes with a number of standard widgets that perform functions specific to the functionality of your WordPress site, such as listing blog categories (Figure 4.3), search features, recent posts, tag clouds, etc.

You can create your own custom widgets easily by placing text or HTML/Java code in what is called a "text" widget. This is how you create most of the widgets and badges you accumulate from the Social Web.

Some custom widgets in our examples include:

- The Flickr badge in Figure 4.5
- The buy-now buttons for books on Figures 4.3, 4.2, and 4.5
- The widgets for sharing on social bookmarking sites in Figures 4.7 and 4.6
- The widgets feeding in blog entries from other sites as in Figures 4.4 and 4.22

For a more detailed discussion of widgets and badges, go to Chapter 9, "Widgets & Badges."

Static Pages

Static pages are the pages of a WordPress site that do not contain blog entries. You can link to these pages from the navigation menu. Figures 4.9 and 4.10 demonstrate static pages. You can have as many pages as you like on your site and it is easy to add and populate them.

Figure 4.9. DaltonPublishing.com, Static Page

Figure 4.10. SocialMediaPower.com, Static Page

Installing WordPress As A CMS

Know the Difference Between Your *Domain* Account and Your *Hosting* Account

When you register your domain name, an account is created for you with the company that sold you the domain name. This account has its own user name and password that you can use to change settings or account information. Just owning the domain name, however, does not mean you have a place to put a Website. You need a hosting account for that.

If you get your hosting account with a different company than the one that sold you the domain name, you need to change what are called "name servers" in your *domain* account that tell the domain name to point to the proper *hosting* account. This is not difficult to do and most hosting companies have good instructions to show you how.

Choosing a Hosting Account for Your WordPress Site

There are some minimum requirements[5] that your hosting account must have in order to run WordPress properly:

- PHP 4.3 or greater
- MySQL 4.0 or greater
- The mod_rewrite Apache module

Apache or Litespeed is also HIGHLY recommended.

Your host will be able to tell you whether or not they meet the requirements.

A word of caution: Some hosting companies may meet these requirements, but if yours is a free account (having shared servers), many WordPress features and plugins will not run properly. Godaddy.com's free account option falls into this category.

WordPress has a few hosting companies they recommend.[6] I use Westhost.com because of their reliability and exceptional tech support.

---

[5]http://wordpress.org/about/requirements/
[6]http://wordpress.org/hosting/

Their personal starter plan runs under $10 a month and is all you will likely need.

Once you have a hosting account that runs WordPress effectively, be sure to point your domain to your new hosting account by changing your name servers, if applicable. Your hosting company can give you instructions for your particular account.

Be Careful of the One-Click WordPress Install Feature Offered by Many Hosts

Installing WordPress as a CMS means that you are going to install it into the root directory as opposed to a subdirectory of your hosting account. Most of the one-click install options only install WordPress in a subdirectory. You also want to have more control over the name of your database for security reasons.

FTP Access

FTP stands for File Transfer Protocol. FTP is the means by which you upload files to your hosting site. You need to use FTP to upload WordPress files if you decide to install it yourself, as well as to upload themes and plugins as we discuss later in this chapter. Luckily, there is a fantastic plugin for Firefox that makes it easy for you to gain FTP access to your site.

First, if you are not using it already, download and install Mozilla Firefox.[7] Next, download and install the plugin FireFTP.[8] Go to Tools on your Firefox task bar and open FireFTP. Create an account to connect you to your hosting account. Contact your host for that information. A good hosting company has tech support readily available to walk you through how to upload files using FireFTP.

One free desktop FTP application is Filezilla.[9] Two good (but not free) applications are WS_FTP[10] and CuteFTP.[11] WS_FTP is best for PCs, while CuteFTP is best for Macs.

---

[7]http://www.mozilla.com
[8]http://fireftp.mozdev.org/
[9] http://filezilla-project.org/
[10]www.ipswitch.com/WS_FTP
[11]www.CuteFTP.com

Installing WordPress

Some of the preliminary steps required to install WordPress can be a bit involved, so we have reserved that topic for Appendix A, "Installing WordPress." This appendix provides a step-by-step installation guide for the do-it-yourselfer. Once WordPress is installed, continue on to the next section.

A Brief Look At The WordPress Dashboard

Figure 4.11 shows a typical WordPress dashboard. From here, you post blog entries, create and edit pages, install plugins and themes, and manage all of the settings of your site.

From the "Write" menu, you can write blog posts, pages, or links. From the "Manage" menu you can manage categories, edit posts and pages, manage your media library, and much more. The "Design" menu is where you customize themes and manage your widgets. The "Comments" menu is for viewing and approving other's comments to your blog posts. To the right are the Settings, Plugins, and Users menus. These are where you manage the overall settings of your site, as well as most of the plugins you install.

Figure 4.11. WordPress Dashboard

Important Initial Settings

Before you start to build your site, there are some important initial settings that should be in place, and tasks that should be performed.

Security Settings

Open source platforms like WordPress can be a target for hackers, but there are precautions you can take to protect your site. We took a couple of these precautions when we first installed WordPress: We gave our database a name other than "wordpress" and gave our tables a prefix other than "wp." These safeguards are a good first step.

The next step is to always keep the latest version of WordPress installed. The developers are continuously adding security fixes and other features. Most of the time, this keeps your site secure—this and good password protection.

In the interest of security, you need to change your administrative user name and password as soon as you have installed WordPress. Sign in to WordPress using the "admin" user name and password that WordPress sent you during the installation.

At the WordPress dashboard, go to "Users" in the upper right corner. Create a new user with the "role" of Administrator. See Figure 4.12. Now, logout of WordPress (upper right of the dashboard). Log back in using the new user name and password. Go to "Users" again and delete the old "admin" user.

The final step to securing your WordPress site is to install the WP-Security Scan plugin,[12] but we will cover that in the "Plugins You Will Want to Install Right Away" section on Page 114.

Other Settings and Tasks to Complete Right Away

Creating a Static Home Page

If you want your front page to serve as a normal home page, you need to complete a couple of preliminary tasks. First, create two pages named

---

[12]http://wordpress.org/extend/plugins/wp-security-scan/

Figure 4.12. Adding a User in WordPress

Add New User

Users cannot currently register themselves, but you can m

Username (required)	newadminuser
First Name	
Last Name	
E-mail (required)	
Website	
Password (twice)	
Role	Administrator

"Home" and "Blog." Refer to the "Building Your Pages" on Page 116 if you do not know how to create pages yet.

Once you have these two pages created, go to "Settings/Reading" and change the settings according to Figure 4.13.

Permalinks

Go to "Settings/Permalinks" and set your permalink structure to anything but the default. This keeps your links optimized for search engines. If you are interested, you can read more about permalinks on the WordPress codex.[13]

There are many other settings to examine and set to your needs, but the ones discussed here should be done before you start testing themes or populating your site.

---

[13]http://codex.wordpress.org/Using_Permalinks

Figure 4.13. WordPress Settings

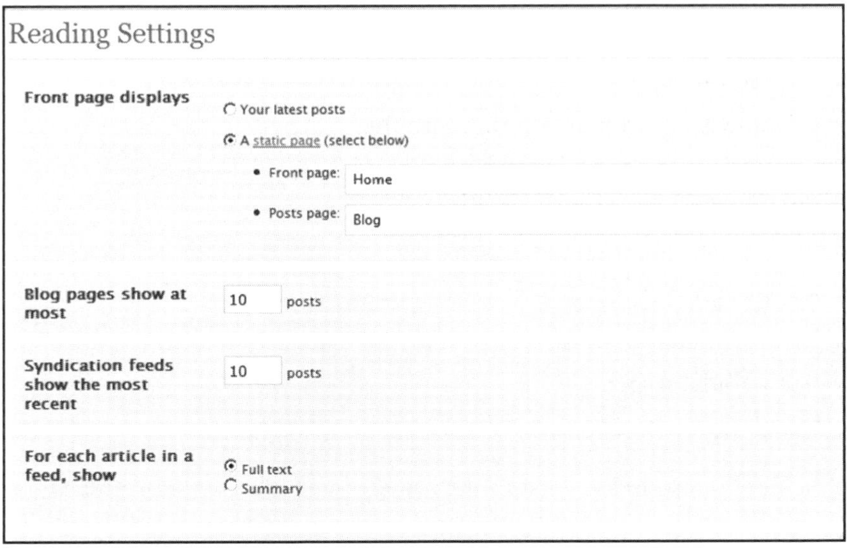

Reading Settings

Front page displays	○ Your latest posts
	● A static page (select below)
	• Front page: Home
	• Posts page: Blog
Blog pages show at most	10 posts
Syndication feeds show the most recent	10 posts
For each article in a feed, show	● Full text ○ Summary

Planning Your Site

Make an *ambitious* list of what you would like to have on your site. Don't hold back on any idea you may have for your site based on an assumption that it will be too difficult or too expensive to implement. Chances are that even if the function is not built into WordPress, somebody has written a plugin to accomplish it.

Search the plugins available for WordPress.[14] They can give you ideas on the types of things you can add to your site. You will discover that you can easily utilize plugins to accomplish seemingly difficult tasks.

Beyond the normal functionality of a Website, I find these are pretty typical functions most entrepreneurs, small businesses, authors, and publishers are looking for:

- Image galleries
- Streaming video
- E-commerce
- Amazon widgets

---

[14]http://wordpress.org/extend/plugins/

- Blogs/Podcasts/Vidcasts
- Random quote generators
- Newsletters
- RSS feed subscription sign up
- Bookmarking/crowd-sourcing buttons
- Surveys
- Mailing list sign-up
- RSS feeds from other sources
- Events listings
- Forms for submissions
- Banner advertising
- Social media newsrooms

You should also make a list of the types of widgets you want to have on your sidebars (see the discussion on sidebar widgets on Page 99).

Once you have the list of features and widgets you want on your site, draw out a plan for where each of them will be placed on your site. This helps you know what to look for in a theme.

Next, make a list of the static pages your site needs to start. These may include an "about" page that tells visitors about you or your site, a gallery or portfolio page, a contact page, etc. You can add as many pages as you need, whenever you like, so just outline the ones you know you need right out of the gate.

Refer to the resource CD for a form that helps you plan your WordPress Website.

Themes

Armed with a thorough plan, move on to choosing a theme. WordPress themes control more that just the look and feel of your site—they ultimately determine your site's functionality.

Look at the figures throughout this chapter. They demonstrate how themes control the number and placement of the sidebars, the placement and behavior of the navigation menus, the layout of the pages, the fonts and colors, and so forth.

It is important that you understand that you can change the theme you use for your WordPress site and that it will not affect the content on your site. This is one of the features that is so appealing about a CMS: You can easily change or update a Website with little effort.

Choosing a Theme

There are many themes to choose from at WordPress.org.[15] There are also many places to purchase themes. A few places I recommend are Template Monster,[16] iThemes,[17] and Premium Themes.[18] You can find more themes by searching Google for "wordpress themes" or by referencing the resource CD.

Use your plan to decide whether you need a one, two, or three-column theme (there are also four-column themes). When in doubt, decide on one more column than you think you need. It is easier to populate an extra column (or remove it) than it is to try and cram too much onto too few columns.

If you are choosing free themes, choose at least 12 themes that you like. You may find that for various reasons you will not be able to use many themes that you choose. Try to make your choice based only on the overall look and feel of a theme, with the idea that the colors, fonts, images, and most anything else can be customized to fit your needs.

Installing Your Theme

Both themes and plugins are installed by first uploading their files to your hosting site using FTP as explained on Page 103. When you find a theme you want to use, download it, unzip the file, and upload the entire directory via FTP to the folder wp-content/themes on your hosting account.

---

[15] http://wordpress.org/extend/themes/
[16] http://www.templatemonster.com/wordpress-themes.php
[17] http://ithemes.com/
[18] http://premiumthemes.net/

Once a theme's files are uploaded, go to "Design" from the WordPress dashboard, and see that it is now listed as an available theme for you to select. Figure 4.14 shows what the panel looks like with several themes available. To select a theme, simply click on it. You may find that once you view a theme with your own content, you no longer like it, which is why I recommend choosing several themes.

Figure 4.14. Installing a WordPress Theme

You can read more about installing and using themes at WordPress. org.[19]

Customizing Your Theme

You may find that you would like a theme if only it had different colors, or the font were larger, or it had different images, etc. Many of those things are easily remedied, so do not give up on a theme too quickly.

Many themes automatically come with options that let you change the colors, fonts, or header images. Even if a theme does not come with such options, all that is required to customize most themes is a little knowledge

---

[19]http://codex.wordpress.org/Using_Themes

of cascading style sheets (CSS). Usually, the changes to a CSS file that you would want to make are minor, so don't be put off by this prospect.

There are good tutorials[20] for using CSS, and the forums at WordPress. org[21] are a fantastic resource. WordPress has a good section on the topic as well.[22]

Plugins

Plugins are what give WordPress its tremendous power and flexibility. Most plugins can be found on the WordPress site[23]. As you browse these plugins, you soon realize that there is little you will not be able to do with your new Website.

Refer to your plan to decide the types of plugins you want to install. For instance, if your plan includes an image gallery, search for a plugin that displays images to your specifications. Sometimes it takes several tries before you find the best plugin for the job. If you cannot find the perfect plugin on the WordPress site, you can do a Google search for plugins to purchase as well.

Installing and Setting Up Your Plugins

Just as for themes, you download a plugin's files, unzip them, and upload them via FTP to the folder "wp-content/plugins." Before you do so, however, read the readme.txt file that came with the plugin. Sometimes a plugin has special instructions for installation.

You can view your uploaded plugins by going to the "Plugins" menu in the WordPress panel. From there, you can activate or deactivate plugins. See Figure 4.15. This screen shot shows a number of plugins that are being utilized for this WordPress site, like a random image generator that changes out the header image of the site on every visit, a shopping

---

[20]http://www.w3schools.com/css/
[21]http://wordpress.org/support/
[22]http://codex.wordpress.org/CSS
[23]http://wordpress.org/extend/plugins/

Figure 4.15. WordPress Plugins Menu

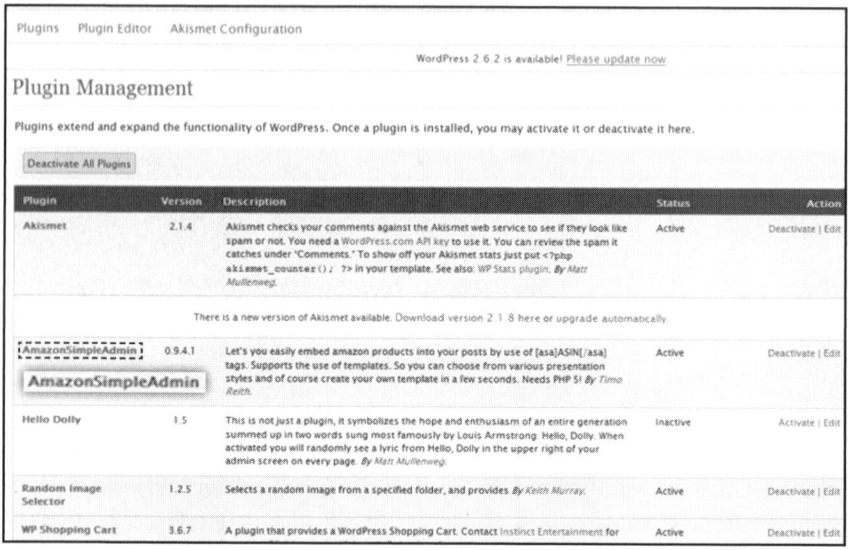

cart plugin that serves as a complete e-commerce solution, and a plugin that lets you easily embed Amazon products into your posts using simple tags. (The Amazon plugin is demonstrated in the following section.)

Once a plugin is activated, read its documentation to learn how to integrate it into your WordPress site. A plugin should not be too complicated to implement. A general rule of thumb is this: If you can't get the plugin to work on the second try, get another plugin to accomplish the task at hand.

A Plugin in Action

Figure 4.16 shows part of a static WordPress page that lists a series of Amazon books. These boxes are pulled from Amazon using a plugin called "AmazonSimpleAdmin" (see Figure 4.15). The plugin allows you to place Amazon books (you can also place other products) in the body of a page or post by placing the book's ISBN between two tags. The plugin then pulls the book's information from Amazon, and displays the information accordingly.

Figure 4.16. AmazonSimpleAdmin Plugin

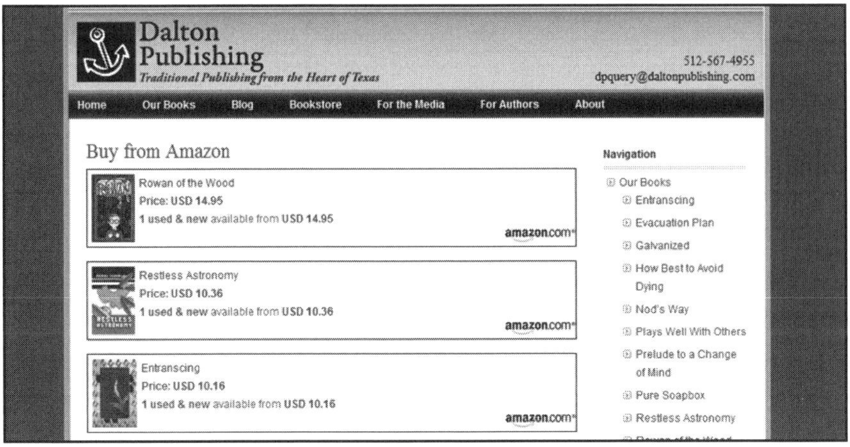

Once the plugin is installed (by uploading and activating as discussed in "Installing and Setting Up Your Plugins" on Page 111), you can use it to embed ISBNs in between tags as follows: [asa]ISBN[/asa].

Figure 4.17 shows how one would embed the ISBNs of three different books using this plugin into a WordPress page (more on creating pages on Page 116). The plugin then pulls the information from each book, and displays it nicely on a WordPress page as seen in Figure 4.16.

Figure 4.17. WordPress Plugins in Action

Hopefully, this demonstrates how to effortlessly implement what may seem like a complicated task.

Plugins You Want to Install Right Away

- Akismet: This plugin comes with WordPress and is used as a spam filter for blog comments.
- WordPress.com Stats:[24] This plugin tracks your blog statistics.
- WP-Security Scan:[25] This is the plugin that was mentioned in the section above on security. It is highly recommended that you install and activate this plugin.
- WordPress Exploit Scanner:[26] This plugin searches the files on your Website, and the posts and comments tables of your database for anything suspicious.
- All in One SEO Pack:[27] This optimizes your site for search engines.

Setting Up Your Sidebars

You create most of the content of your sidebars using sidebar widgets. As discussed on Page 100, there are standard widgets as well as "text" widgets that you can populate with your own content. These text widgets can contain HTML, JavaScript, Flash, or plain text. Some of the plugins you install may also come as ready-made widgets you can place on your sidebars.

Figure 4.18 shows the WordPress dashboard for placing widgets (go to "Design/Widgets" to get there). As you can see, there are many standard widgets to choose from: Pages, Archives, Links, etc. To place a widget on a sidebar, just click on "add" next to the widget. You can position them however you like as well. The number of sidebars available will depend on your theme.

Figure 4.18 shows the widget panel corresponding to the left sidebar in Figure 4.19. The top widget is a text widget that contains the code to display the Widgetbox.com widget (the "Get My Widget for your site" button). The next widget is a standard "Links" widget that displays the list of links that appear underneath the Widgetbox widget.

---

[24] http://wordpress.org/extend/plugins/stats/

[25] http://wordpress.org/extend/plugins/wp-security-scan/

[26] http://wordpress.org/extend/plugins/exploit-scanner/

[27] http://wordpress.org/extend/plugins/all-in-one-seo-pack/

Figure 4.18. Managing Widgets in WordPress

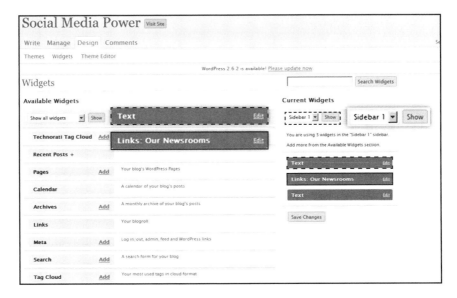

Figure 4.19. Sidebar Widgets in WordPress

In the right sidebar of Figure 4.19, there are a number of text widgets that display content from other sites or perform functions.

Figure 4.20 shows the admin area where the HTML code is placed to create the "text" widget that displays the social media primer banner at the top of the sidebar (see Figure 4.19 on Page 115). We discuss this process at greater length in Chapter 9, "Widgets & Badges."

Figure 4.20. Sidebar Widgets in WordPress

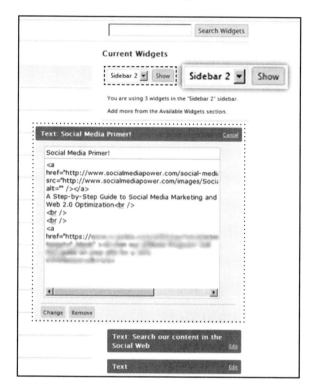

Building Your Pages

The static pages of your WordPress site can contain the same content as any regular Website page (HTML page). You can create pages that contain simple text or pages as complex as fully interactive image or video galleries, and beyond.

A Basic Page

Creating the pages of your WordPress site is a simple process. For a page that only contains text, go to "Write/Pages." Put the name of your page as the title, the content of the page in the body area, and click "publish." Figure 4.21 shows the "About" page depicted in Figure 4.22. Note that the page is automatically added to your navigation menu, if your theme has one.

Figure 4.21. Creating a Page in WordPress

The above is really an oversimplified example of a WordPress page. There are many settings you can use to make your page closer to how you would like it to look or behave, like whether you will allow comments, the order of the page in the navigation menu, whether it will have images, or what its title and description will look like to search engines. Again, refer to WordPress[28] for more complete documentation.

---

[28] http://codex.wordpress.org/Pages

Figure 4.22. SocialMediaPower.com, Static Page

More Advanced Pages

As mentioned before, a WordPress page can accommodate just about anything a regular HTML page can. The example on Page 101 demonstrated how using plugins can transform a WordPress page into anything from a gallery to a shopping cart. Figure 4.23 shows the HTML view of a WordPress page. You could, therefore, design your page in a WYSIWYG editor like Dreamweaver, and paste the resulting code into your WordPress page. The code in Figure 4.23 produces the home page shown in Figure 4.24.

Figure 4.23. Creating an HTML Page in WordPress

Figure 4.24. SocialMediaPower.com

Custom Page Templates

Notice how each of the pages we have demonstrated so far has the same sidebars, headers, etc. as the rest of the site. But what if you want a page that is different, like one with no sidebar, a different sidebar, or a different page header? That is not a problem with most themes as long as you are willing to do a little bit of coding.

Figure 4.25 shows a page from the same site as Figure 4.24, but with no sidebar. This page required a wider body area to accommodate the portfolio and was accomplished by creating a custom page template that did not include the PHP code that included sidebars. To learn how to create custom page templates go to the WordPress documentation.[29] There are also many themes that come with their own custom page templates.

---

[29] http://codex.wordpress.org/Pages#Creating_Your_Own_Page_Template

Figure 4.25. SocialMediaPower.com, Static Page

Posting Blog Entries

Now that your site is in place, you can start adding blog posts to keep it dynamic and interactive. Add blog posts by going to "Write/Posts." Refer to Chapter 3, "RSS Feeds & Blogs" for following good blogging guidelines and creating optimized blog posts.

This Chapter On The Resource CD

- Further Reading
- Linkable Resources
- Fillable Forms:
    › Planning Your WordPress Website, with Diagrams

5 Podcasting, Vidcasting, & Webcasting

A podcast is a series of audio or video files that is distributed over the Internet. What distinguishes a podcast from just any audio or video file you can download or stream from the Internet is that a podcast can be syndicated and subscribed to. This is because a podcast, like a blog, is an RSS feed. A podcast is really just a blog composed of episodes of audio or video entries rather than text, and can be subscribed to like any blog/feed. You can even add podcast entries to an existing blog, rather than having a stand alone podcast.

Read Chapter 3, "RSS Feeds & Blogs," before proceeding, since most of the tools and tactics covered in that chapter apply to podcasts as well. Chapter 4, "Building a WordPress Powered Website," also provides a review of RSS feed and blogging technology.

A podcast includes both audio and video files. There are other terms like vidcast and vlog that refer to video feeds, but in this book the term podcast refers to both types of files. All of the examples in this chapter are for audio files, but the same process applies equally to video files unless stated otherwise.

The general plan for creating and promoting your podcast looks something like this:

1. Record and prepare a podcast episode (either audio or video).
2. Upload the episode to the Internet.
3. Publish the episode to a blog, Website, or service.
4. Create your podcast feed.
5. Burn your podcast feed to FeedBurner.
6. Promote your podcast on your Website or blog, and in podcast directories.
7. For each new podcast episode, repeat steps 1, 2, and 3.

What Will Your Podcast Be About?

Before you create your first episode, you should be clear about the purpose of your podcast. Will you be recording interviews, lectures, or panel discussions? Clips of your own music? Reciting excerpts from your book? Reading stories for children? Or just recreating existing blog posts as podcast episodes? What is the premise of the podcast?

When people subscribe to your podcast they will have an expectation of consistency as to the topics your episodes will cover. So planning ahead at this stage is important.

Publishing Options For Your Podcast

Using a Blogging Platform

If you have an existing blog, this is a natural choice for publishing your podcasts. All you need to do is add podcast episodes similar to how you add blog posts. Even if you only post podcasts and not blog posts, a blogging platform like WordPress is still the best solution, since all of the technology is already built in. There are also many good podcasting plugins for WordPress[1] that will help you streamline the process.

---

[1] http://wordpress.org/extend/plugins

Publishing to Your Website

A podcast is an RSS feed, so to publish a podcast to your Website, you need to know how to create an RSS feed. Read about this in Chapter 3, "RSS Feeds & Blogs" and in Appendix B, "Creating Your Own RSS Feed," which also includes a section on podcasts.

You can also use software like FeedForAll to create your podcast feed. See the "Using Software to Create Your RSS Feed" section on Page 57.

Using a Service

There are a number of good services out there that can help you record, publish, and promote a podcast. Audio Acrobat[2] is one of them; HipCast[3] is another.

If you do not plan to have a blog any time soon, but still want to publish a podcast, using a service is a good solution.

Creating And Uploading Podcast Episodes

Preparing the Script and Key Terms

Below is a typical podcast script. You can get royalty-free music for your podcast episodes at a number of sites on the Internet.[4] Always make sure that the music you use is royalty-free and offered freely for use in podcasts, and give the author credit. This script outline can also be found on the resource CD.

- Opening (30-60 seconds)
  - › Introduce the podcast as a whole.
  - › This should be the same for each episode.
  - › Mention the name of the podcast, what its purpose is, and the URL where it can be found.
  - › Introduce yourself and who you are.
  - › Introduce the topic of the episode.

[2] http://www.audioacrobat.com/
[3] http://www.hipcast.com/
[4] http://www.podsafeaudio.com/

> › Mention the episode number.
> › Introduce guests if you have any.

- Opening Jingle (30 seconds)
- Main Topics (6 to 12 minutes)
  > › Depends on the type of episode you are recording.
  > › An informational podcast is typically only six minutes long.
  > › A panel or interview could be as long as twelve minutes.
- Intermission (30 seconds)
  > › Break up longer episodes with an intermission.
  > › Use music for the intermission.
- Closing (2 minutes)
  > › Thank your guests if you have any.
  > › Thank the audience for listening.
  > › Announce the next episode topic.
  > › Repeat the podcast URL.
- Closing Jingle (60 seconds)

Make a list of the best key terms for each episode and repeat these key terms at every opportunity that feels natural in your script. Of course, you can write the script first and extract the best (most repeated) key terms for use in the metadata and landing page of the episode (more about that later).

Recording Episodes

There are many programs you can buy or download for audio or video recording. Audacity®[5] is a good freeware choice for recording audio. You can download, install, and begin using this software in about 30 minutes. You need to get a decent microphone for your computer first or the quality of your podcasts will suffer. USB microphones seem to have higher ratings than others.

Once you have your script written, start Audacity, and record your podcast. Figure 5.1 shows an example script open in one window, and Audacity in another. It really is as easy as hitting the record button and talking into your mic. You can monitor your voice levels with the graphics and pause at any time and resume.

[5] http://www.audacity.sourceforge.net

Figure 5.1. Creating a Podcast Episode Using Audacity

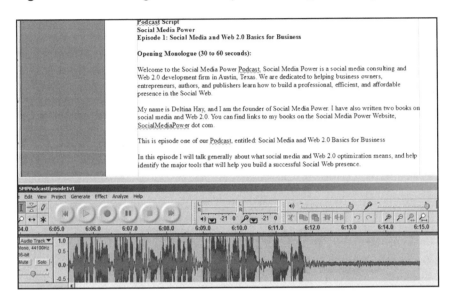

Adding music is easy, too. Figure 5.2 shows our finished podcast episode in one Audacity window, and a royalty-free music MP3[6] in another. To

Figure 5.2. Creating a Podcast Episode Using Audacity

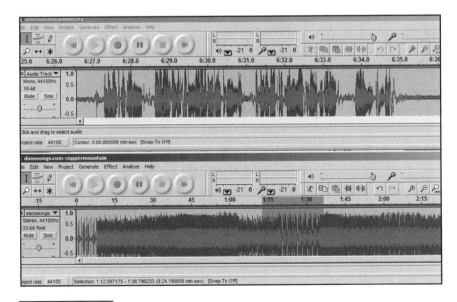

---

[6] http://danosongs.com/

copy part of the music into your podcast, just select the portion you want and paste it into your podcast where you want it to play.

Once your podcast episode is recorded, save it as an MP3 file. Go to File/ Export as MP3 to do this in Audacity. Figure 5.3 shows the export box. Be sure and complete every option in this box. This is the "metadata" of your audio file and is important for optimization (see the "Optimizing Your Podcast" section on Page 130). You want to repeat the key terms you generated in the "Preparing the Script and Key Terms" section on Page 123. Repeat key terms in Title, Artist, Album, and Comments.

Figure 5.3. Creating a Podcast Episode Using Audacity

Uploading Episodes

The next step is to upload your MP3 file to your hosting site. Using FTP is the preferred method for getting your files onto your site (see Page 103). Figure 5.4 shows how we have uploaded our example podcast to a folder on our hosting site called "podcasts." We created this folder at the main level of our site, so that the direct link to our podcasts will always be   http://www.socialmediapower.com/podcasts/nameofpodcast.mp3. (Whenever you create a folder on a hosting site, and place a file in the folder, you are also creating a link to that file that can be accessed via the Internet, as demonstrated in the previous example.)

Figure 5.4. Uploading a Podcast Episode

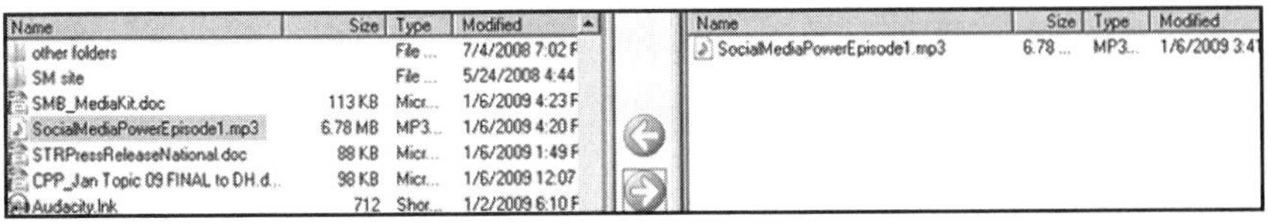

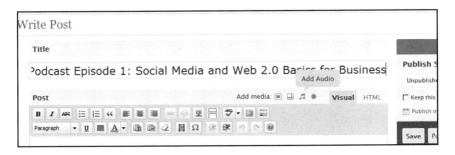

If you are using a service to create and host your podcast, however, they may have different uploading procedures.

Publishing Your Podcast

If you are using a service like Audio Acrobat (see the "Publishing Options For Your Podcast" section on Page 122), you should follow their guidelines for publishing your podcast episodes.

To a Blogging Platform

Figure 5.5 shows the WordPress posting interface. Click on the audio icon to the left of "Add media" as shown. From here you can post your podcast episode just like you would a regular blog post, only you provide the link to the actual episode file (see Figure 5.6). You created this link when you uploaded the podcast episode in "Uploading Episodes" Page 126.

Figure 5.5. Publishing a Podcast to a Blogging Platform

Part of optimizing your podcast is to have its landing page (in our case the blog entry) contain the key terms associated with the podcast episode

Figure 5.6. Publishing a Podcast to a Blogging Platform

(see the "Optimizing Your Podcast" section on Page 130). Once the link to the podcast episode is posted, include a description that uses these valuable key terms. Use the key terms as tags and utilize whatever SEO plugins you have in place to optimize the entry. Remember that this is still a blog post, so apply all of the optimization skills you learned in Chapter 3, "RSS Feeds & Blogs." See Figure 5.7.

Note that on Figure 5.7, one of the categories that is assigned for this post is "podcasts." This is how we distinguish the podcast episodes from the other posts in WordPress. Recall in Chapter 3 how to use categories to generate separate feeds (see Page 81). This "feed" constitutes the entire

Figure 5.7. Publishing a Podcast to a Blogging Platform

podcast, so that every time a post is saved with that category assigned, it will become an episode of the podcast.

Figure 5.8 shows how this method of posting will look on your site. When a visitor clicks on the link they will be able to download or play the episode. There are other ways of displaying your podcast, though. For instance, you can use plugins[7] that allow you to embed audio or video players directly into your posts.

Figure 5.8. Publishing a Podcast to a Blogging Platform

To a Website

For SEO purposes, each episode of your podcast should have its own landing page. That is, each episode should reside on its own HTML or PHP page, so that it has a unique URL. On this landing page, you want to write a description of the podcast episode that includes all of the key terms you established in "Preparing the Script and Key Terms" on Page 123. Your landing page, then, will look very similar to the blog post created in the previous section (Figure 5.8), with a description and a link to the podcast episode.

Once your landing page is created, you need to add the episode to your RSS feed by adding a new item with an enclosure element (see Appendix B, "Creating Your Own RSS Feed") or to FeedForAll if you are using it to manage your feeds.

---

[7] http://wordpress.org/extend/plugins/podcasting/

Optimizing Your Podcast

First, read the "Optimizing and Promoting Your Blog and RSS Feed" section on Page 72. Since your podcast is also an RSS feed, apply most of the tactics discussed in that section.

Podcasts can be optimized for search engines and podcast directories by consistently using the same key terms within the podcast itself, in the metadata (see the "Recording Episodes" section on Page 124) of the audio and video files, and on the page that the podcast resides (the landing page). As you create your podcast and podcast episodes, keep these three optimization points in mind:

1. Many audio and video search engines now use speech recognition to identify key terms within podcasts. So make sure you write each episode to include your best key terms, and that you use these same key terms in the file's metadata and on the landing page of each podcast episode.

2. You add the metadata for each podcast episode when you save it as an MP3 file (see the "Recording Episodes" section on Page 124). Repeat key terms from the actual spoken episode in this metadata.

3. The page where each podcast episode resides is called its landing page (see the "Publishing Your Podcast" section on Page 127). Again, make sure you repeat your best key terms on this page, and especially repeat terms that are spoken in the podcast episode.

Burning to FeedBurner

Once your podcast is published, you want to burn it to FeedBurner and optimize it. Go to your FeedBurner account, or create one if you don't have one yet. Before proceeding, read the entire "FeedBurner" section on Page 76.

Figure 5.9 shows how we burn our Social Media Power podcast feed example. The feed URL we use is based on the WordPress category ID for "podcasts" that we assigned to our podcast entry above. Refer to burning feeds using WordPress categories on Page 81. Note that the box is checked that says "I am a podcaster." This lets FeedBurner know to look for an audio or video file at this feed URL. In the next step you are

Figure 5.9. Burning a Podcast to FeedBurner

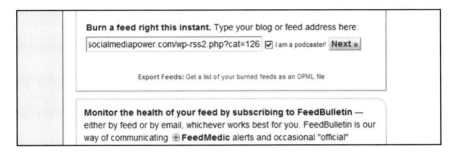

given an option to change the name of the feed FeedBurner creates for your podcast (see Figure 5.10).

Figure 5.10. Burning a Podcast to FeedBurner

Figures 5.11 shows the screen in the next step toward burning your podcast feed. This step is very important—this is where you optimize the feed for iTunes and Yahoo!. Do not skip anything in this step and use your best key terms in the summaries and search keywords areas.

Figure 5.11. Burning a Podcast to FeedBurner

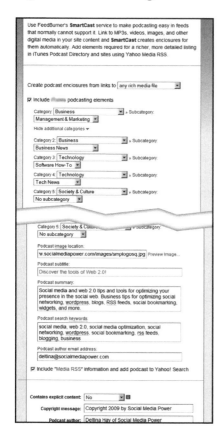

Since FeedBurner knows that this is a podcast, some of the settings are different than the settings covered in the previous chapter. For instance, Figure 5.12 shows the "PingShot" options for our podcast feed. The services listed here are specifically for podcasts, so select all of them.

Figure 5.12. Burning a Podcast to FeedBurner

Headline Animator	PingShot
Display rotating headlines	
BuzzBoost	Most web-based feed reading services will check for updates on their own time.
Republish your feed as HTML	Give 'em a push with PingShot. Choose the services you want to ping, and we'll
SpringWidgets Skin	notify them when you publish new content.
Email Subscriptions	
Offer feed updates via email	When I publish new content in my feed, notify these services...
PingShot	
Notify services when you post	✓ ODEO — Play Download and Create Podcasts
FeedCount	✓ My Yahoo — a customizable web page with news stock quotes weather and many
Show off your feed circulation	other features
Chicklet Chooser	

Helping Visitors Subscribe

People subscribe to podcast feeds the same way they subscribe to any other RSS feed (see Chapter 3, "RSS Feeds & Blogs"). You can subscribe to a podcast using the usual feed readers (Google Reader, MyYahoo, Pageflakes, etc.) but also through specialized readers called "podcatchers." These services specialize in indexing only podcasts.

Make it easy for visitors to your Website or blog to find your podcast feed. Figure 5.13 shows the FeedBurner "Chicklet Chooser"—read more about this in the "FeedBurner" section on Page 80. Create a separate button for your podcast feed on your site (separate from your regular blog or RSS feed).

Figure 5.13. FeedBurner Chicklet chooser.

Once you have generated and copied the code from the Chicklet Chooser, place it onto your Website or blog, and make it clear that this feed is to your podcast (see Figure 5.14).

Figure 5.14. Podcast Chicklet on a Website

Figure 5.15 shows what a visitor sees when they click your FeedBurner chicklet. Notice that there are a number of podcatchers as choices. As you can see from Figure 5.16, the process for subscribing to your podcast feed using Google Reader is no different than subscribing to a regular feed. What *is* different is that Google recognizes the feed as a podcast, so subscribers can play it in an embedded player from their Google Reader account (see Figure 5.17).

Figure 5.15. Podcast Chicklet on a Website

Figure 5.16. Subscribing to a Podcast

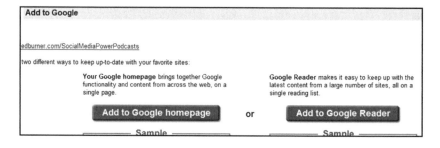

Podcast Directories

In addition to the feed directory sources listed in the previous chapter, there are a number of podcast directories for submission of podcasts. Check the resource CD for an extensive list of podcast directories.

Figure 5.17. A Podcast Subscription in Google Reader

Webcasting

A Webcast is an online broadcast, and usually consists of a series of uploaded videos. They can be viewed either on Webcasting sites or embedded into your Website or blog.

Webcasts are also called channels. YouTube lets you create channels that you can regularly add videos to. See Chapter 8, "Media Communities," on how to create these channels.

Some popular Webcasting sites are blogTV[8] and blip.tv.[9] Note that these are also social networking sites, so use the tactics from Chapter 6, "Social Networking & Micro-Blogging," to optimize your presence in these sites.

Services such as Webcast2000[10] and Webcasting.com[11] can help you create and maintain your own Webcast as well.

---

[8] http://www.blogtv.com/
[9] http://www.blip.tv/
[10] http://www.webcast2000.com/
[11] http://www.webcasting.com/

This Chapter On The Resource CD

- Further Reading
- Linkable Resources
- Example Podcast
- Fillable Forms:
    › Podcasst Script Outline

6 Social Networking & Micro-Blogging

Social networking is one of the most powerful social media strategies you can implement. Most social networking sites allow you to create a personal profile page to post information about you or your business, invite people to join your network, join groups, blast messages and events, connect with other people, and much more.

These networking sites are effective outlets for finding new customers and readers, but it is easy to find your message spread thin if you don't choose the right strategy. Many businesses settle for sparse profiles on various sites, never discovering the other powerful marketing tools many of these social networking platforms have to offer—most of them for free. To avoid the scattershot approach, choose three or four social networking sites that best fit your business and invest the time to maximize your presence in them.

In this chapter we first take a thorough look at Facebook, currently the fastest growing social networking site, and an ideal first choice for anyone or any business wanting to get a solid foothold in the Social Web. We also highlight some other social networking sites, show you how to build your own social network, and finally, outline a plan that you can implement for whichever sites you choose to add to your social networking strategy.

Facebook

Below is an overview of the most basic functions of the Facebook platform. Most social and professional networking sites have these same functionalities in one way or another.

Posting or Publishing

Posting is what you do to add items to your profile or "feed." Posts can include a brief status update (a quick "What's on your mind?" post), photos, videos, events, notes, etc.

The Feed

Often called a mini-feed, this is where you can view lists of posts that others in your network have added to their profiles (and where they view yours). This is also where you can connect with others by commenting on their posted entries. You can even filter your feed by friend lists, photos, links, etc.

The Wall

Your "wall" is where all of your own posts reside. You can see your friends' walls by visiting their profile page. You can also leave messages on people's walls.

Applications

Applications are add-ons that Facebook or other developers have created to work within the Facebook platform. There are many types of applications. They range from book sharing applications to games to news feeds. You can use applications to help connect with other people within the Facebook community, so find and participate in applications where you believe your target audience is active.

Groups

Anyone can create a Facebook group. They are a way for you to connect with other people around a common interest.

People Search

This feature lets you search Facebook for people you may know. Facebook also recommends people you may know based on your existing friends and geographic region.

Messages and Requests

People can leave you messages, send requests to be their friends, join groups, attend events, and more.

Pages and Advertising

You can create Facebook pages for your business or book (see the "Facebook Pages" section on Page 146), or place highly targeted ads within the Facebook community. It is important to note that Facebook pages are meant for businesses, while your Facebook profile should be created for you, as an individual.

The Facebook Home Page

Figure 6.1 shows my Facebook home page. From this page, I can:

- Post status updates (see the "What's on you mind?" box in Figure 6.1)
- View and search groups (Figure 6.2)
- View and post events (Figure 6.3)
- Add Facebook pages, or see stats on my existing pages (Figure 6.4)
- Create a targeted advertisement (Figure 6.5)
- Add or browse applications (Figures 6.6 and 6.7)
- Check friend and group requests (Figure 6.8)
- Find people and invite them to my network (Figure 6.9)
- Read or send messages and invitations (Figure 6.10)

Figure 6.1. A Facebook Home Page

Figure 6.2. Facebook Groups

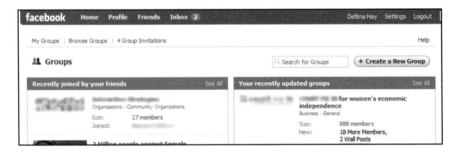

Figure 6.3. Facebook Events

Figure 6.4. Facebook Page Statistics

Figure 6.5. Facebook Advertising

Figure 6.6. Accessing Facebook Applications

Figure 6.7. Browsing Facebook Applications

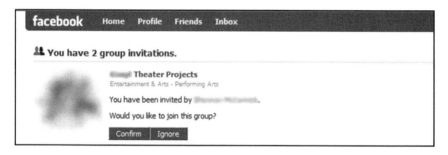

Figure 6.8. Facebook Requests

Figure 6.9. Find People in Facebook

Find people you know on Facebook

Your friends on Facebook are the same friends, acquaintances and family members that you communicate with in the real world. You can use any of the tools on this page to find more friends.

Find People You Email   Upload Contact File

Searching your email address book is the fastest and most effective way to find your friends on Facebook.

Your Email: [   ]
Password: [   ]
               [Find Friends]

Also from my Facebook home page, I can see and comment on what my network of friends and colleagues are up to (see Figure 6.1. Page 140). Through the news feed, I can see the photos, links, videos, events, and other items they have posted. In addition to being able to filter the feed by photos, links, and other items, I can also filter this feed using my own friend lists (on Figure 6.1 those are "Personal" and "Business").

Figure 6.10. Messages in Facebook

The feed filters I have in place are on the left sidebar in Figure 6.11. You can create your own friend lists by clicking on the "Friends" tab.

I can post many types of items to my page easily. Figure 6.11 shows a couple of ways I can post. The first image shows me posting a link. The second shows me using the GoodReads application to recommend a book.

Figure 6.11. Posting to the Facebook News Feed

The Facebook Profile

Figure 6.12 shows my Facebook profile. From this page, I can:

- Publish stories; add links, photos, videos, and notes to my own "wall" (Figure 6.13)
- Update my profile (Figure 6.14)
- Manage applications (Figure 6.15)
- Add additional tabs to my profile (depending on which applications I have added) (Figure 6.15a)

Figure 6.12. Facebook Profile

Figure 6.13. Post to Facebook Wall

Figure 6.14. Updating Facebook Profiles

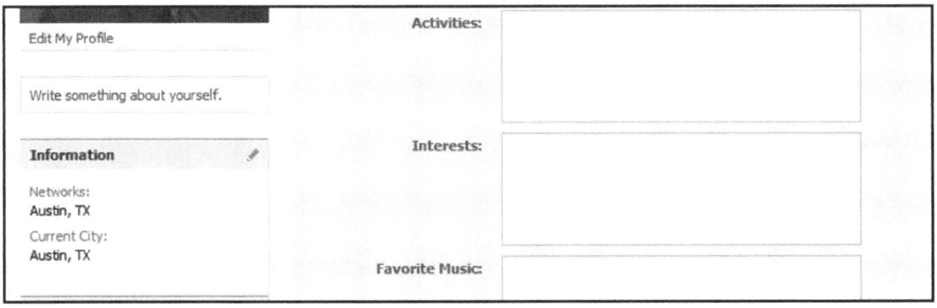

Figures 6.15 & 6.15a. Managing Applications/ApplicationTabs

This is also where others can see what is on my wall, leave me messages, comment on my entries, or write to my wall.

Your profile page will likely look different, including the applications and tabs you have added, but the basic options remain the same. Be certain to fill out your profile completely. Figure 6.14 shows some of the options available to you in the "Personal Information" section once you click the "Info" box from your profile page. Use and reuse your key terms often in this area.

There are a number of settings you can control on your Facebook profile (click the "Settings" button), including importing stories from your blog and other social accounts like Digg.com and Delicious.com. See Figure 6.16. This figure shows how to enter your blog's feed URL to import blog posts into your Facebook profile.

Figure 6.16. Facebook Profile Settings

Facebook Pages

Facebook pages are specifically for marketing a business, product, or personality. They offer a way for a business to represent itself to the Facebook community in an authentic way. Facebook users can search pages the same way they search for people within the network community. Facebook offers these pages to businesses at no charge.

Figure 6.17 shows the search results for "social media wordpress." A Facebook search shows all search results, or a breakdown of results by people, pages, applications, or groups. Our search yields Social Media Power's Facebook page as well as their application. When we click on

Figure 6.17. Facebook Search Results

the "pages" tab, we see only the pages that match our search (see Figure 6.18).

Figure 6.18. Facebook Pages Search Results

As an added bonus, Facebook pages are indexed in search engines. Figure 6.19 shows a Google search for "Dalton Publishing." Notice their Facebook page listed second, as well as their MySpace page listed fourth.

Figure 6.19. Google Search Results With Facebook Pages

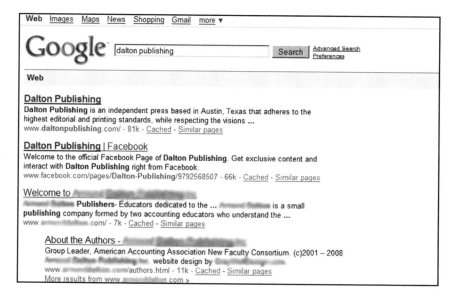

Creating Facebook Pages

Once you have an account and have completed your profile, log in to Facebook, and go to the "Advertising" link at the bottom of your Facebook profile page, or go directly to the Facebook business link.[1] See Figure 6.20.

Figure 6.20. Facebook Services for Business

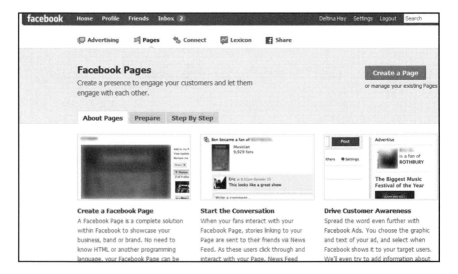

Choose the best category for your business, book, or product (see Figure 6.21). The three main categories are: local business; brand or product; and artist, band, or public figure. You can choose a subcategory as well. If you offer a number of different services or products, you may want to

Figure 6.21. Creating a Facebook Page

[1] http://www.facebook.com/business/

create several pages. For instance, if you are a publisher, you may want to create a main page for your publishing company using the "brand or product" category and individual pages using the "Artist, Band, or Public Figure" category for each of your authors.

Choosing the name of your Facebook page is very important. Figure 6.22 shows where to do this. You are limited to around 65 characters, so make them count. The name of your Facebook page determines how well your page performs in searches.

Figure 6.22. Creating a Facebook Page

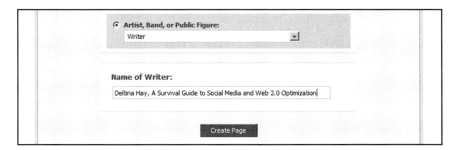

Figure 6.23 shows a newly created Facebook page. The next step is to input detailed information about your business or product. Click on "add information" on your new page to do this (see Figure 6.23).

Figure 6.23. Creating a Facebook Page

The category you chose in the previous step determines what type of information you can enter. Figure 6.24 shows the information options for the "Artist, Band, and Public Figure" category, whereas Figure 6.25 shows the "Brand or Product" options.

Figure 6.24. Creating a Facebook Page

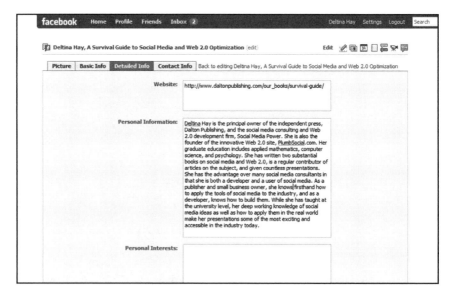

Figure 6.25. Creating a Facebook Page

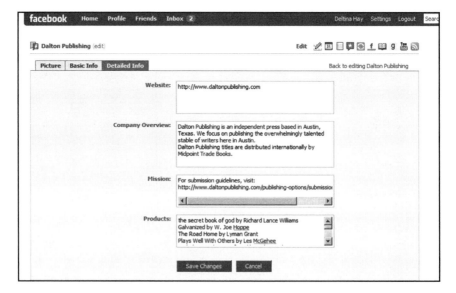

Regardless of the category you choose, prepare the information you enter here ahead of time. Use your preparation worksheet (refer to Chapter 2, "Preparation," or the "A Social Networking Strategy" section at the end of this chapter on Page 174) to populate your page with all of your best information and key terms. You may only have a few seconds to get a reader's attention, so put your best key terms forward.

At this stage, click on every tab and fill each box thoroughly, reusing your key terms often. Be certain to upload an image to the "Picture" tab as well (see Figure 6.26). Figure 6.27 shows what good, detailed information looks like on a Facebook page.

Figure 6.26. Creating a Facebook Page

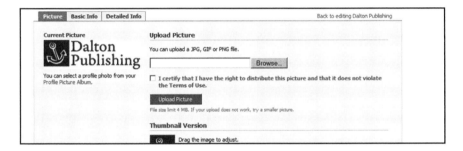

Figure 6.27. Example of Facebook Page Information

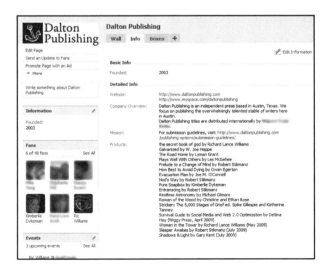

Once you input your detailed information, you can customize or remove the built-in applications for your page. Figures 6.28 and 6.29 show these applications. Clicking on edit beside any one of these gives you more information about what they are and how to use them. Click on "view page" to see these applications in action on your page.

Figure 6.28. Facebook Page Built-in Applications

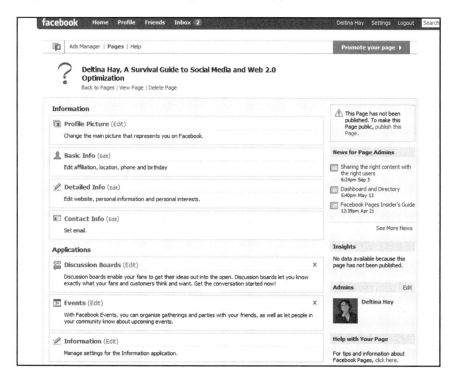

As an example, click on "edit" beside the "Notes" application. You can add manual notes to your page or, as seen in Figures 6.30 and 6.31, you can import a blog that feeds your latest blog posts onto your Facebook page using this application.

There are many more applications you can add to your page. Click on "More Applications" at the bottom of the edit page (Figure 6.29) or go to the Facebook application directory.[2] Add applications that help represent your company and/or your products in your own unique way.

---

[2] http://www.facebook.com/apps/

Figure 6.29. Facebook Page Built-in Applications

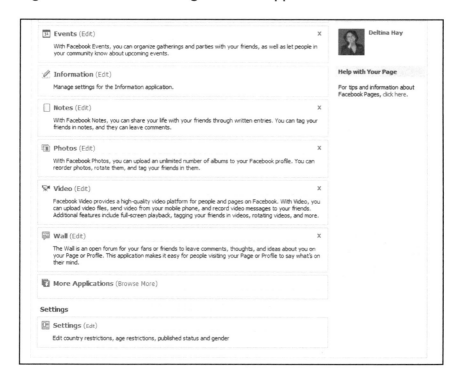

Figure 6.30. Importing a Blog to Facebook Notes

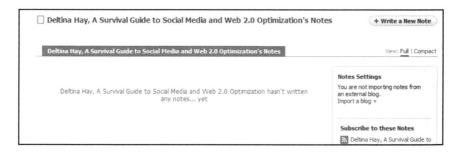

Applications are not difficult to install and are usually very easy to set up. A general rule of thumb when choosing an application is that if you can't figure out how to set it up after the second try, find another one. There is often more than one application out there that can accomplish the same task.

Figure 6.31. Importing a Blog to Facebook Notes

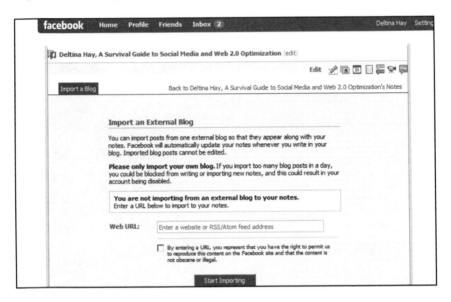

Browse or search the application directory for applications that make sense to implement for your business or product. Figure 6.32 shows the "Boxes" tab of Dalton Publishing's Facebook page.[3]

On this Facebook page, Dalton Publishing utilizes the following applications:

Book Share Books[4]

This application lets readers share their favorite books with their friends, as well as rate them and comment on them. This is a perfect application for a publishing company wanting to showcase their books.

My Flickr[5]

Display photos from your Flickr account using this application. These photos can include logos, book covers, photos from author events, etc. You are provided many options of how to display the photos, too.

---

[3] http://www.facebook.com/pages/Dalton-Publishing/9792568507
[4] http://apps.facebook.com/bookshare/
[5] http://apps.facebook.com/myflickr/

Figure 6.32. Dalton Publishing's Facebook Page

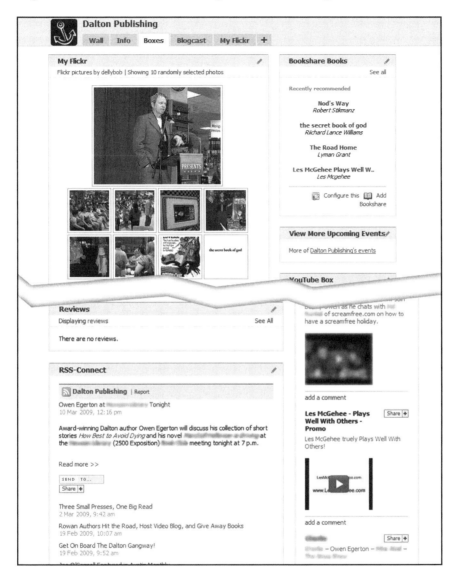

YouTube Box[6]

Allows visitors to play your YouTube videos right on your Facebook page. This is handy for book trailers or promotional videos.

RSS-Connect[7]

This is a nice application that allows you to display RSS feeds on your Facebook page. It is a convenient way for Dalton Publishing to display the feeds from their main site, as well as to their authors' newsroom feeds.

By implementing these applications, Dalton Publishing has created an interactive page that also gives their visitors a personable look into their business. You can find many applications that can do the same for your business.

Once your page is ready, don't forget to publish it. You will see a message in the upper right corner as you prepare your page that says "This Page has not been published…" Click on "publish this Page" in that box so that your Facebook page can be seen by others.

Figure 6.33 shows the "wall" of Dalton's Facebook page. This is similar to a regular Facebook profile in that Dalton can post items and others can comment on them. This is also where most of the built-in applications appear (see Page 138). Also from here, you can send updates to all the fans of your page, promote your page with an ad, and manage page settings.

---

[6] http://apps.facebook.com/videobox/

[7] http://apps.facebook.com/rss-connect/

Figure 6.33. The Wall of a Facebook Page

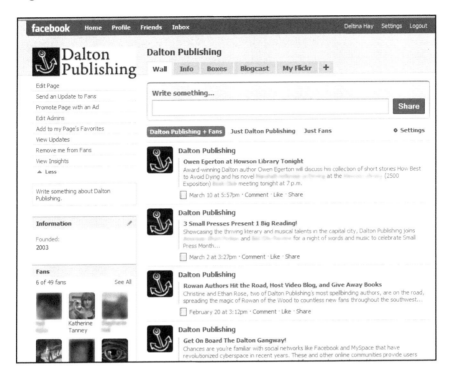

Other Social Networking Sites

There are many social and professional networking sites out there. What you want to do, however, is find the ones that are the best fit for you or your business. Once you decide to use a particular social networking site, apply the same process as we did in our Facebook example by filling out your profile thoroughly, joining groups, and looking for applications and other features that can help make your presence representative of you, your book, or your business.

Highlighted below are examples of different types of networking sites. An extensive list of social networking sites can be found on the resource CD.

MySpace

MySpace[8] is like a combination of a Facebook page and a Facebook profile. Their Terms of Use do not exclude businesses from creating MySpace profiles, so you can build your profile as your business alone if you wish. However, you might consider creating a MySpace profile both for yourself, or a key member of your company, and for the company itself.

Figure 6.34 shows Dalton Publishing's MySpace profile.

They use similar applications to the ones they use on their Facebook page:

Happy Flickr[9] to import images to their MySpace profile from their Flickr account.

RSS Reader[10] to import blog entries and RSS feeds from their own and their authors' blogs.

YouTube Favorites[11] to highlight their favorite YouTube videos.

You can find MySpace applications by going to "More/Apps Gallery" while editing your profile, or directly to the application gallery.[12]

Once you have an account with MySpace, fill out your profile completely using your best key terms. Figure 6.35 shows part of Social Media Power's profile to demonstrate how you can use and reuse key terms.

---

[8] http://www.myspace.com
[9] http://profile.myspace.com/Modules/Applications/Pages/Canvas.aspx?appId=100261
[10] http://profile.myspace.com/Modules/Applications/Pages/Canvas.aspx?appId=107266
[11] http://profile.myspace.com/Modules/Applications/Pages/Canvas.aspx?appId=110982
[12] http://apps.myspace.com/index.cfm?fuseaction=apps

Figure 6.34. Dalton Publishing's MySpace Page

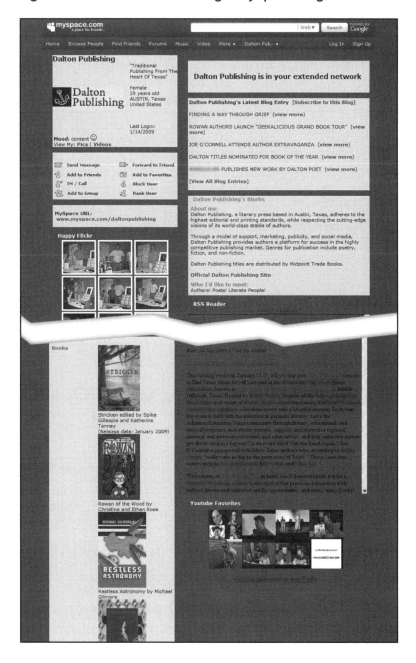

Figure 6.35. Completing a MySpace Profile

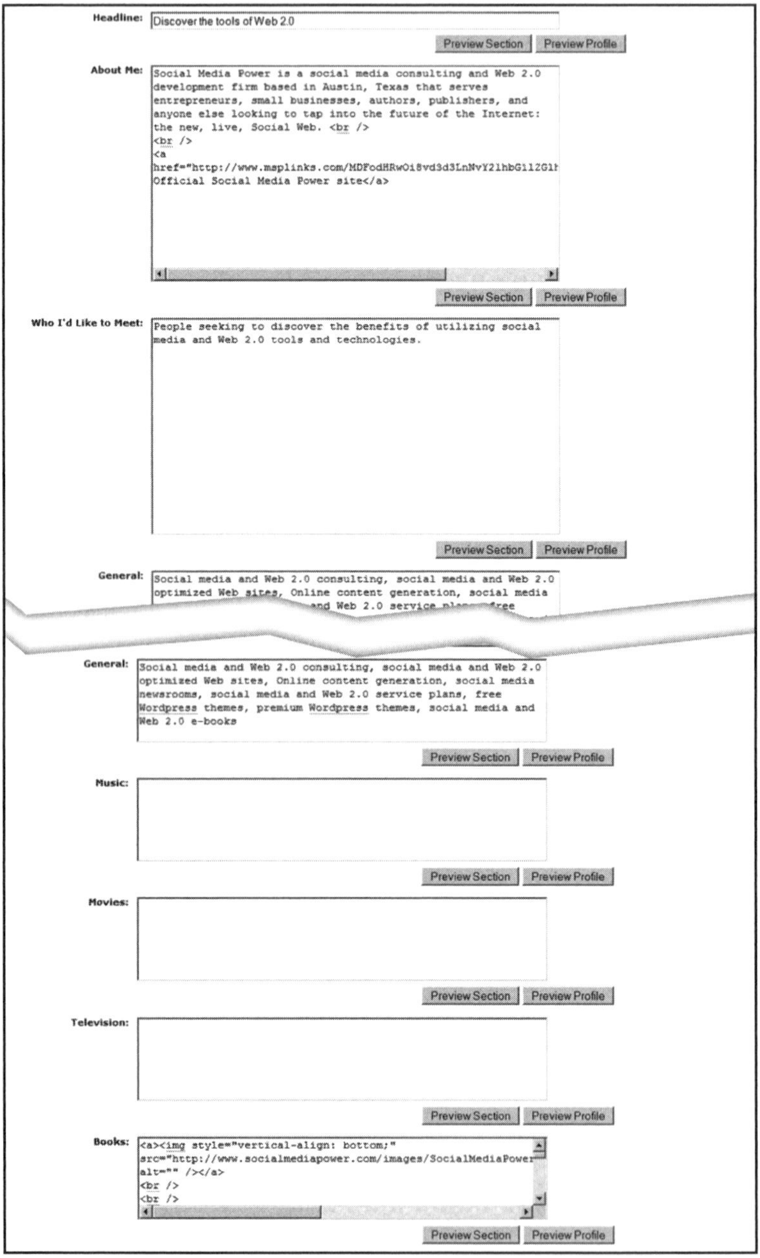

Notice that in MySpace profile boxes, you can use HTML tags to style the content on your page and make it more interactive. In Figure 6.35, Social Media Power uses the link tag "<a href..." to embed links to their Websites and books, and the line space tag, "< /br>" to help make their content more readable.

You can also add CSS styling to your "About Me" box to customize the look and feel of your MySpace page. There are a number of good tutorials that can help you learn how to customize your MySpace page layout[13].

LinkedIn

LinkedIn[14]is more of a professional networking site than a social one. As you can see from Figures 6.36 and 6.37, a LinkedIn profile is more focused on professional experience and expertise.

Figure 6.36. A LinkedIn Profile, Top

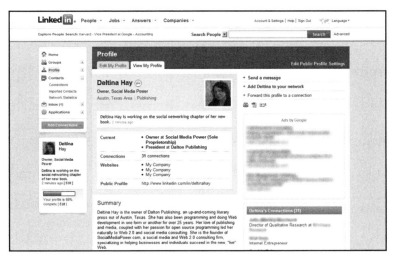

This networking site is a great tool for people wanting to connect with other professionals, or for those seeking professional positions. It is also ideal for consultants and service firms seeking clients.

---

[13] http://www.squidoo.com/myspace_layouts
[14] http://www.linkedin.com

Figure 6.37. A LinkedIn Profile, Bottom

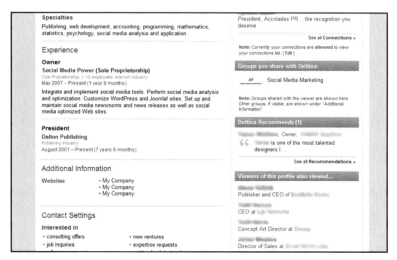

Just like other networking sites, you can add applications, join groups, post quick updates, and search for and interact with other people (see Figure 6.36). One thing that is more specific to LinkedIn, however, is the ability to recommend others in your network. You can ask others to recommend you and your services, or others may ask the same of you.

Twitter

Twitter[15] is considered a micro-blogging platform. It is a bit of a hybrid between blogging and social networking. This basic concept of combining blogging and interactivity has become so popular that, as we saw in both Facebook and LinkedIn, many of the other networks now have this same feature built in.

The basic premise of Twitter is for people to stay in touch through quick, frequent answers to one simple question: What are you doing? Figure 6.38 shows this simple concept in action. When you "follow" people in Twitter, you are notified through email or your mobile device whenever they post an entry. You can also place badges on your Website or blog that keep you updated (see Figure 6.39).

---

[15] http://www.twitter.com

Figure 6.38. A Twitter Home Page

Figure 6.39. Twitter Badges

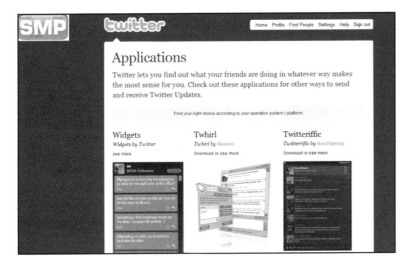

Twitter has intentionally kept its platform simple, and that has lent to its popularity. Figure 6.40 demonstrates the simplicity of a Twitter profile. You can also add a mobile device as your preferred method of notification (see Figure 6.41). Be sure and upload an image of you or your business logo so your followers have a visual way of associating your presence.

Figure 6.40. Twitter Profile

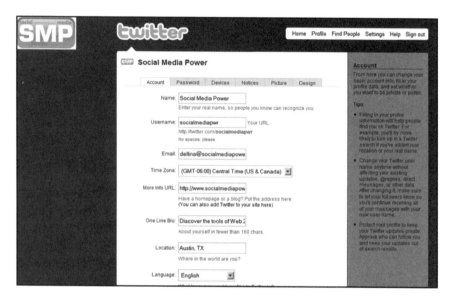

Figure 6.41. Mobile Devices to Twitter

A few Twitter applications can be found on the Twitter site (see Figure 6.39), but many more are located at the Twitter fan wiki.[16]

---

[16] http://twitter.pbwiki.com/Apps

Twitter is the most popular micro-blogging sites. As a result, the number of people who you can follow becomes overwhelming. Visit the Twitter fan wiki for applications that can help you filter entries and friends into more manageable chunks. There are even applications that you can place on your computer's desktop to help you keep up with your favorite updates. WeFollow[17] is a directory that can help you find people to follow as well.

It is important to remember that building a strong foundation in the Social Web is not about how many thousands of friends or followers you can gather, rather, it is about improving your reach to the people who are actually in your target market. Therefore, a good strategy is to choose carefully who you follow on Twitter and other such sites. You can get a good idea about a person by taking a brief look at their profile before deciding to follow them, so take that few seconds to do so.

Social Bookmarking and Media Communities

Though considered social bookmarking sites (see Chapter 7, "Social Bookmarking & Crowd-Sourcing"), Delicious.com [18] and other bookmarking sites like StumbleUpon [19] naturally evolve into social networking sites. As conversations and connections develop around common bookmarks, so too does your network within these communities.

The same evolution happens within media communities like Flickr[20] and YouTube[21] (see Chapter 8, "Media Communities"). Since conversations and connections develop around different multimedia items like images and video, communities naturally form as a result.

Apply the same tactics and strategies to these sites as you do to the other networking sites discussed in this chapter.

---

[17] http://wefollow.com/
[18] http://delicious.com
[19] http://www.stumbleupon.com
[20] http://www.flickr.com
[21] http://www.youtube.com

Niche Social Networking Sites

A good social networking strategy includes establishing a healthy presence in one or more of the staple networking sites like Facebook, MySpace, LinkedIn, and Twitter, coupled with a presence in a couple of niche sites that put you in front of potential clients and affiliates in your area of expertise.

You can find these sites by searching Google or by researching where other people in your industry are putting their efforts.

Here are a few example strategies to help you along:

Publishers and Authors

- Facebook
- MySpace
- Twitter
- LibraryThing[22]
- GoodReads[23]
- Shelfari[24]

Tech Consulting Firms

- Facebook
- MySpace
- Twitter
- LinkedIn
- Mashable[25]
- Slashdot[26]

Entertainment Firms:

- Facebook
- MySpace

[22] http://www.librarything.com
[23] http://goodreads.com
[24] http://www.shelfari.com
[25] http://www.mashable.com
[26] http://www.slashdot.org

- Twitter
- Bebo[27]
- EntertainMyUSA[28]

Real World Examples:

- Dalton Publishing[29]
- Hidden Lands of Nod[30]
- Digital Growth Strategies[31]
- Women and Mutual Funds[32]
- ComedySportz[33]

Creating Your Own Social Network

If you have a large readership or following who tend to have a lot to say to each other, you might consider creating your own social network. Custom social networks are also handy for corporate teams and educational classes.

There are a number of ways to create a social network. Joomla![34] and Drupal[35] are two CMSs you can use to do so, but Ning.com[36] is the easiest. Ning is a free service where you can build a very functional Web-based social networking site, complete with forum, blogging, and file sharing capabilities. The free version contains Google ads, but for a small monthly fee, Ning removes the ads for you.

---

[27] http://www.bebo.com

[28] http://www.entertainmyusa.com/

[29] http://testsite.plumbsocial.com

[30] http://stikmanz.plumbsocial.com

[31] http://dgs.plumbsocial.com

[32] http://womenandmutualfunds.plumbsocial.com

[33] http://csz.plumbsocial.com

[34] http://www.joomla.org

[35] http://www.drupal.org

[36] http://www.ning.com

In a few short steps you can create a functional network. The first step is to create the network by giving it a name and a URL (see Figure 6.42). Use your key terms within this name and URL.

Figure 6.42. Creating a Social Network in Ning

The next step is to give the network a bit more information (Figure 6.43). Of course, you want to repeat your key terms wherever you can in this step, too.

Figure 6.43. Creating a Social Network in Ning

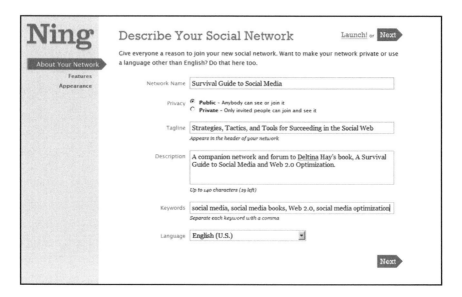

Figure 6.44 shows the third step, which is to add and position features for your network.

Figure 6.44. Creating a Social Network in Ning

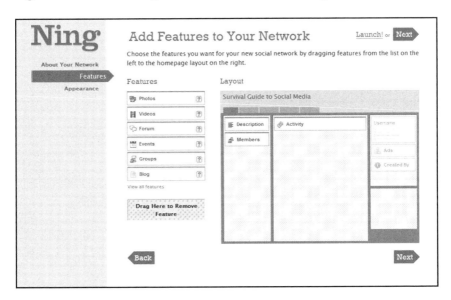

The final step as seen in Figure 6.45 is to choose a theme and customize your network.

Figure 6.45. Creating a Social Network in Ning

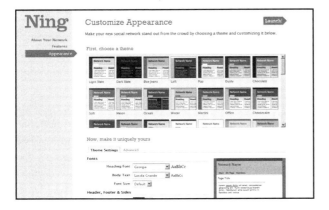

The completed network is shown in Figure 6.46. Clicking on "Manage" brings you to all of the other ways you can further customize your network (see Figure 6.47).

Figure 6.46. A Completed Ning Network

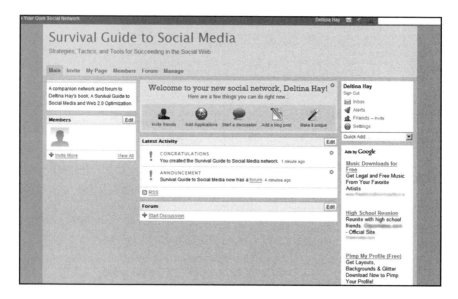

Figure 6.47. Customizing a Ning Network

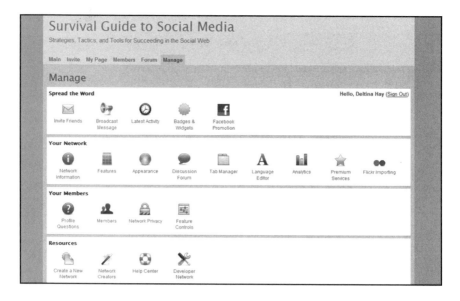

Dalton Publishing's Ning network, The Dalton Gangway (Figure 6.48), is a place for authors and fans to connect, and for Dalton's authors to share marketing and other ideas with each other. As you can see, there are many ways of making a Ning social network your own, from custom modules for importing photos from Flickr, to highlighting your other Social Web tools, to listing links of resources.

Figure 6.48. Dalton Gangway Ning Network

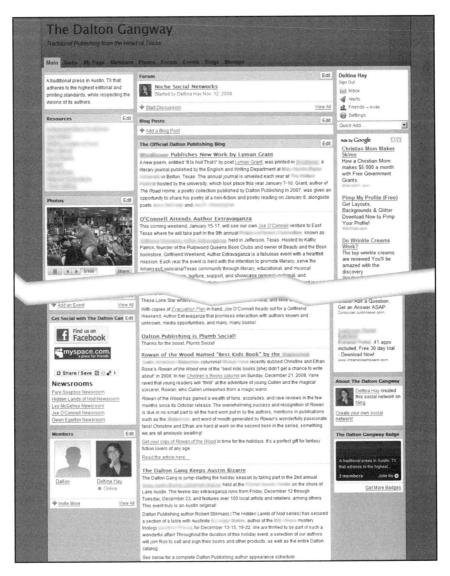

Figure 6.49 shows how to create a badge for promoting your Ning network on your Website or blog. You can encourage other members to promote your network, too, by offering ways for them to create custom badges directly from the network (see Figure 6.49).

Figure 6.49. Creating a Ning Badge

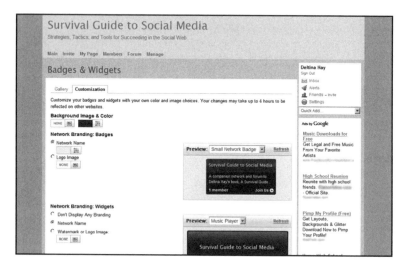

Promoting Your Social Networking Presence

Promote your social networking presence wherever you can, especially on your Website or blog (see Figure 6.50). Here are some additional examples:

- Dalton Publishing[37]
- The Hidden Lands of Nod[38]
- Digital Growth Strategies[39]
- ComedySportz [40]

Most social networking sites offer badges or other tools that you can use to promote your presence on their sites. Here are some examples:

---

[37] http://testsite.plumbsocial.com
[38] http://stikmanz.plumbsocial.com
[39] http://dgs.plumbsocial.com
[40] http://csz.plumbsocial.com/

Figure 6.50. Badges Promoting a Social Web Presence

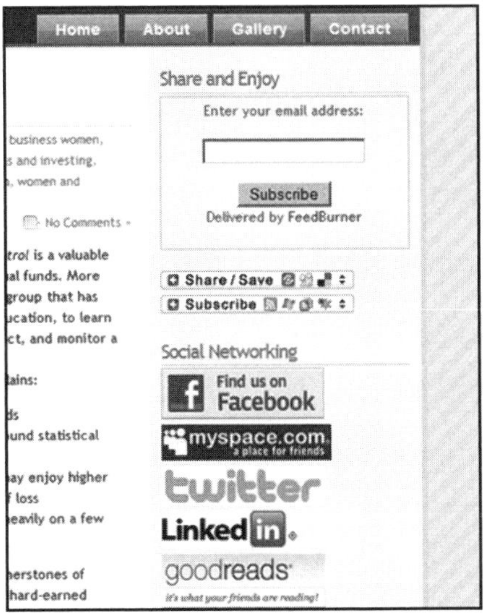

Facebook

You can promote your Facebook page with ads within Facebook,[41] or by posting a Facebook badge on your Website or blog. Facebook has a promotional guidelines area on its site[42] where you can download badges and images to promote your profile or page.

Twitter

Figure 6.39 on Page 163 shows some of the badges you can use to promote your Twitter presence.[43] These badges can offer running updates of your Twitter entries, or entries from others you are following.

LinkedIn

LinkedIn offers nice, professional looking badges. You can find them by going to the "Edit My Profile" area (see Figure 6.51).

---

[41] http://www.facebook.com/advertising
[42] http://www.facebook.com/pages/manage/promo_guidelines.php
[43] http://twitter.com/downloads

Figure 6.51. Badges for Promoting a LinkedIn Presence

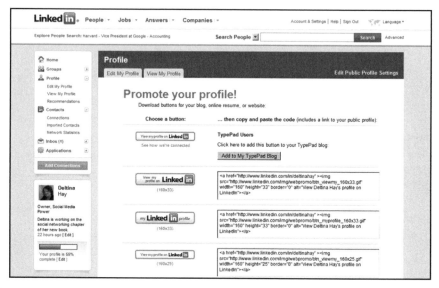

Ning

As we saw in the "Creating Your Own Social Network" section on Page 172, there are a number of badges you can create to promote your own social network (see Figure 6.49 on Page 171).

A Social Networking Strategy

Follow these steps for each social or professional networking site you join:

- Read and follow the site's Terms of Use.
- Complete your profile using prepared material, including your best key terms.
- Upload a profile image or logo when available.
- Search for applications to enhance or customize your presence.
- Integrate other social tools and sites into your presence (like Flickr images or YouTube videos).
- Invite friends and colleagues to join your network. Do not invite people just for the sake of inviting them; only invite people you think can benefit from a specific community.

- Choose your friends wisely; do not just add anyone who asks; check out their profile first.
- Join groups relevant to your area of expertise or interest.
- Promote your page or profile on your Website or blog.
- Get to know the network features: Explore all of the features of the networking platform and implement each of them that make sense for you or your business.
- Do not turn your back on your investment: Keep your social networking presence dynamic by contributing to it frequently.

If you have not competed the tasks in the "Preparation" chapter, prepare the following worksheet before you go forward with your strategy:

- Key Terms
  - › Start with a list of your best key terms and weave them into the rest of your worksheet items.
  - › Key terms are one, two, or three-word terms that you can imagine someone using as search terms if they were searching for your business or book in a search engine.
- General Information
  - › Your name
  - › Business or book name
  - › Email addresses
  - › URLs
  - › Instant Messaging screen names
  - › Other social networking profile URLs
- Biographical and Descriptive Information
  - › Short bio (50 words)
  - › Longer bio (100 words)
  - › Short company or book description (50 words)
  - › Longer company or book description (100 words)
  - › Business mission statement
- Products
  - › List of books and other products

These worksheet items are based on building a profile and a page in Facebook. If you choose a different social networking site, look at some completed profiles on which to base your worksheet items. This worksheet is also available on the resource CD.

This Chapter On The Resource CD

- Further Reading
- Linkable Resources
- Fillable Forms:
    › Social Networking Strategy Worksheet
    › Social Networking Preparation Worksheet

7   Social Bookmarking & Crowd-Sourcing

Social Bookmarking

Social bookmarking is a way for you to save your favorite blogs and Websites in a public space the same way you might save them using your own Web browser. The concept is simple, but its power is enormous.

Imagine that you have saved (or bookmarked) all of your favorite Websites and blogs to a central place online and tagged them with specific terms so you could easily search and find them later. Imagine further that you could then see how thousands of other users have tagged the same sites and that you could view all of the sites that they tagged. From this process we get "folksonomy"—the taxonomy of the Internet in terms of its users.

Instead of allowing search engines to provide you with the "supposed" best matches for your search terms, you can go to a social bookmarking site, search using those same terms, and find the top sites tagged (and commented on) by users just like you. You can pull up a site on one of these bookmarking sites and have access to everyone who has tagged the site, and if they have made their bookmarks public, you can even look at all of the other sites those users have tagged. There really is no end to the resources and readers you can access via social bookmarking.

Social Bookmarking in Action

Figure 7.1 shows the front page of Delicious.com,[1] one of the most popular social bookmarking sites. This front page features some Websites people have recently saved to their own delicious bookmarking accounts.

Figure 7.1. Delicious.com* Home Page

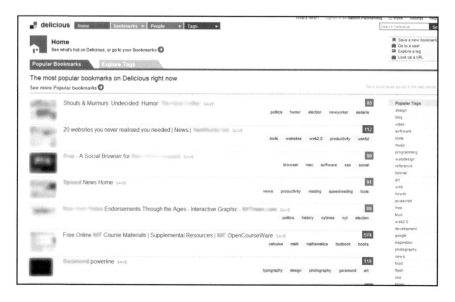

From here you can enter search terms that return resulting Websites that other members have "tagged" with those same search terms. Figure 7.2 demonstrates this. When the term "books" is searched, we get the results shown. All of these results were bookmarked by other users and tagged with the term "books." Click on any of these links, and you are taken to the respective Website, just like in traditional search engines.

The number to the right of each site listed shows how many people have bookmarked that site. If you click on that number you see a list of all of those people (see Figure 7.3). Figure 7.3 shows a general list, but if you click on the "Notes" tab, you see the comments that others entered when

[1] http://delicious.com

Figure 7.2. Searching Delicious.com

Figure 7.3. Viewing Who Has Bookmarked a Site in Delicious.com

they originally bookmarked the site (see Figure 7.4). You also see a list of the most popular tags that users have used to describe the site.

Figure 7.4. Viewing Comments in Delicious.com

This is where the concept of "folksonomy" is demonstrated. You not only see the comments other people have made on a particular site, you also get the additional terms they used to tag it. You can further expand your search on those tags, so your search results are influenced by real people's classification of the Web, not on a machine's.

Furthermore, you can click on another user to see all of the sites that he or she has bookmarked (as long as they have made them public). Figure 7.5 shows the bookmarks for Dalton Publishing, an independent press in Austin, Texas. We found their bookmarks, and hence their Website, only two clicks away from the very general search term "books" that we started with—this would be nearly impossible in a traditional search engine.

Figure 7.5. Dalton Publishing's Bookmarks

Hopefully, you see how powerful these sites can be in helping you reach millions of potential readers you may not have reached otherwise.

Using Social Bookmarking Sites

To get started, get an account with Delicious.com. Once you have an account, the service walks you through how to add a button to your browser's task bar so you can bookmark sites easily.

Figure 7.6 demonstrates how you would bookmark a site using Delicious.com from a Firefox browser. When you come across a site you want to bookmark, just click on the "post to delicious" button on your browser's task bar—you then see a screen similar to Figure 7.6. Here is where you enter your chosen "tags" and your notes to the site you want to bookmark. Make these descriptive, since this is what attracts others to your account if they happen to come across your notes on this particular site.

Figure 7.6. Bookmarking a Website to Delicious.com

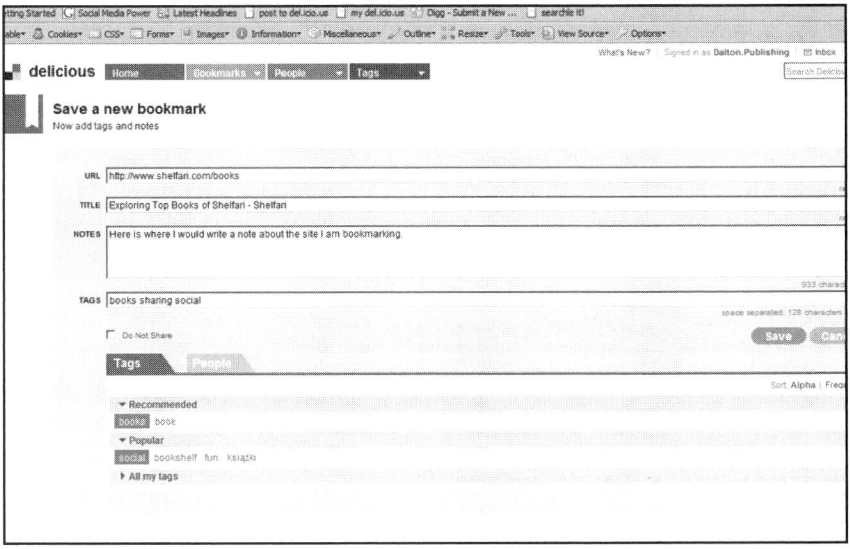

Once you have bookmarked many sites, you can search them just like you search the entire Delicious site—based on tags. Figure 7.5 shows the bookmarks for Dalton Publishing. Figure 7.7 shows only Dalton Publishing's bookmarks that are tagged with the term "socialmedia."

Figure 7.7. Dalton Publishing's Bookmarks, Tagged

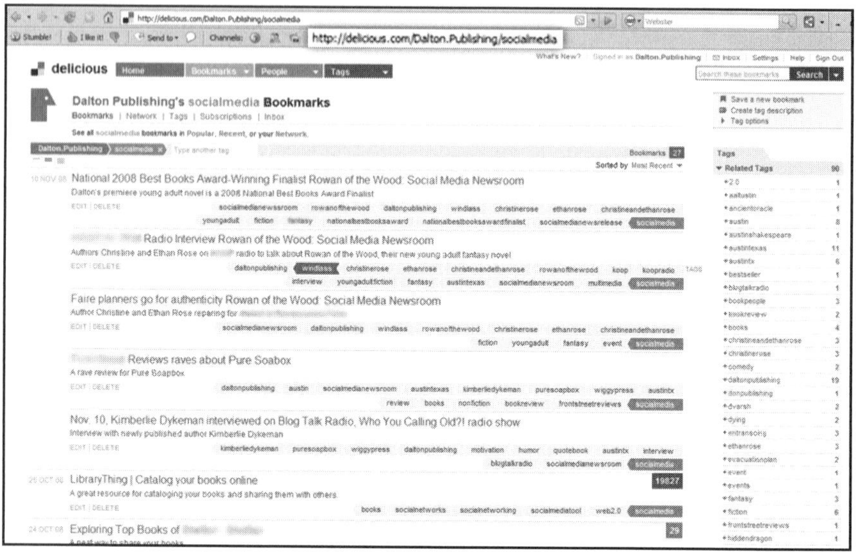

A Social Bookmarking Strategy

The first thing to do is get a good feel for a number of social bookmarking sites. There are some popular sites listed at the end of this chapter and on the resource CD. Choose a couple that represent your interests. If you do not feel inclined to do the research, I recommend starting with Delicious.com, Technorati, and StumbleUpon. Using these three sites should give you a broad reach into the world of social bookmarking.

Before you begin using a bookmarking site, however, become familiar with their guidelines. Some sites are much more stringent than others about bookmarking your own sites, or representing a business of any sort. It is best to go forward informed rather than risk getting a reputation for ignoring the rules, or worse, getting banned from a site.

As you develop your social bookmarking strategy, keep in mind that the Social Web is about interacting, sharing, and collaboration—not self promotion. Bookmark, tag, and comment on sites that interest you, and connect with others with similar interests. You will be amazed at how many people you ultimately reach. There is nothing wrong with bookmarking your own Web pages or blog posts, as long as the site allows it; just balance those contributions with others.

I know I sound like a broken record on this point, but fill out your profiles completely! You don't want to go through the trouble of bookmarking a bunch of sites, only to have others not even know how to find *your* Website if they find your bookmarks engaging enough to click through to your profile.

Create a list of your best key terms to use as tags and use them as often as they apply to the sites you bookmark. Use your best tags within the descriptions you give each of your bookmarked sites as well.

Many of the social bookmarking sites have developed social networking characteristics as well. If available, you should join groups that are relevant to your area of expertise or interest and subscribe to email updates for those groups.

Purpose-Built Delicious Pages

When you create your Delicious.com account, the link to your bookmarks look something like this: http://delicious.com/your.account, where "your.account" is the username you chose when you created your account. When you bookmark a Website and "tag" it, you in essence create another URL that looks like this: http://delicious.com/your.account/tag.

For example, on Figure 7.7 notice the URL at the top of the browser: http://delicious.com/Dalton.Publishing/socialmedia. This is there because we searched for all bookmarked sites in Dalton Publishing's account with the tag "socialmedia."

Now, imagine that you can create a URL for any collection of sites you want by just bookmarking the sites in Delicious.com using a common tag. These are called "purpose-built Delicious pages."

Rather than tagging your favorite sites blindly, think about how you might tag them intentionally to create your own purpose-built pages that contain a collection of related sites. For instance, you could create links to several pages like this:

- delicious.com/your.account/company.name
- delicious.com/your.account/public.relations
- delicious.com/your.account/client.name

- delicious.com/your.account/competition
- delicious.com/your.account/book.title
- delicious.com/your.account/author.name

You can then use links to those URLs in the body of your Websites, blogs, news releases, etc.

Book publishers and companies with many advocates can especially benefit from these pages. A publisher could collect sites relevant to each of its authors and book titles, and use links in each author or title's respective press releases, media pages, or by the authors themselves on their own Websites or blogs.

The best demonstrated use of purpose-built pages are within social media newsrooms and news releases—see Chapter 10, "Social Media Newsrooms."

Other Popular Social Bookmarking Sites

Technorati[2]

"Technorati was founded to help bloggers to succeed by collecting, highlighting, and distributing the online global conversation. As the leading blog search engine and most comprehensive source of information on the blogosphere, we index more than 1.5 million new blog posts in real time and introduce millions of readers to blog and social media content."

—Technorati.com

StumbleUpon[3]

"StumbleUpon helps you discover and share great websites. As you click Stumble!, we deliver high-quality pages matched to your personal preferences. These pages have been explicitly recommended by your friends or one of 6 million+ other websurfers with interests similar to you. Rating the sites you like automatically shares them with like-minded people – and helps you discover great sites your friends recommend."

—StumbleUpon.com

---

[2] http://www.technorati.com
[3] http://www.stumbleupon.com

Searchles[4]

"Searchles is a highly scalable 'social search' platform that showcases expertise, enables collaboration with peers and instantly captures it in searchable knowledge indexes. The platform is a hybrid, combining aspects of 'social bookmarking' and 'social networking' technology with analytical 'social search' capability. You decide who influences your discovery efforts, when and how through networks of trust you create—no other bookmarking or social search site lets you do that!"

—Searchles.com

Crowd-Sourcing

A *crowd-sourced* news site allows its users to determine the popularity of a news story, blog entry, or Website through various types of voting or rating systems. Most of these sites also have certain social aspects, allowing users to connect to others with similar interests. Connections between users are usually made through the conversations that ensue around a particular story, blog post, or Website.

This system gives news-searchers an alternative to what is served up to them by the regular news sites. It offers a way for searchers to see how other people rate stories and what they have to say about them. This concept of user-rated content is what has been coined "crowd-sourcing."

Crowd-Sourcing in Action

Digg[5] is an example of a crowd-sourced news site since it encourages people to "digg" the stories they like, which will in turn bring the most "dugg" stories or blog posts closer to the front page of the site. Each news site has its own unique twist on this concept.

---

[4] http://www.searchles.com
[5] http://www.digg.com

Figure 7.8 shows the front page of Digg. All of the stories listed have been added by users, and "dugg" by other users—some of the most popular of these stories will show up on this front page. Digg's front page offers a number of general areas (like Technology, World & Business, Science, etc.) to click on for more specific news to fit your interests. It also offers crowd-sourced videos and images.

Figure 7.8. Front Page of Digg.com

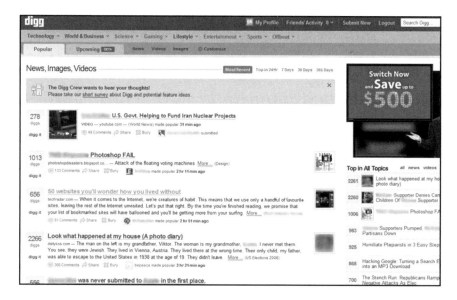

Search crowd-sourced news sites the same way you search other news sites or search engines. Figure 7.9 shows the search results for the search term "business social networking." The search results will show stories,

Figure 7.9. Search Results on Digg.com

blogs, and Websites other users have added that fit the search criteria along with how many people have "dugg" each result—this number is to the left of each result in Figure 7.9.

You see a few additional ways to filter or sort your search results as well. For instance, you can choose to see only the stories that made it to the front page of Digg, or all stories, or you can order the search results by "the best match," "the most diggs," etc. (see Figure 7.10).

Figure 7.10. Filtering Searches in Digg.com

Once you find a story of interest, you can go directly to the story, read others' comments on the story, or see the other users who dugg the story. Figure 7.11 shows a few of the comments other users posted on the first

Figure 7.11. Comments on Submissions to Digg.com

story listed in Figure 7.9. From here, you can connect with others by adding comments of your own or going to another user's profile (see Figure 7.12). If you find their profile interesting, you might want to visit one of their Websites or explore other stories they have dugg.

Figure 7.12. User Profile on Digg.com

Using Crowd-Sourced News Sites

Once you have an account with a crowd-sourced news site, you can add your own content and/or rate existing content. Continuing with Digg as an example, to add a story to the news site, you can go to Digg.com and click on the "Submit New" button at the top right of the page (see Figure 7.8 on Page 186).

Figure 7.13 shows the first screen you see when you submit a new link to the site. Pay close attention to the submission guidelines listed to the left. Each crowd-sourced site has its own submission guidelines. Become familiar with them before you submit.

Figure 7.13. Submitting to Digg.com

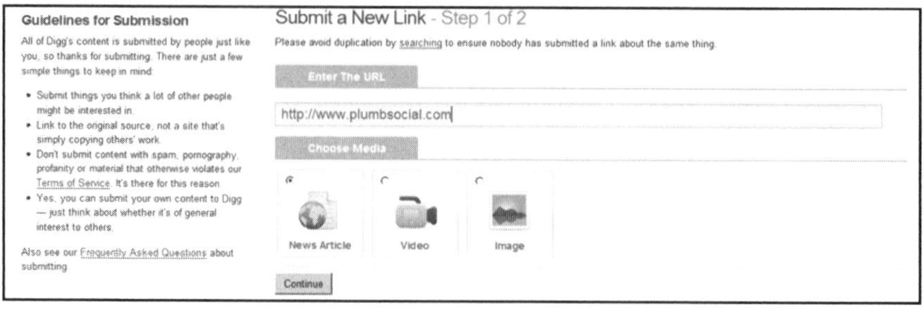

Figure 7.14 shows the next step, which is to enter a title and description for your submission. Just as you did with social bookmarking entries, use as many of your best key terms in each title and description as you can. You also need to choose a topic (category) to place your submission in during this step.

Figure 7.14. Submitting to Digg.com.

Once you submit your entry at the second step above, Digg then searches all of its existing entries for duplicates. It then presents a list of possible sites that might be a match to your submission. If it has already been added to Digg by another user, you can still digg it, but it will retain the title and description given by the original submitter. If your submission is original, you see a screen like Figure 7.15.

For convenience, you can digg stories on the fly right from your browser by installing a button on your browser's task bar.[6]

To digg a story that you find interesting while you are browsing the Digg site, just click on "Digg it" to the left of the story. Likewise, if you would like to comment on a story, click "comments" just under the story's title. See Figure 7.8, on Page 186.

---

[6] http://digg.com/tools/

Figure 7.15. Submitting to Digg.com

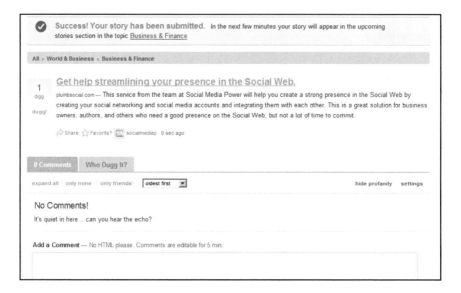

A Crowd-Sourcing Strategy

Crowd-sourced news sites are different from social bookmarking sites in that they focus on sharing news and information *about* stories, Websites, and blogs, as opposed to sharing bookmarks *to* Websites or blogs. As a result, you want to use a different strategy for these sites than you would social bookmarking sites.

There are a lot of crowd-sourced news sites out there, so you may want to explore a number of the sites we mention at the end of this chapter or on the resource CD to get a feel for them. You should be able to choose a few sites that are good fits for your message.

As always, fill out your profiles completely so that others can find their way to you easily.

Add some of your more newsworthy blog posts, Web pages, or online press releases to each of your chosen crowd-sourced news sites. Pay close attention to each site's submission guidelines and do not add information that does not adhere to their guidelines or is not a good fit for the site. When considering whether to add something to one of these sites, ask yourself if it is something *you* would find newsworthy, and if you would *naturally* share it with others. Just like with social bookmarking sites, be sure to offset your own content by contributing other content as well.

You will get a natural following of readers from these sites if you contribute regularly and engage in the conversations that happen around topics of interest. The advantage to this strategy is that you can hone in on your target audience by seeking out and commenting on topics relevant to your product, book, or message.

Many of these sites have also added social networking features, so explore any additional ways the sites may offer to connect, such as groups.

Other Popular Crowd Sourcing Sites

reddit[7]

"[R]eddit is a source for what's new and popular on the Web—personalized for you. Your votes train a filter, so let reddit know what you liked and disliked, because you'll begin to see recommended links filtered to your tastes. All of the content on reddit is submitted and voted on by users like you."

—reddit.com

Mixx[8]

"You find it; we'll Mixx it. Use YourMixx to tailor the content categories, tags, specific users and groups, and we'll deliver the top-rated content as chosen by you and people who share your passions. So go ahead and whip up your own version of the Web. Just tell us how you like it Mixxed and we'll deliver the best the Web has to offer—morning, noon and night."

—Mixx.com

Gabbr[9]

Gabbr.com [is] a community based social networking news site. Gabbr. com allows you to take advantage of a number of useful Web based features in a social context….The latest news from agencies like CNN, Reuters, the Associated Press and BBC are accessible through Gabbr

---

[7] http://www.reddit.com
[8] http://www.mixx.com
[9] http://www.gabbr.com

and updated in real time. The top headlines in the blogosphere are also readable through Gabbr's interface. But you don't just read the news at Gabbr, you interact with other users by contributing to the discussion. Users can comment on any story through Gabbr to be a part of the news story."

—Gabbr.com

Preparation And Tracking Your Progress

Use a sheet like Figure 7.16 to list the Web pages and blog posts you plan to add to bookmarking and crowd-sourced news sites, along with some of your best key terms as tags, and descriptions that also include those key terms.

If you have a lot of content you plan to add, or if you are doing bookmarking and crowd-sourcing for your clients, you may want to keep a record of your additions to these sites (see Figure 7.17).

Fillable versions of these worksheets are available on the resource CD.

Figure 7.16. A Form for Organizing Submissions

Company Name: Social Media Power			
URL	Title	Description	Tags
http://www.socialmediapower.com/articles/social-media-news-releases-explained/	Social Media News Releases Explained	A thorough explanation of social media news releases, with links to examples.	social media, social media newsroom, social media news release, social media optimization, Web 2.0
Http://www.socialmediapower.com/2008/08/28/the-30-minute-facebook-application/	The 30-minute Facebook Application	Learn how to further optimize your presence in the social Web by creating your own Facebook application in 30 minutes or less.	social media, social networking, facebook, facebook applications, web 2.0
http://www.socialmediapower.com/2008/06/02/top-9-wordpress-plugins/	Top 9 Most Useful Wordpress Plugins	A list of essential plugins for anyone looking to optimize their Wordpress site for social media and Web 2.0	social media, wordpress, plugins, social media optimization, social bookmarking, SEO, social media tools, Web 2.0
http://www.socialmediapower.com/articles/social-media-newsrooms-the-ultimate-web-20-tool-for-your-business/	Social Media Newsroom: The Ultimate Web 2.0 Tool for Your Business	A social media newsroom is one place to send the media, prospective clients, book reviewers, or anyone who wants to know all about you, your business, or your book. It is the ultimate Web 2.0 tool for your business.	social media, social media newsroom, web 2.0, social media tools, web 2.0 tools, social media optimization

A Note On Making Your Content Sharable

Hopefully this chapter has demonstrated for you how important it is for you to make your own content easily shared on social bookmarking and crowd-sourcing sites. Refer to Chapter 3, "RSS Feeds & Blogs," Chapter 12, "Pulling It All Together," and Chapter 9, "Widgets & Badges" for more information on how to do this.

Figure 7.17. A Form for Tracking Activity

Company Name: Social Media Power			
Date	**Original URL**	**Bookmarking Site**	**Bookmark URL**
11/11/08	http://www.socialmediapower.com/artic les/social-media-news-releases-explained/	Delicious	http://delicious.com/social.media.power/socialmedianewsrelease
		Digg	http://digg.com/tech_news/Social_Media_News_Releases_Explain ed
11/11/08	Http://www.socialmediapower.com/200 8/08/28/the-30-minute-facebook-application/	Delicious	http://delicious.com/social.media.power/facebookapplications
		Digg	http://digg.com/tech_news/The_30_minute_Facebook_Application
11/11/08	http://www.socialmediapower.com/2008/06/ 02/top-9-wordpress-plugins/	Delicious	http://delicious.com/social.media.power/wordpress
		Digg	http://digg.com/tech_news/Top_9_Most_Useful_WordPress_Plugin s
11/11/08	http://www.socialmediapower.com/articles/s ocial-media-newsrooms-the-ultimate-web-20-tool-for-your-business/	Delicious	http://delicious.com/social.media.power/socialmedianewsrooms
		Digg	http://digg.com/tech_news/Social_Media_Newsrooms_A_Web_2_ 0_Tool_for_Your_Business

This Chapter On The Resource CD

- Linkable Resources
- Fillable Forms:
  - › Social Bookmarking Strategy
  - › Crowd-Sourcing Strategy
  - › Social Bookmarking & Crowd-Sourcing Submission Form
  - › Social Bookmarking & Crowd-Sourcing Tracking Form

8 Media Communities

Media communities are social sites where you can save, share, and comment on multimedia items. It is yet another way Internet users have found to connect with one another—by finding similar interests around images and videos.

In addition to increasing your exposure in the Social Web, adding your images and video to media communities can have other advantages. There are many open source applications that tap into the power of these sites to offer you a host of features you can add to your blog or Website, features like image and video galleries, portfolios, or sidebar widgets. With proper planning, you can even see better search engine placement for your images and video files by adding them to media communities.

Image Sharing Sites

Image sharing sites are a way for you to get some serious mileage out of your photos and other images. With the right strategy, you can maximize the ways in which potential clients and readers can find you through your posted images in the Social Web.

Image Sharing in Action

Flickr[1] is probably the most popular site on the Internet for sharing images. Flickr offers a place for you to share your images with others, as well as a platform for organizing and linking to your images.

Figure 8.1 shows the Flickr account for Dalton Publishing. This opening screen shows the most recently uploaded images.

Along the right are the sets of images Dalton has created. A "set" is a collection of related images. You can create up to three sets with a free Flickr account, or unlimited sets with a "pro" account. A pro account

Figure 8.1. A Typical Flickr* Account With Sets

---

[1] http://www.flickr.com

runs $25 a year. Dalton creates a set for each of their books, for each significant event they host, and for a few miscellaneous collections of images—like one for all of their book covers. Figure 8.3 shows a set of images. You can reach this screen by clicking on any set.

Figure 8.3. A Flickr Set

By clicking on a specific image, you can see more detail for that image, like the tags and descriptions assigned to it when it was uploaded (see Figure 8.4). If you click on a specific tag, you can view all the other images

Figure 8.4. Flickr Image Detail

that Dalton Publishing associated with that tag. Figure 8.5 shows all of the images tagged with the term "dalton publishing."

Figure 8.5. Tagged Images in Flickr

When you upload images, you can make them public so that anyone can view them, or private so that only people who are your "friends" on Flickr can see them. Public images can be viewed and commented on by anyone. Figure 8.6 shows how you might comment on an image.

Figure 8.6. Commenting on an Image in Flickr

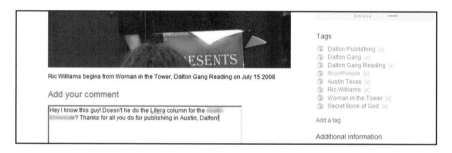

*All Flickr images reproduced with permission of Yahoo! Inc. ©2009 Yahoo! Inc. Flickr is a registered trademark of Yahoo! Inc. Figure 8.2. There is *no* Figure 8.2.

Using Image Sharing Sites

Uploading and Optimizing Your Images

Once you have an account, uploading images to sites like Flickr is easy. However, just because it is easy is no reason to go to it without a plan. Read the "Image Sharing Strategy" section on Page 206, and go forward with a good plan so you can maximize the effectiveness of using these communities.

Figure 8.7 shows one of the options you can use to upload images to your Flickr account. You can reach this menu by signing in to your account and clicking "Upload Images and Video." There are three steps to this process:

1. Choosing your images

2. Uploading your images

3. Giving your uploaded images good titles, descriptions, and tags.

You can upload several images at a time as shown in Figure 8.7. Just select each image you want to upload and click "open."

Figure 8.7. Uploading Flickr Images

On the next screen (Figure 8.8) you can perform batch operations, like assigning tags to each image, adding all the images to a specific set, even adding a new set on the fly. In our example, we are uploading photos taken from one of Dalton Publishing's author events. Therefore, we want to "tag" each image with the author's name, the book title, and the event name. In this case, the author has three books in a series, so our tags include the title of each book, as well as the series name.

Figure 8.8. Batch Operations on Uploaded Flickr Images

Figure 8.9 shows the titles and descriptions that we assigned to each image. We make a point to use the author's name, the event name, and at least one of the book titles in each title and description. Note that when you upload an image, Flickr will automatically use the name of the file as the title. You want to be sure and change the title to one that uses several good key terms as we did in our example. Figure 8.10 shows Dalton Publishing's "photostream" along with the new set to the right, and the recently uploaded images.

There is a great tool called the "Flickr Uploadr" that you can download to your desktop. The tool allows you to upload to Flickr right from your desktop by dragging and dropping images into the tool. Figure 8.11 shows

Figure 8.11. Flickr Tools Menu

flickr
Signed in as Dalton Publishing   Help   Sign Out

Home   You   Organize   Contacts   Groups   Explore   Search

Help / Tools

There are loads of ways for you to upload to Flickr, in addition to the web-based upload form. Try out one of these tools to get your photos or video online quickly and effectively.

m.flickr.com

Do you use a mobile phone?
You can upload straight to Flickr by email, or using one of our cool partner services.
Check out the Flickr Mobile Tools.

Upload by email

Figure 8.9. Assigning Titles and Descriptions to Images

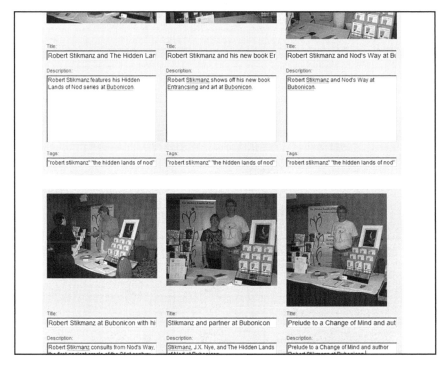

Figure 8.10. Uploaded Images in Flickr Photostream

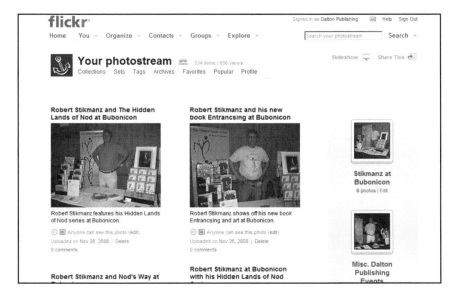

the download screen used to access the tool. You can reach this screen by clicking on "help/tools" at the bottom of your main photostream page, or by going to this link: http://www.flickr.com/tools/.

Creating Badges

From the tools screen in Figure 8.11, you can create a Flickr badge. A Flickr badge is a widget that you can place on your Website or blog that displays images from your Flickr account as a small gallery. Figure 8.12 shows a Flickr badge in the right sidebar.

Figure 8.12. Flickr Badge and Gallery on Website

On the right sidebar of the tools screen is a link to "build a badge." There are a few steps to creating your badge: First, choose what type of badge you want, then choose which images to include; then you choose layout options and colors, and finally, copy the code to place on your site or blog.

The first step is to choose whether you want to create an HTML badge or a Flash badge (Figure 8.13). A Flash badge offers some movement to an

Figure 8.13. Creating a Flickr Badge

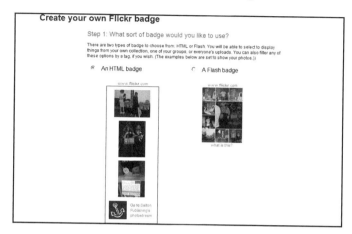

otherwise static site, while an HTML badge is static, but takes less time to load.

Figure 8.14 shows the next step, which is to choose which images you want in your badge—all of them, images tagged with a certain key term, or images in a specific set.

Figure 8.14. Creating a Flickr Badge

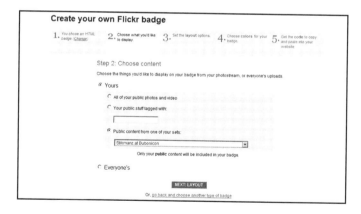

If you chose to create an HTML badge, the next screen (Figure 8.15) allows you to choose certain layout options like number of images, size of images, etc. If you chose a Flash badge you go directly to the color options screen.

Figure 8.15. Creating a Flickr Badge

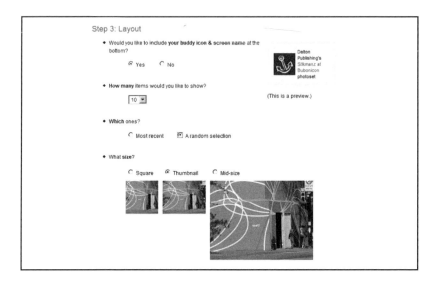

Figure 8.16 shows the color options screen. You can enter hex numbers for your colors if you know them, or use the color picker.

Finally, in the next step, the code for your badge is generated (Figure 8.17). Copy this code and place it anywhere you want in the body of your site's HTML code or as a sidebar widget on your WordPress blog.

Figure 8.16. Creating a Flickr Badge

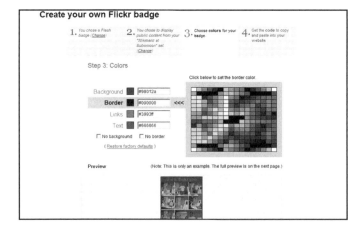

Placing the code from Figure 8.17 into a sidebar widget (see Page 99) produces the Flickr badge on that WordPress site's sidebar as seen on Figure 8.12 on Page 202.

Figure 8.17. Copying Flickr Badge Code

Galleries and Adding Flickr Images to Blog Posts

One reason it is a good idea to organize your images in sets is that there are many plugins for WordPress and other applications that rely on sets to help you create galleries. Figure 8.12 on Page 202 shows a gallery from a WordPress site that was created using the plugin called "Flickr Tag."[2] This plugin allows you to easily create galleries using your Flickr sets, as well as embed your Flickr images into your blog posts and pages.

Figure 8.18 shows the code that is used to create a gallery from Flickr sets using Flickr Tag. Each of your Flickr sets has a number, which are the numbers you see in the code. For instance, the "Stikmanz at Bubonicon" set we just created is shown in Figure 8.19. If you look at the address in the browser, you see the set's number, which is why the images for that set show up in the gallery as shown in Figure 8.12 on Page 202.

---

[2]http://wordpress.org/extend/plugins/flickr-tag/

Figure 8.18. Using the Flickr Tag Plugin for Galleries

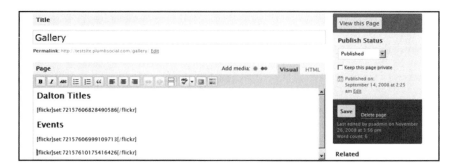

Figure 8.19. Finding a Flickr Set Number Using Your Browser

Figure 8.20 shows how you can use the tool to embed images into blog posts or pages simply by clicking on the image (or set) you want to add.

Another good application for WordPress, as well as for a traditional Website, is Simple Viewer.[3] Once you have Simple Viewer installed, you can use an add-on called Flickr Viewer to import your Flickr images into your gallery.

Image Sharing Strategy

- Get an account with the image community of your choice and fill out your profile completely (see Figure 8.21). Remember that this may be the only chance you get to make an impression on potential clients or readers.

---

[3]http://www.airtightinteractive.com/simpleviewer/

Figure 8.20. Using the Flickr Tag Plugin to Embed Images

Figure 8.21. Using Key Terms in Flickr Profiles

- Gather the images you can upload right away. This may include:
  › Logos
  › Head shots of company principals
  › Author photos
  › Book covers
  › Event photos
- Prepare a main key term list to use as tags for every image. This may be your company name, principal name, author name, book title, home city, etc.
- For each image you want to upload prepare:
  › A list of key terms to use as tags in addition to your main key term list.
  › A short title that uses at least two key terms.
  › A description that uses several key terms.
- Use a form like Figure 8.21.1 so you will be prepared when uploading images. A printable version of this form is available on the resource CD.

- Pull images from your account onto your blog and/or Website:
  - › As a badge or widget
  - › As an image gallery
- Connect with others by browsing images and commenting.

Figure 8.21.1 Prep Form for Image Communities

Image Community Upload Form			
Image Name	Title	Description	Tags
Stikmanz2-bubonicon8-24-008	Robert Stikmanz and The Hidden Lands of Nod at Bubonicon	Dalton Publishing author, Robert Stikmanz, features his Hidden Lands of Nod series at Bubonicon.	dalton publishing, robert stikmanz, the hidden lands of nod, prelude to a change of mind, entrancing, bubonicon
Stikmanz2-bubonicon-8-23-008	Robert Stikmanz and his new book Entrancing at Bubonicon	Dalton Publishing author, Robert Stikmanz, shows off his new book Entrancing and art at Bubonicon.	dalton publishing, robert stikmanz, the hidden lands of nod, nod's way, entrancing, bubonicon

Other Image Sharing Communities

While searching for a list of photo sharing sites, I came across an interesting chart by Chris Silver Smith called "Comparison of Image Sharing Sites for Potential SEO Benefit".[4] This chart lists the sites and how they will benefit your SEO placement.

Video Sharing Sites

Many claim that video is the future of the Internet. That may be true, and if it is, YouTube and other video sharing sites are where you want to have a good presence when that future comes. Even if you do not have video of your own to upload, you can take advantage of these sites by building galleries from videos others have uploaded or by connecting to others by commenting on their videos.

Using Video Sharing Sites

Uploading and Optimizing Your Videos

Figure 8.22 shows the front page of YouTube.[5] From here you can search and watch videos or upload your own if you have an account. Clicking the "Upload" button in the upper right of this screen yields the Video Upload screen shown in Figure 8.23.

---

[4]http://silvery.com/PhotoSharingComparison.html
[5]http://www.youtube.com

Figure 8.22. YouTube Home Page

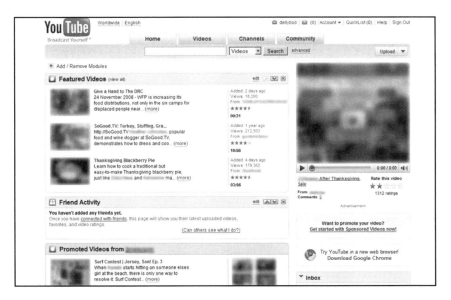

Figure 8.23. YouTube Video Upload Screen

When uploading video clips, follow the same guidelines as you do for uploading images: Prepare a list of key terms and use them as tags and in the body of a video's title and description. YouTube also requires that you choose a category for your uploaded videos.

You can optionally add a date and a Google map to the location where your video was taken, as well as "Sharing Options" that include whether you want others to be able to comment, embed, or syndicate your videos. See Figure 8.24.

Figure 8.24. YouTube Uploaded Video Options

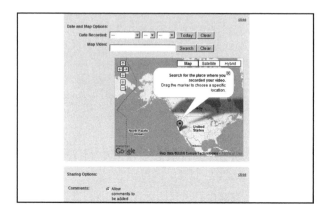

Channels, Favorites, Quicklists, and Playlists

Your public page in YouTube is called your "channel." Figure 8.25 shows Dalton Publishing's channel. Get to this page by clicking on your username (dellybob in our example). You can edit your channel settings including descriptions, colors, which videos to display, and more by clicking "Edit Channel" from this page.

Add "Favorites" to your account on the fly as you browse the videos on YouTube. Others can browse your favorites on your channel page. See Figure 8.25.

You can add a video to your "Quicklist" if there is a little plus sign in the lower left of the video when you are browsing. Quicklists are good tools for saving groups of videos temporarily until you are ready to build a playlist with them.

"Playlists" are collections of videos that you can arrange in a specific order, share with others, or embed as galleries on your blog or Website.

To edit your channel, favorites, quicklists, and playlists, go to your account overview page (Figure 8.26). Reach this page by clicking "Account" from the upper right menu of the YouTube home page when you are signed in.

Figure 8.25. YouTube Channel

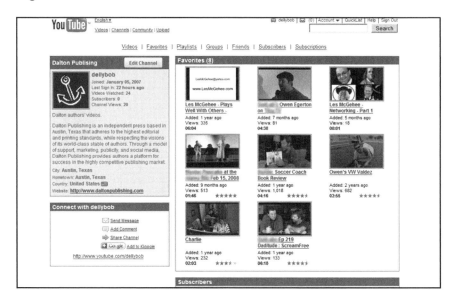

Figure 8.26. YouTube Account Overview Page

Embedding Videos and Galleries

Each public video on YouTube has an embed code that you can copy and paste into your Website or blog posts. See upper right area of Figure 8.27. You can also copy links if you don't want to embed the entire video.

Figure 8.27. YouTube Individual Video Detail

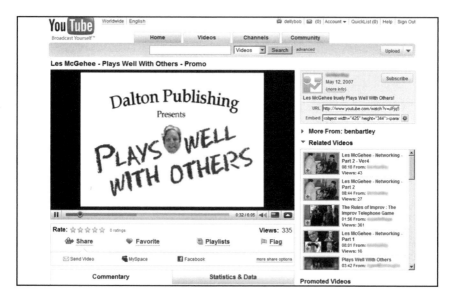

The easiest way to embed galleries is with playlists, since each YouTube playlist you create has its own embed code. To add a new playlist, go to your account menu and click on playlists (see Figure 8.26). Figure 8.28 shows a playlist from the Dalton account called "Gary Kent." When you

Figure 8.29. Adding Videos to YouTube Quicklist

Figure 8.28. YouTube Playlist Detail

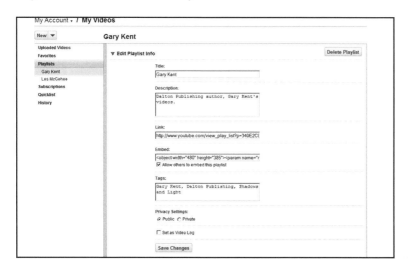

add playlists, use the same strategy as when adding individual videos. Use your best key terms as tags and in titles and descriptions.

Figure 8.29 shows a search on the key terms "Gary Kent." From this page, we use the little plus signs in the left corner of the videos that we want to save to add them to our quicklist.

Once we have all the videos in our quicklist that we want, we go back to our account page and click "Quicklists." See Figure 8.26 on Page 211. From here, you can select all or some of the videos in a quicklist and add them to a playlist. We added all of the quicklist videos to the Gary Kent playlist. See Figure 8.30.

Back at the accounts/playlist page (Figure 8.28), we copy the embed code for the playlist and embed it in a page on our WordPress site. Figures 8.31 and 8.32 show the embedded code and the resulting video gallery.

YouTube has a nice handbook[6] with some good pointers on creating and uploading videos.

---

[6]http://www.youtube.com/t/yt_handbook_home

Figure 8.30. Adding Videos to YouTube Playlist

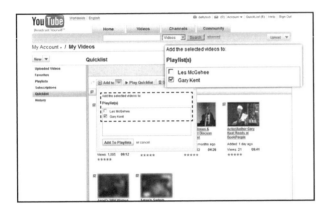

Figure 8.31. YouTube Gallery Code Embedded

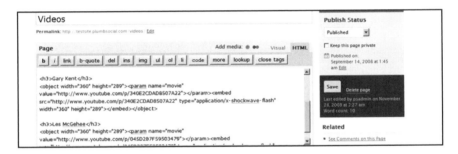

Figure 8.32. Resulting Gallery From YouTube Embed Code

Video Sharing Strategy

- Get an account with the video community of your choice and fill out your profile completely (see Figure 8.25 on Page 211). Remember that this may be the only chance you get to make an impression on potential clients or readers.

- Gather and prepare the video clips you plan to upload. YouTube accepts video files from most digital cameras, camcorders, and cell phones in the .AVI, .MOV, .WMV, and .MPG file formats.

- Prepare a main list of key terms to use as tags for every clip. This may be your company name, principal name, author name, book title, home city, etc.

- For each video you want to upload prepare:
  - › A list of key terms to use as tags in addition to your main key term list.
  - › A short title that uses at least two key terms.
  - › A description that uses several key terms.
  - › A YouTube category.

- Use a form like Figure 8.33 (replace "Image Name" with "Video Name") so you will be prepared when uploading video clips. A printable version of this form is available on the resource CD.

- Determine the organization of your account:
  - › Decide which playlists to create in your account by person's name, by company, by authors, by book titles, by product, etc.
  - › Create titles, descriptions, and key terms to use as tags for each playlist.
  - › Browse YouTube videos to add to your playlists.
  - › Create galleries on your Website or blog using the embed code from your playlists.

Figure 8.33 Prep Form for Video Communities

Image Community Upload Form			
Image Name	Title	Description	Tags
Stikmanz2-bubonicon8-24-008	Robert Stikmanz and The Hidden Lands of Nod at Bubonicon	Dalton Publishing author, Robert Stikmanz, features his Hidden Lands of Nod series at Bubonicon.	dalton publishing, robert stikmanz, the hidden lands of nod, prelude to a change of mind, entranscing, bubonicon
Stikmanz2-bubonicon-8-23-008	Robert Stikmanz and his new book Entranscing at Bubonicon	Dalton Publishing author, Robert Stikmanz, shows off his new book Entranscing and art at Bubonicon.	dalton publishing, robert stikmanz, the hidden lands of nod, nod's way, entranscing, bubonicon

Searching And Search Engine Placement

You search images in Flickr and videos in YouTube using search terms just as you do in a search engine like Google. Your search results return images or videos that have your search terms in their title or description.

Figure 8.34 shows a search in Flickr on the terms "publishing austin." In the results are a number of the images from Dalton Publishing's Flickr account, specifically, the ones with the terms "publishing" and "austin" in the images' file names.

Flickr displays details on each image that is returned in a search. The first image displayed from the search in Figure 8.34, for instance, shows:

- The file name: "Dalton Publishing display at BookPeople in Austin, Texas"
- Who posted the image: by "Dalton Publishing"
- What tags it was assigned: Tagged with "austintexas, bookpeople, daltonpublishing"
- When it was taken and when it was uploaded

Figure 8.35. Exploring Tags in Flickr

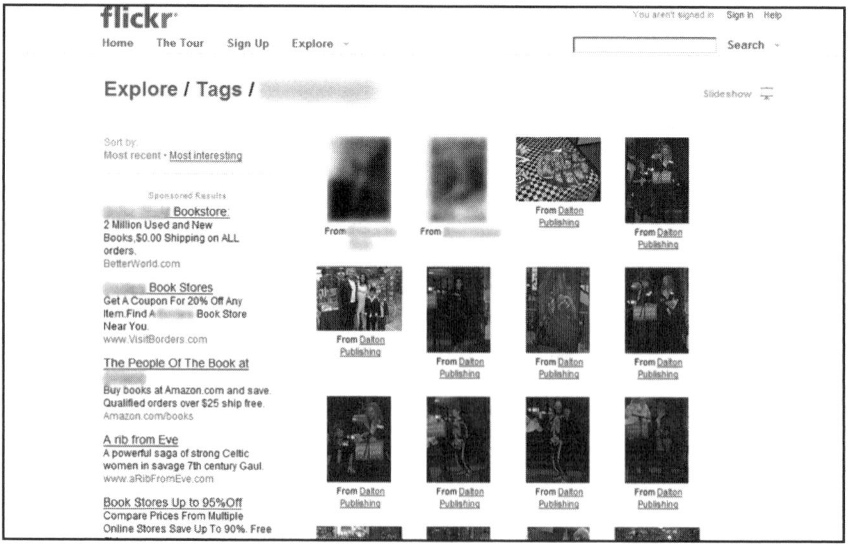

- Links to more photos by the poster of the image, or to their profile: "See Dalton Publishing's photos or profile"

Figure 8.34. Search Results in Flickr

From here, you can further explore images by clicking on the tags that others have assigned to their uploaded images. By clicking on the "bookpeople" tag in our example, we get the results as shown in Figure 8.35. This shows all of the images in Flickr that are tagged with specific terms, not just the images of a particular user, thus further expanding and honing your search results.

It is during such a search that others may happen upon your profile. Figure 8.21 on Page 207 shows Dalton Publishing's Flickr profile. Be sure and fill in your profile completely; it is how other users will ultimately find their way back to your blog, Website, or products.

An added perk to using Flickr is that your images also get good placement in the Yahoo! search engine. Searching Yahoo! Image search using the same terms we used in the previous example, we will see some of the same results. See Figure 8.36.

Figure 8.36. Fickr Images in Yahoo!* Search Results

Figure 8.37 shows a search in YouTube using the term "les mcgehee" who is one of Dalton Publishing's authors.

Like Flickr, Youtube displays details on each video that is returned in a search. These details include the name of the video, part of the description, when the video was added, who uploaded the video, how many times it has been viewed, how the video has been rated by others, and the video length.

From the search result's screen, one can watch a video, link to the profile of the person who added the video, and search under the same terms for channels and playlists that include the videos.

Notice in Figure 8.38 that there are two video playlists that Dalton Publishing has added to. This is another way people can find you in a video community search.

---

*All Yahoo! images reproduced with permission of Yahoo! Inc. ©2009 Yahoo! Inc. YAHOO! is a registered trademark of Yahoo! Inc.

Figure 8.37. Search Results in YouTube

Figure 8.38. Playlists in YouTube Search Results

Figure 8.39 shows a search using the same terms ("les mcgehee") in Google video search. Just as with Flickr and Yahoo! Image search, one is most likely to see the videos from YouTube listed first in a Google video search.

Figure 8.39. YouTube Videos in Google Search Results

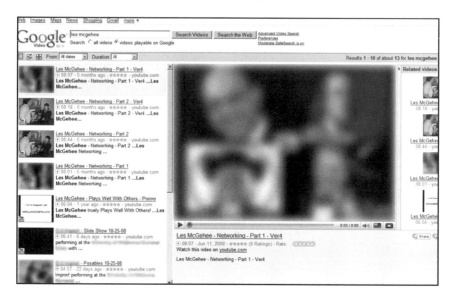

Connecting With Others

Do not forget that the purpose of media sharing communities is for people to connect with each other through a shared medium like images and video. You can reach a lot of potential clients and readers by becoming a part of such communities, but you need to take the time to connect.

This Chapter On The Resource CD

- Further Reading
- Linkable Resources
- Fillable Forms:
  - › Image Sharing Strategy
  - › Prep Form For Image Communities
  - › Video Sharing Strategy
  - › Prep Form For Video Communities

9 Widgets & Badges

Figure 9.1 shows a sidebar from Dalton Publishing's social media Website. On this Web page are many widgets and badges. From the top down, they are:

- A widget from FeedBurner.com that helps visitors subscribe to the site's RSS feed via email
- A widget from AddtoAny.com that visitors can use to subscribe to Dalton's RSS feed in many different feed readers
- A widget from AddtoAny.com that visitors can use to share or bookmark Dalton's site in social bookmarking or crowd-sourcing sites
- A number of badges—from Facebook to Shelfari—that lead a visitor to Dalton's profiles on their respective sites
- A widget from Flickr.com that imports and highlights images from Dalton's Flickr account
- A widget from Upcoming.org (not visible) that imports and lists Dalton's upcoming events

Figure 9.1. Widgets on a Website

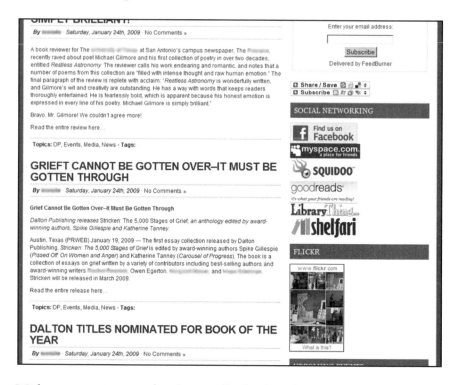

Widgets are snippets of code, usually displayed graphically, that can be used to syndicate content, for example RSS feeds, or to add interactive features that users can drop onto their own blogs or Websites. Widgets are often customizable by the user and typically offer ways for users to pull information from the widget's originating site.

In the example above, for instance, each of the widgets demonstrated were created by going to a social site (like Flickr.com), finding where they offer widgets, customizing the widget to display specific images along with color and size options, copying the code, and placing the code within the Dalton Website via the WordPress widget panel (see Page 115).

Though the terms widget and badge are often used interchangeably in the Web 2.0 community, a badge is typically just an icon or logo that has a link back to its source, which serves as a way of displaying one's membership or presence in a community on the Social Web. Widgets are also referred to as "Gadgets." You may have installed a gadget or two on your desktop if you use Windows Vista. To avoid confusion, we will refer to all of them as widgets, unless their source refers to them otherwise.

Widgets come in different styles and levels of complexity. Some are simple links back to their source, others are as complex as mini search engines you can implement on your own site. They also vary in user friendliness. Most widgets, though, are simple to install and set up. This is what makes them so successful.

Individual widget installation varies, but, generally, the process is as follows:

1. Discover where a site offers its widgets or badges.
2. Choose the type of widget you want to generate from the source site.
3. Set widget options, and, if applicable, customize the look and feel of the widget.
4. The source populates the widget with your profile information (if applicable) and your customizations.
5. The source then generates the code for your widget.
6. Copy the generated HTML, JavaScript, or Flash code.
7. Place the resulting code onto your Website or blog where you want the widget to appear (see Page 254).

The examples highlighted in the following sections of this chapter demonstrate the level of complexity of widgets, as well as real world examples of how to install and use them.

Highlighting Your Social Web Presence

Some widgets help you show off all of the places you are in the Social Web. Some of these are just small icons that you download from a particular social site and place on your Website or blog with a link back to your profile or page. Other widgets pull information from your profile or from profiles you are connected to within a specific community.

Social Networking

In Chapter 6, "Social Networking & Micro-Blogging," we showed you several examples of using badges and widgets to promote your social networking presence. See Page 173 for one such example.

Here are a few, more specialized examples:

Twitter

From the Twitter/Apps menu, you can find a number of widgets to use on your Website, blog, or social networking sites (see Figure 6.41, Page 161).

Figure 9.2 shows the "Widgets by Twitter" widget options. With this widget you can display your Twitter updates or integrate Twitter into some of your other social networking sites.

Figure 9.2. Twitter Widgets

Figures 9.3 and 9.4 shows some of the screens used while integrating your Twitter account with your Facebook account. Figure 9.5 shows the resulting application page on Facebook.

Figures 9.3 and 9.4. Creating a Twitter Widget For Facebook

Figure 9.5. Twitter Widget on Facebook

Figures 9.6 and 9.7 show one way to create widget code to place on a Website or blog that displays a Twitter widget. Figure 9.8 shows the result once the code is pasted onto the Social Media Power Website.

Figures 9.6 & 9.7. Making a Twitter Widget

Figure 9.8. Twitter Widget On a Website

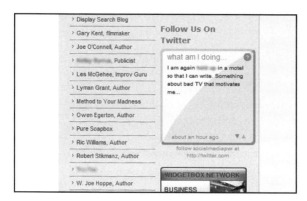

LinkedIn

LinkedIn offers a nice widget that displays your public profile as a sort of digital business card. Login to your LinkedIn account and go to Tools/ Developers at the bottom of the page. Figure 9.9 shows a few of the available widgets you can install on your Website.

Figure 9.9. LinkedIn Widgets

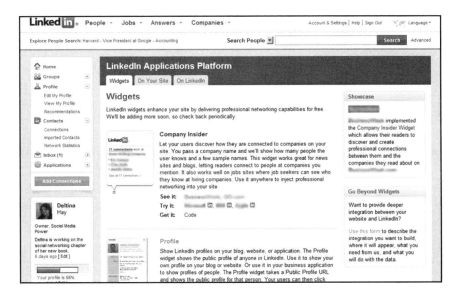

Figure 9.10 demonstrates the "Profile" widget. LinkedIn widgets are a little more involved than some of the others, but once they are set up, they work just fine. Follow the instructions carefully, and you should have no problem, or have your Webmaster help you.

Figure 9.10. Creating LinkedIn Widgets

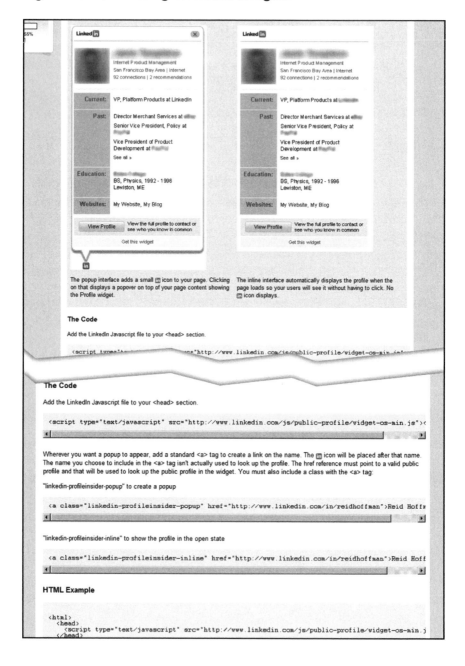

Figure 9.11 shows an example of this widget on the "About Us" page on the Social Media Power Website.

Figure 9.11. LinkedIn Widget On a Website

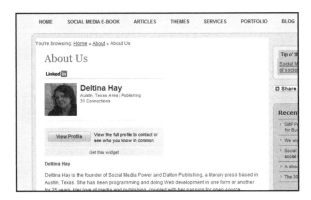

Shelfari

This niche social networking site has a stylish widget that displays your favorite books on a graphic bookshelf. Log in to your Shelfari account and go to My Shelfari/More/My Widgets. Figure 9.12 shows the first screen you see. Figure 9.13 shows the next screen. If you are planning to place the widget on one of the social sites listed (Facebook, MySpace, etc.), then click on the corresponding icon.

Figure 9.12. Creating a Shelfari Widget

Figure 9.13. Creating a Shelfari Widget

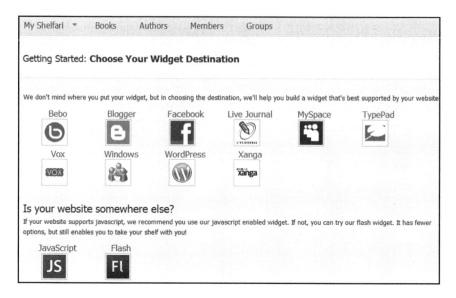

We want to place the widget on a Website, so we choose the JavaScript option. Figure 9.14 shows a list of filtering options used to select the books you wish to display on our bookshelf widget.

Figure 9.14. Creating a Shelfari Widget

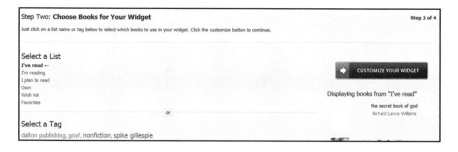

The next screen (Figure 9.15) shows ways you can further customize the widget. Once it is customized, copy the code and place it on the Website.

Figure 9.15. Creating a Shelfari Widget

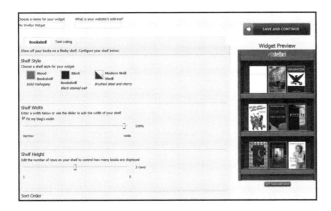

Figure 9.16 shows the resulting widget displayed on Dalton Publishing's social media Website.[1] Figure 9.17 shows the pop-up info box that shows when a visitor rolls over a book image.

Figure 9.16. Shelfari Widget On a Website

Figure 9.17. Shelfari Widget On a Website

Ning

Ning widgets can show off your own profile and list others in your network as well. Figure 9.18 shows what such a widget looks like in the development stage.

Figures 9.18. Creating a Widget For Ning

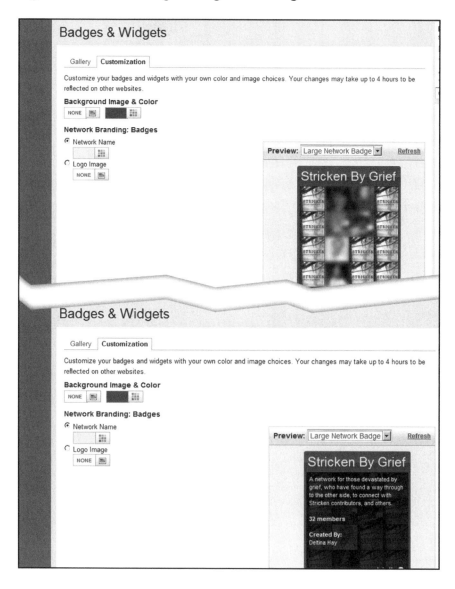

Media Communities

Chapter 8, "Media Communities," shows you how to create and install a Flickr badge, which is a widget that pulls images from your Flickr sets onto your Website or blog. See Page 202.

That chapter also shows you how to embed a YouTube gallery onto your Website. See Page 214. You can make your own YouTube widget by creating an embedded player and simply adjusting the size of the player to fit your sidebar.

You can find more widgets for Flickr, YouTube, and other media communities in widget sharing communities (see the "Widget Communities" section on Page 254) or as WordPress plugins (see the "Using Widgets in WordPress" section on Page 249).

Other Social Sites

You are likely to have many more sites that you want to highlight on your Website or blog. Some sites do not make their widgets or badges easy for users to find. To find available widgets for a site, first do a site-wide search using the search terms "widgets" or "badges." If that yields nothing, try searching the site's help area. If that still reveals nothing, try searching Google for "sitename widgets." If you were searching for YouTube widgets, for instance, you would search using the term "YouTube widgets."

Sharing And Syndicating Your Content

In Chapter 7, "Social Bookmarking & Crowd-Sourcing," we discuss improving your Social Web presence by contributing to social bookmarking and crowd-sourcing sites. We also discuss the importance of integrating an RSS feed or blog into your Web presence in Chapter 3, "RSS Feeds & Blogs." In this section we look at some widgets that encourage others to subscribe to your RSS feed and to share your site on social bookmarking or crowd-sourcing sites.

Feed Widgets

Chapter 3, "RSS Feeds & Blogs," shows you how to use feed widgets to promote your blog or RSS feed using FeedBurner chicklets and email widgets. See Page 80. There are many more user-friendly ways to encourage people to subscribe to your feed. Some of them even give your feed some extra exposure in the Social Web.

Here are a couple of specific examples:

Blidgets

The widget community Widgetbox[2] offers a feed widget called a "blidget." This blidget is a customizable widget that allows users to display your feed on their site. Read more about widget communities on Page 254.

Get an account with Widgetbox, then click on the "Make a Blidget" button (see Figure 9.19).

Figure 9.19. Creating a Widgetbox Blidget

---

[2] http://www.widgetbox.com

On the next screen enter your RSS feed or blog URL (see Figure 9.20). Refer to Chapter 3, "RSS Feeds & Blogs," on Page 77 if you do not recall how to find your feed URL.

Figure 9.20. Creating a Widgetbox Blidget

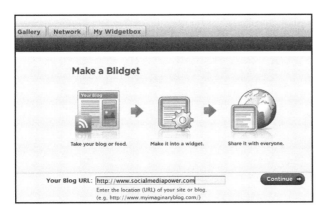

Figure 9.21 shows how you can customize your new feed widget, including adding an image, titles, tags, and a description. Use and reuse your best key terms whenever you can while creating your blidget.

Figure 9.22. Creating a Widgetbox Blidget

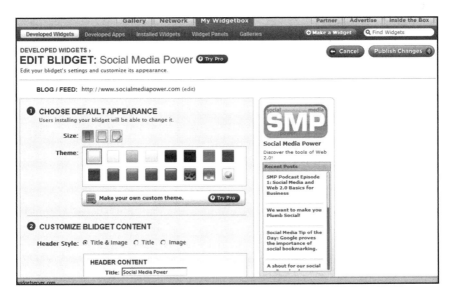

Figure 9.21. Creating a Widgetbox Blidget

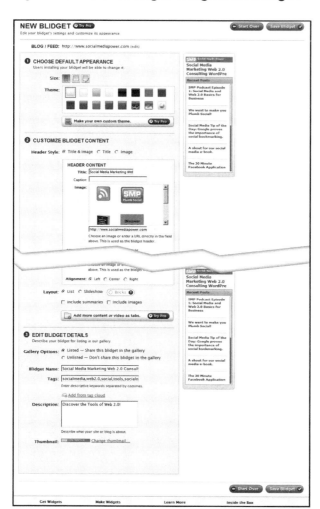

Figure 9.22 on Page 235 shows the finished blidget for Social Media Power. Widgetbox blidgets like the one we just created are free, but they also offer a pro version for around $30 a year that allows you to design custom themes for your blidget, among other features.

Once your blidget is complete, promote it on your Website or blog. Log in to Widgetbox and go to "My Widgetbox." Here you see all of your widgets, including the blidget you just created (see Figure 9.23). Click on the title of your blidget and go to "Promote Your Blidget." From here

Figure 9.23. Creating a Promo Widget For a Blidget

you create a widget that you can place on your site or other social sites that prompt people to get your feed as a customizable widget for their site.

Figure 9.24 shows how you can customize this widget for your site by changing the color and dimensions.

Figure 9.24. Creating a Promo Widget For a Blidget

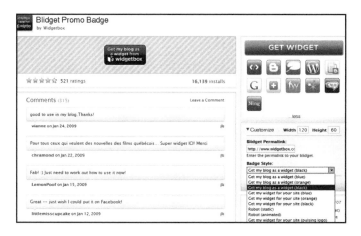

Once it is ready, copy the code to place on your site or another social site just as you would any other widget (see Figure 9.25).

Figure 9.25. Creating a Promo Widget For a Blidget

Figure 9.26 shows the respective widget on the Social Media Power Website. When a visitor clicks on this widget, they can subscribe to the feed and display it on their own site after customizing it.

Figure 9.26. Widgetbox Widgets in Action

Figure 9.27 shows where the visitor is taken when they click to get the widget.

Figure 9.27. Widgetbox Widgets in Action

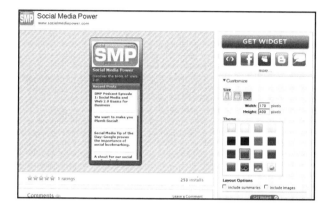

Figure 9.28 shows the feed widget or blidget displayed on another site that has subscribed to it.

Figure 9.28. Widgetbox Widgets in Action

AddtoAny

Figure 9.29 shows another convenient feed widget from AddtoAny[3] (see the button that says "Subscribe"). We saw this feed widget in action in Chapter 3, "RSS Feeds & Blogs." When a user clicks on this widget they can subscribe to your feed in many different feed readers.

Figure 9.29. AddtoAny Widget

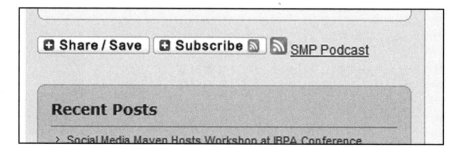

To create this feed widget, go to AddtoAny.com and click "Get the Subscribe Button" (see Figure 9.30). You do not need to have an account with them to get your button code.

Figure 9.30. Creating an AddtoAny Subscribe Widget

---

[3] http://www.addtoany.com

Figure 9.31 shows all of the options available to customize this feed widget. Enter a title for your feed and your feed URL, choose the look and feel of your widget, and click "Get Button Code" to generate the code for the widget.

Figure 9.31. Creating an AddtoAny Subscribe Widget

A few other sites that offer feed widgets are Clearspring,[4] SpringWidgets,[5] AddThis,[6] netvibes,[7] and Google Gadgets.[8]

Social Bookmarking and Crowd-Sourcing

In Chapter 7, "Social Bookmarking & Crowd-Sourcing," we mention the importance of making your site easy for others to add or share in these vital areas of the Social Web. Listed here are a few widgets that you can use on your Website or blog to accomplish this goal.

---

[4] http://www.clearspring.com/
[5] http://springwidgets.com/
[6] http://addthis.com/
[7] http://eco.netvibes.com/submit/editor
[8] http://www.google.com/webmasters/gadgets/

AddtoAny

In addition to their feed widget, AddtoAny has a nice widget that helps visitors bookmark or share your site on their preferred social bookmarking or crowd-sourcing sites. Figure 9.27 on Page 239 shows this widget in action (see the "Share/Save" button). Figure 9.32 shows another version of this widget, one that pops up when it is rolled over.

Figure 9.32. AddtoAny Popup Sharing Widget

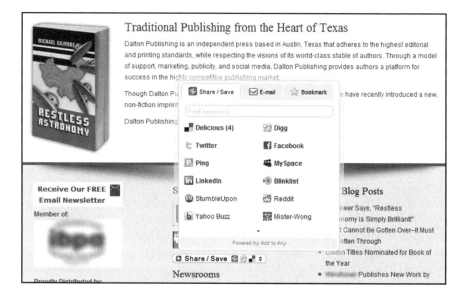

To create your share widget, go to AddtoAny.com and click "Get the Share/Save Button" (see Figure 9.30 on Page 240).

Figure 9.33 shows all of the options available to customize this widget. Enter your Website name and URL, choose the look and feel of your widget, and click "Get Button Code" to generate the code for the widget.

ShareThis

ShareThis is more robust than some of the other share widgets. Figure 9.34 shows the options available for this widget. One of the things that distinguishes this widget is that, in addition to giving your visitors a way to share your site in the Social Web, it offers visitors a way to post your site to their social networking profiles or blog (see Figure 9.34).

Figure 9.33. Creating an AddtoAny Sharing Widget

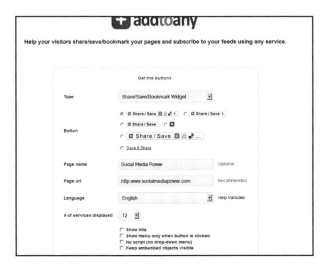

Figure 9.34. ShareThis Widget

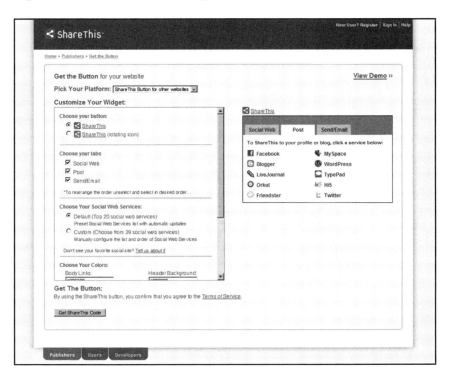

Making Your Site More Interactive

Some widgets help optimize your Website or blog for Web 2.0 by making your site more interactive. These include widgets that help visitors find you in other places on the Social Web, suggest related content that your readers may find helpful, or offer customizable search tools. Following are some examples:

Digg.com

You can display Digg[9] news stories on your site using Digg widgets. Figure 9.35 shows the screen for creating a Digg widget. You can filter stories for this widget by topic, author, or any number of other ways.

Figure 9.35. Digg.com Widgets

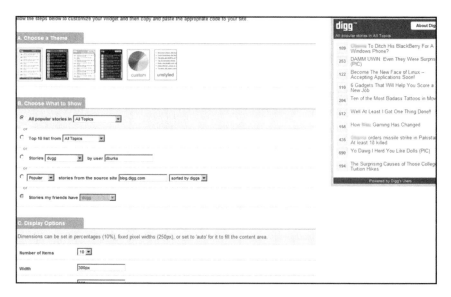

Delicious.com

Figure 9.36 shows a widget offered by the social bookmarking site, Delicious.com. This widget displays your Delicious bookmarks as a tag cloud. When one of the tags in the "cloud" is clicked, the visitor will

[9] http://digg.com/add-digg

be taken to all of your bookmarked sites on Delicious.com with that respective tag.

Figure 9.36. Delicious.com Widget Example

Lijit

The Lijit[10] "wijit" is an approach to letting your readers search your content all over the Social Web, as well as your network's content. It is sort of like creating your own search engine for your readers, where you determine the sites that are included in the engine.

Figures 9.37 and 9.38 show this widget in action. When a user enters a search term into the widget on the Social Media Power Website (Figure 9.37), a resulting search screen pops up (see Figure 9.38). This search platform has a number of tabs that allow the user not only to search the Social Media Power Website, but to search every site in their "network" using the same search terms.

Once you have an account, you choose your content sources (what the search engine considers your "network") and input all of your profile information. You can then customize your search "wijit" and place it on your site for your readers to use.

[10] http://www.lijit.com

Figure 9.37. Lijit Search Widget

Figure 9.38. Lijit Search Widgets Results

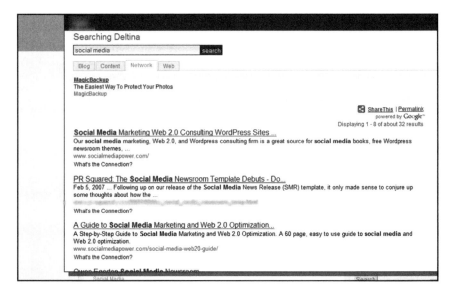

Sphere

The Sphere Contexual widget[11] offers a way for visitors to view articles or blogs that are related to your content from *within* your content. The Sphere Related Content widget is a plugin specifically for blogs. You can place it at the end of your blog posts to offer readers an opportunity to view related content. See Figure 9.39.

---

[11] http://www.sphere.com/tools

Figure 9.39. Sphere Contexual Widget

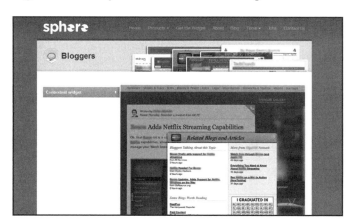

Google and Facebook Connect

Some of the next-generation Web tools that you can read more about in Chapter 11, "More Social Tools," allow Internet users to carry their social networking connections around with them as they surf the Web. These widgets offer ways for you to allow users to login to your site using their existing Google or Facebook IDs, and to share information from your site with others in their network.

Promoting Products And Making Money

Offering products for sale or placing ads on your site can be a simple process using widgets. Here are two examples:

Amazon

You can feature your own or others' products using Amazon widgets on your Website or blog. Amazon offers referral fees for direct sales that result from your use of their widgets, too. Amazon widgets vary in size and complexity, but all of them are easy to set up and customize.

Figure 9.40 shows the range of widgets available at Amazon. The best strategy for choosing the widget that is best for your site is to pop one open and play around with it a bit. You can offer simple, sidebar widgets for your products (Figure 9.41) or use individual widgets to build an entire store on your site (Figure 9.42).

Figure 9.40. Amazon Widgets

Figure 9.41. Amazon Widget Example

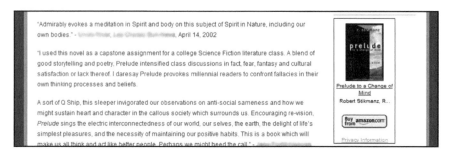

Figure 9.42. Amazon Widget Example

Google Ads

No doubt you have seen Google ads on many sites you have visited. These ads can produce some decent income for sites with a lot of traffic. Figure 9.43 shows a couple of different options for Google AdSense members. In addition to the typical sidebar and header ad widgets that Google offers, you can install your own mini search engine on your site, and generate income from it.

Figure 9.43. Google Adsense Widgets

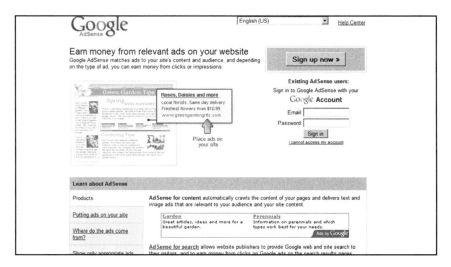

Using Widgets In WordPress

In Chapter 4, "Building a WordPress Powered Website," we discuss that plugins are one of the features that give WordPress and other content management systems their tremendous power and flexibility. We also talk about plugins that can be used as "sidebar widgets" and how easy they are to set up and position on your WordPress site or blog. To activate a sidebar widget that is a WordPress plugin, install the plugin, then go to Design/Widgets and pull the widget onto your sidebar, as explained on Page 99 of the aforementioned chapter.

Widgets in WordPress can exist on the sidebars, inside of pages, or directly in blog posts. We demonstrate each scenario below.

Widgets in Sidebars

Having "widget-ready" sidebars is a huge convenience when it comes to placing widget code onto your site. Let's look at an example that demonstrates one of the widgets we created in a previous section and see how easy it is to place onto a WordPress sidebar.

From the WordPress dashboard, go to Design/Widgets. Figure 9.44 shows that the Social Media Power WordPress site has four sidebars to work with. We want to add a widget to Sidebar 2.

Figure 9.44. Creating a Sidebar Widget in WordPress

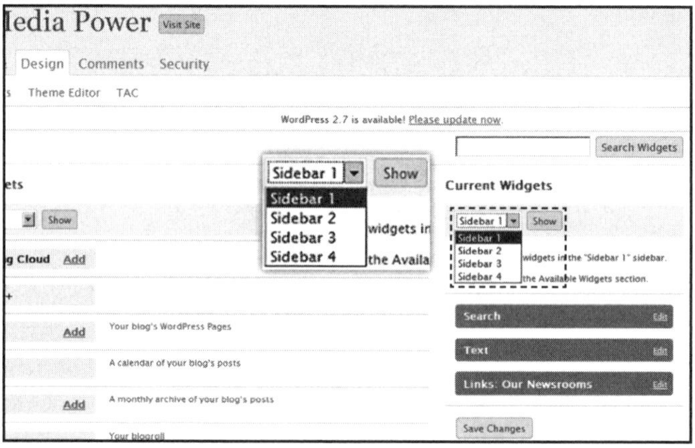

Refer back to the "Highlighting Your Social Web Presence/Social Networking" section on Page 226 where we created a Twitter widget. Figure 9.7 on that page shows the step where we copy the Twitter widget code to place on our site. Continuing with that example, we copy the code onto our clipboard and return to WordPress.

We now need to add a "Text" widget to place our code into. Text widgets are empty widgets that you can populate with whatever code you like. We click on "Add" to the right of the word Text and our new, blank widget appears (see Figure 9.44).

Then, we click on "edit" next to the new Text widget, and paste the Twitter widget code in the body of the text box. We add the title "Follow Us On Twitter" and we are done, so we click "change" to save the widget, and "Save Changes" to save the changes to the sidebar. See Figure 9.45.

Figure 9.45. Creating a Sidebar Widget in WordPress

We want our Twitter widget above our Google Connect widget, though, so we drag our new widget up above the Google widget (see Figure 9.46).

Figure 9.46. Creating a Sidebar Widget in WordPress

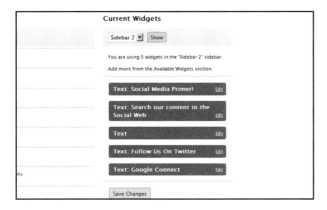

Figure 9.47 shows the finished Twitter widget on our WordPress site.

Figure 9.47. Twitter Widget On a WordPress Site

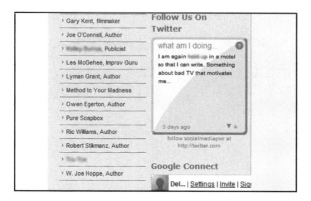

Widgets in Pages

A good example of placing a widget inside a WordPress page is the Shelfari widget we demonstrated in the "Highlighting Your Social Web Presence/Social Networking" section on Page 229.

Once the code is copied (see Figure 9.15 on Page 231) we place it on the page where we want the widget to appear. Manage/Pages brings us to the page editor, and clicking on the page title "About" takes us to the page we want to add the widget code to. Figure 9.48 on Page 253 shows where we added the code, and Figure 9.16 on Page 231 shows the finished product.

Widgets in Posts

Some widgets live directly inside your blog posts so that readers can perform actions on individual posts, like sharing posts in social networking and crowd-sourcing sites.

As an example, the AddtoAny share widget, as demonstrated in previous sections, can also be added to individual blog posts so that readers can bookmark or share just a single post if they wish. This is accomplished by installing and activating the AddtoAny bookmark button plugin.[12]

---

[12] http://wordpress.org/extend/plugins/add-to-any/

Figure 9.48. Shelfari Widget Code On a WordPress Page

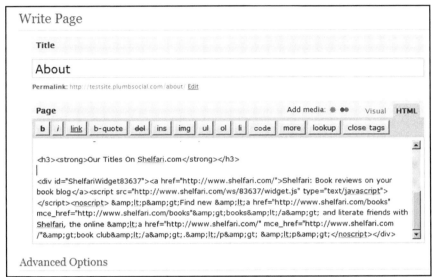

Once this plugin is installed and activated, the button appears in your posts automatically. Refer to Chapter 4, "Building a WordPress Powered Website," if you do not recall how to install and activate plugins.

Figure 9.49 shows the widget in action. When the "Bookmark" button is clicked within a particular post, the post can be saved or shared by the user to any number of social sites (see Figure 9.50).

Figure 9.49. Adding a Widget to WordPress Posts

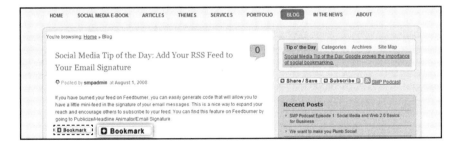

Figure 9.50. Adding a Widget to WordPress Posts

Placing Widgets In Other Websites

Since there are countless ways of creating traditional Websites, it is impossible for us to cover all of the ways you might place widget code into your Website's code. If you maintain your own Website, you already have a good idea of how and where to place widget code so that a widget displays where you want it on your site.

If you have a developer who maintains your Website but who does not do your social media optimization, it is probably best for you to generate and copy the widget code yourself, send them the code, and tell them where you want the widget to appear on your site.

Widget Communities And Directories

In the Feed Widgets section above, we demonstrated the "blidget." This feed widget is one of the features of the Widgetbox widget community.

Widget communities are sites where widget developers can highlight their widgets and others can install and use them. They usually have a user-friendly platform in which to create widgets of your own and a way for you to add them to the community. Other users can then install your widget on their sites like we saw in the blidget demonstration earlier in the chapter.

Some of these communities offer stats on how your widget is doing, like number of views and installs. See Appendix C for more information.

If you are searching for a widget to accomplish something specific, these communities are a good place to search. You can also find talented developers in these communities to create custom widgets for you.

Here are a few widget communities to check out:

- Widgetbox[13]
- Clearspring[14]
- SpringWidgets[15]

You can also use widget directories to find widgets to place on your Website, blog, or personal page (like iGoogle or netvibes).

Here are a couple of widget directories to check out:

- netvibes ecosystem[16]
- Google Gadget directory[17]

Creating Your Own Widgets

As we demonstrated with the Widgetbox blidget in the Feed Widgets section above, creating your own feed widget is not a difficult task. Of course, you need to have a blog or RSS feed in place to do so. A feed widget is an easy way for you to become part of widget communities, and also offers your feed additional exposure.

You can create your own widgets to accomplish just about anything you want. Widgets can be valuable, viral marketing tools if they become popular. If you have a good idea for a widget, there are a number of ways you can proceed.

As discussed in the previous section, most widget communities have user-friendly platforms for creating widgets. Or, if you do not have the skills to create one yourself, you are likely to find a good widget developer in one of these communities to do it for you.

---

[13] http://www.widgetbox.com
[14] http://www.clearspring.com
[15] http://springwidgets.com/
[16] http://eco.netvibes.com/widgets
[17] http://www.google.com/ig/directory

Some platforms (Clearspring and Widgetbox for instance) let you create "Remote" widgets that do nothing more than display an existing Web page. This is a quick and easy way for you to create a widget of your own.

Google Gadgets[18] is also a good platform for creating widgets. Many of the other platforms import and convert Google Gadgets for you, so you can get more mileage out of your widget. Google even provides examples of popular gadgets[19] that you can freely use as templates for your own. You can also search the Google Gadget directory for ideas.[20]

You can create widgets (or "Applications," as they are usually called) specific to particular platforms, like Facebook.[21]

There are some specialized skills involved for creating anything but the most basic widget. A basic knowledge of XML (see Appendix B), HTML, and JavaScript are typically required.

If you want to take the plunge, see Appendix C for a demonstration of how to build a widget of your own.

Working Widgets Into Your Strategy

Chapter 12, "Pulling It All Together," discusses the importance of integrating and streamlining your Social Web presence as much as possible. Widgets are an integral part of this process. By utilizing the types of widgets discussed in this chapter, especially the ones that help social tools work together, you will be well on your way.

A Good Plan to Follow

- Use widgets and badges to show your site visitors where you are in the Social Web
- Use widgets that pull images, video, events, books, and other information from media or other communities you are a part of onto your site

---

[18] http://www.google.com/webmasters/gadgets/
[19] http://code.google.com/apis/gadgets/docs/legacy/gs.html#GGE
[20] http://www.google.com/ig/directory?synd=open
[21] http://developers.facebook.com/)

- Add widgets to your site that can add interactivity—but only if it makes sense to do so
- Implement widgets to highlight your products offered for sale on other sites like Amazon
- Add RSS feed widgets to help visitors subscribe to your content
- Use widgets to help visitors share your site on social bookmarking and crowd-sourcing sites
- Place social bookmarking and crowd-sourcing widgets at the end of your blog posts to make each individual post easy for others to share
- Create your own widget if it makes sense to do so
- For security reasons, only install widgets from trusted sources

This plan is recreated on the resource CD.

Do Not Clutter Your Site

Only add widgets to your site that you believe will benefit your visitors or are essential to your presence; don't place them just for the sake of placing them. Sites can start looking cluttered and disorganized when they have too much on their sidebars.

If you have a substantial Social Web presence that you want to highlight, consider creating a separate social media portal just for that purpose. See Plumb Social[22] for ideas.

This Chapter On The Resource CD

- Further Reading
- Linkable Resources
- Fillable Forms:
    - › Working Widgets Into Your Strategy Worksheet

---

[22] http://www.plumbsocial.com

10 Social Media Newsrooms

What Is A Social Media Newsroom?

Imagine having just one place where you can tell the media, prospective clients, book reviewers, or anyone who wants to know all about you, your business, or your book exactly what they need to know. A place where they can:

- View all your major media coverage
- See all of your past and present new releases
- Look up all of your past and future events
- Read and link to all of your book reviews
- See and link to all of the places you are present in the Social Web, including any widgets or badges you may have available
- Download multimedia material like photos, company logos, podcasts, vidcasts, etc.
- View bios on each key person in the company, along with links to their social or business networking profiles like LinkedIn, Facebook, Myspace, Second Life, etc.

- Check out your own purpose-built Delicious page linking to other sites relevant to your business.
- Subscribe through RSS feeds to any portion of information on the site.
- Share any content on the site with their friends or colleagues via email or by posting to social bookmarking indexes like Delicious or Digg with one click
- Send you an instant message using AIM, Yahoo Messaging, MSN, Skype, etc.
- Link directly to your latest blog posts
- Search the site or the entire Web using either Google or Technorati
- Link to other blogs or Websites that are relevant to your message
- See all Technorati tags related to your content
- Comment directly on your media coverage, news releases, and events

That marvelous place is a Social Media Newsroom (SMNR). Similar to a traditional online newsroom, it lists media coverage, news releases, events, media contact information, and so forth, but it also includes social media and Web 2.0 elements that allow visitors to share and interact with its content.

The SMNR fulfills the traditional purpose of a newsroom while taking advantage of the tremendous indexing opportunities social bookmarking and RSS feed services like Technorati, Delicious.com, Digg, and FeedBurner provide. Imagine that every entry made in your newsroom (*all* of your media coverage, news releases, bios, photos, vidcasts, podcasts, events, etc.) was not only indexed in Google and all of the other search engines, but also in popular bookmarking and RSS feed services, making your content accessible to millions of Social Web users. This is the true power of the SMNR for entrepreneurs, small businesses, authors, and small presses—it offers unprecedented exposure at next to no cost.

This fantastic exposure is a byproduct of the original reason the SMNR was created, but it has grown beyond a mere electronic repository. Originally designed by Todd Defren of SHIFT Communications,[1] the social media newsroom has become the blueprint for the new media—a media that understands multimedia and wants a one-stop shop for every

---

[1] http://www.shiftcom.com

bit of material they will need for their coverage. This new media wants something that is fully downloadable and print ready, easily shared with their colleagues, with links and searches that will lead them directly to more relevant information. More important, though, they want a place that welcomes their comments and invites interactivity. They want to be able to talk back, to create a true media exchange.

Do You Need A Social Media Newsroom?

A social media newsroom is for individuals or businesses that tend to get or want to get a lot of media coverage, or who put out news releases on a regular basis. Even if you or your business do not fit into either of these categories, but you are building an impressive presence on the Social Web, you may consider building one just to highlight that fact and show off your presence. However, I do not recommend building a newsroom unless you have the resources to keep it up-to-date.

If you already have a Website with most of these features, you might wonder why you need a newsroom. First, a newsroom tells the members of the media and prospective clients that you are making a *serious* effort to make their jobs easier. A social media newsroom is akin to a news release in that standardization is essential to allow for easy navigation and content extraction by the media.

Second, as mentioned earlier, a social media newsroom (if built using a platform such as WordPress) means that each entry in your newsroom, from a news release to a simple image, can be automatically indexed in search engines, RSS feed indexes, and social bookmarking services, since each entry is added as a separate entry that can be given its own key terms. This means someone can find your site by running into your company logo image, by searching for a blog on the subject of your business expertise, by looking up relevant sites tagged in Technorati or Delicious.com, or by searching for RSS feeds.

But a social media newsroom should not replace your existing Website. You still want a place for blogging and to have a more traditional place to present other information. You will also do all of your "selling" on your Website. Your SMNR is not a sales tool. Your newsroom is meant to be a neutral place to present all of your media materials—just like a mega-news release.

Building Your Social Media Newsroom

It is best to build your newsroom using a blogging or CMS platform such as WordPress, Typepad, Joomla!, or Drupal. Doing so means your site will have built-in RSS feed support and be widgetized (widgets and badges from other social sites are easy to place on the site). I prefer to use WordPress.

Install WordPress (or other CMS) and Your Theme

It is recommended that you read Chapter 4, "Building a WordPress Powered Website," before continuing. You may also want to refer to the newsroom examples depicted at the end of the chapter as you continue.

The first step is to install WordPress (see Appendix A) and choose a theme. You can use any suitable theme, but using a theme that is specifically designed for newsrooms can save you a lot of work. Go to the resource CD for a list of recommended WordPress newsroom themes.

Next, install and prepare your theme (see Chapter 4, "Building a WordPress Powered Website, Page 109).

Design the Functionality of the Theme

When designing the layout of your newsroom, keep in mind that the site needs to stay "flat." By that, I mean that there is no navigation within or off the main page. One purpose of the page is to truly make all of your media available in one place, at a glance. Note that in most of the examples featured in this chapter the main sections of the newsroom are scrollable content boxes. This allows any number of items to be placed in these sections without needing to incorporate navigation. This rule does not apply to the "Social Media" section or if you build your own social media news releases (see Page 271).

The best way to control which entry appears in which respective content box is to use WordPress categories. In other words, each entry in the newsroom is actually a blog entry or "post," and assigning this post to a specific category will determine which content box the post will appear in.

If you are comfortable altering cascading style sheets and changing a modest amount of PHP code, then your can learn how to create your own scrollable, category-driven content boxes in WordPress[2]. A theme designed specifically for newsrooms, however, should already have this functionality, or something similar, built-in.

You want to create the following categories in WordPress (depending on which sections you choose to maintain):

- Media (for media coverage you have received)
- News (for news releases)
- Reviews (for book reviews)
- Events
- Team (for team members or authors)
- Multimedia (for multimedia gallery items)
- Social Media (for social badges, widgets, etc.)

You also want to make sure that your multimedia items, such as audio and video, do not take the visitor away from the newsroom, unless it is from a badge or widget within your "Social Media" section. You can install plugins that will allow them to watch or listen on the spot, or only offer a download option.

Another thing to keep in mind when choosing or designing your theme is to keep it clean. Use a simple theme with no built-in images save for your logo or book cover image in the header. And keep the colors as neutral as possible. The *content* is what you want your visitors to notice.

Set Up Your Newsroom Sections

Next, set up, but do not yet populate, the following main sections in your newsroom (each of these sections should have respective categories as described above):

- Media Coverage: a section offering direct links to online sources or to PDFs of media coverage your company or book has received.
- News Releases: a section listing links to traditional or Social Media News Releases (see Page 271).
- Events: a section to list events your company is hosting such as book signings, etc.

---

[2] http://www.empoweredbywordpress.com

- Book Reviews (or another industry-specific section): a section offering direct links to online sources or to PDFs of reviews your company or book has received.

- Social Media: a section with links to all of the other places you are in on the Social Web. This section should also list badges or widgets from other social sites such as a Flickr badge, an Upcoming.org widget, a Facebook widget, etc.

- Multimedia: a section to hold images, audio/video clips, PDF documents, etc. This section contains your company logo, book cover, author/CEO photos, sales sheets, flyers, brochures, etc.

- Team or Author: a section containing biographies on each key person in the company, along with links to their social or business networking profiles like Facebook, LinkedIn, etc.

- Add other main sections as your industry demands. There may even be sections here that do not apply to your industry. The main thing is to make certain you have a WordPress category created for any main section you require.

In addition to the main sections, you want to include:

- A section to list RSS feeds that allow visitors to subscribe to individual sections of the room, like media coverage, news releases, or book reviews—or to all of the items in the newsroom

- A way for readers to share the content of the site, using:
  - › email
  - › social bookmarking sites like Delicious.com, Technorati, StumbleUpon, etc.
  - › crowd-sourced news sites like Digg, Mixx, Propeller, etc.

- A small section for instant message indicators for key media contacts using AIM, Yahoo Messaging, MSN, Skype, etc. The "IM Online" WordPress plugin is useful for this.

- The ability for visitors to search the site or the Web using either Google or Technorati

- Links to other blogs or Websites that are relevant to your message

- A section of links to blogs or RSS feeds of key company personnel or of major clients

- Technorati tag cloud. There are a number of good plugins for this. Search the plugin section on WordPress.org.
- If you have video clips that are relevant to your message, you may want to feature them toward the top of the newsroom.

Preparing to Populate Your Newsroom

Use the following list to gather all of the information you need to populate your newsroom and to complete any preparatory tasks. There is also a worksheet on the resource CD.

Folders

Create the following applicable folders to hold the items for the "main" sections of your newsroom (add a folder for any additional "main" sections you add to your newsroom) as well as a general folder for miscellaneous images:

- yoursite.com/newsroom/media
- yoursite.com/newsroom/news
- yoursite.com/newsroom/multimedia
- yoursite.com/newsroom/events
- yoursite.com/newsroom/reviews
- yoursite.com/newsroom/socialmedia
- yoursite.com/newsroom/images

This will help you keep your content organized and you will always know where to upload and link to the items you need.

Icon Set

Choose a multimedia icon set and upload it to your "image" directory. This set should include icons to represent news items, podcasts, video clips, PDFs, DOCs, etc. They will look something like the icons in Figure 10.1. The best way to get a complete set is to purchase one from a royalty-free photo stock site like istockphoto.com. The prices are quite reasonable.

Figure 10.1. Internet Icon Set From istockphoto.com

Preparing Documents, Images, and Other Multimedia Items for Your Newsroom

For each image you plan to place in your newsroom:

- Create a print-ready PDF version:
  - › Large jpg files often give errors when opening in browsers, so to guarantee you have good, printable versions of your images, save them as PDF files.
- Create a small, thumbnail version:
  - › These are the images that will be visible on your newsroom. You want your newsroom to load quickly, so do not place large image files on it. Always place small, thumbnail images that can be clicked on if there is a need to download a larger image.
  - › Thumbnail images should be jpg or gif, and be no more than 200 pixels wide and 72 dpi. The easiest way to create these in PhotoShop is to resize and use the "Save for Web" option.
- Upload each version to its respective directory.

For each video clip or podcast you plan to place on your newsroom:

- Try to keep the file size under 10 megabytes.
- Even if you have a thumbnail image to represent a specific podcast or video, use an image from your icon set to represent the item. This helps to keep multimedia items distinct and consistent for your users.
- Upload each file to its respective directory.

For each document you plan to place on your newsroom:

- If possible, convert all documents, presentations, etc. to PDF documents.
- Use images from your icon set to appropriately represent your documents (whether PDF, Word Doc, etc.).
- Upload each file to its respective directory.

A note on file names: Develop a naming convention for the files you create that uses only alpha characters. Instead of john_doe_headshot.jpg, you might consider JohnDoeHeadshot.jpg. This can save you a lot of grief later on. It is also a good idea to use at least one good key term in each file name.

Gather the Following Images, Documents, Links, or HTML Code for the Main Sections of Your Newsroom

For each team member or author you want under the "Team" or "Author" section:

- Headshot image
- Brief bio (PDF version)
- Link to blog
- Links to networking profiles in LinkedIn, Facebook, MySpace, Twitter, etc.

For the social media section gather widgets, badges, or links to:

- Facebook pages
- MySpace pages
- Squidoo lenses
- Twitter accounts
- Flickr accounts
- YouTube accounts
- Upcoming.org account
- Social bookmarking accounts like Delicious, Technorati, etc.
- Purpose-built Delicious pages (see Page 183)
- Second Life locations
- Other social sites you have a presence in

Multimedia:

- Logos
- Book cover art
- Executive or author photos
- Press kits and sales sheets (as PDFs)
- Podcasts (downloadable only)
- Video clips (downloadable only)
- Book trailers
- White papers you would like to permanently feature (as PDFs)
- PowerPoint presentations (converted to PDFs)
- Brochures (as PDFs)
- Other promotional or relevant multimedia items

For each item that will be featured in the "Media Coverage" section of your newsroom:

- A small logo from the media source cited
- A short lead-in to the story featured
- A link to original story or PDF version of the story cited

For each item that will be featured in the "News Releases" section of your newsroom:

- The main title and date of the news release
- Create a social media news release (see the "Social Media News Releases" section on Page 271)
- A link to the full news release if hosted on a third party site like PRWeb

For each item that will be featured in the "Reviews" section of your newsroom:

- A small logo from the review source cited
- A short lead-in to the featured review
- A link to or a PDF version of the review cited

For each item that will be featured in the "Events" section of your newsroom:

- A short lead-in to the event
- A link to more information or map to the event

Repeat for any other "main" sections you create for your newsroom.

Gather the following additional information:

- Media contact information: name, telephone number, and email address
- RSS feeds for blogs belonging to key team members or authors
- Links to blogs/sites you regularly read or reference related to your industry

Complete the Following Preparatory Tasks

FeedBurner

Get a FeedBurner account for your newsroom and follow the instructions on Page 76 to "burn" the main feed to your newsroom.

Once you have a FeedBurner feed for the main newsroom, burn a feed for each main section. This will mean that users can subscribe only to posts that you place in specific sections of the newsroom. As an example, a publishing company might have a separate feed for an author's reviews that the author can then display on his or her own Website. Similarly, if a member of the press is only interested in your current news releases, he could subscribe only to that category. Refer to the "Burning More Than One Feed" section on Page 81.

Optimize each of these feeds by following the guidelines in Chapter 3, "RSS Feeds & Blogs."

Purpose-Built Delicious Pages

We discussed purpose-built Delicious pages in Chapter 7, "Social Bookmarking & Crowd-Sourcing," on Page 183. A social media newsroom is the perfect venue for this application of social bookmarking.

List your most relevant Delicious pages on your social media newsroom. If you have not created them yet, here are some tags to consider:

- delicious.com/your.account (link to main page)
- del.icious.com/your.account/public.relations
- del.icious.com/your.account/client.name
- del.icious.com/your.account/competition
- del.icious.com/your.account/book.title
- del.icious.com/your.account/author.name
- del.icious.com/your.account/business.name
- del.icious.com/your.account/product.name
- del.icious.com/your.account/principal.name

Technorati

Create a Technorati account and "Claim" your newsroom when it is ready. It is a good idea to do the same thing in some of the other top social bookmarking sites as well (see Chapter 7, "Social Bookmarking & Crowd-Sourcing"). Start saving favorite blogs in Technorati, limiting them to blogs that are relevant to your newsroom.

Instant Messaging Services

Establish an account with at least one instant messaging (IM) service from the following: AIM, ICQ, IRC, Jabber, MSN, Skype, Yahoo!. I recommend using Yahoo! Messenger in WordPress, as it leads to fewer errors than some of the other services.

Populating The Newsroom

Once all of the preparation is complete, you can begin populating your newsroom. Many of the smaller sections and lists contain static information that you can input once into the sidebars, such as the contact information, the links to blogs, links within the social media section, etc. Use the examples at the end of this chapter as a guide.

The items within the main sections, however, will need to be entered as individual blog posts or entries, with the proper categories assigned to each so that they appear only in their proper sections.

Refer to the "Optimizing and Promoting Your Blog and RSS Feed" section on Page 72, and apply the same principles to your newsroom entries. This ensures that each entry gets maximum exposure in the Social Web, as well as in the search engines.

Social Media News Releases

A social media news release is essentially a traditional news release that is social media and Web 2.0 optimized. In short, the release encourages interactivity, is easily shared in the Social Web, and contains other Web 2.0 elements.

Generally, these elements include:

- Multimedia items such as downloadable images, audio/video files, or PDF/DOC files
- A way for readers to comment directly on the news release content
- An obvious and easy way for readers to bookmark the news release in social bookmarking sites or to share it via email
- Technorati tags and links to purpose-built Delicious pages (see Page 270)

Creating Social Media News Releases

You can create your own social media releases or use a service like PRWeb[3] (see the resource CD for a list of additional services).

As mentioned earlier, a social media news release is just a traditional release with added elements. You do not need to change your present format except to insert some additional sections. Figure 10.2 shows an example.

---

[3] http://www.prweb.com/

As you can see, this release contains all of the traditional sections of a news release, but also includes the following sections:

Figure 10.2. Social Media News Release

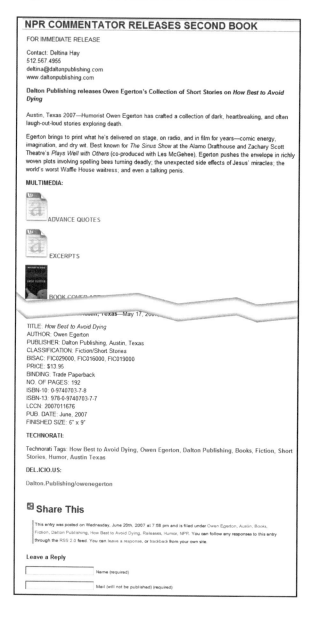

Multimedia Section

Figure 10.3 shows an example of a multimedia section. You want to offer the following downloadable items, prepared as explained beginning on Page 264:

- PDF or Word documents:
  - › Book excerpts
  - › White papers
  - › Advanced reviews
  - › Brochures
  - › Any document that will enhance or expand on the subject matter contained within the release
- Images:
  - › Author photos
  - › Company executive photos
  - › Book cover art
  - › Company logos
- Podcasts and video clips

Figure 10.3. News Release Multimedia Section

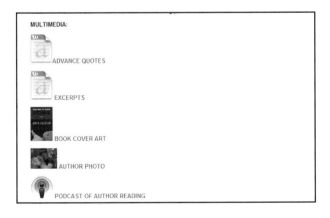

Technorati Tag Section

Use this section to list links to Technorati pages that are tagged with a list of key terms relevant to your release (see Figure 10.4). Read more about Technorati in Chapter 7, "Social Bookmarking & Crowd-Sourcing," Page 184.

Figure 10.4. News Release Multimedia Section

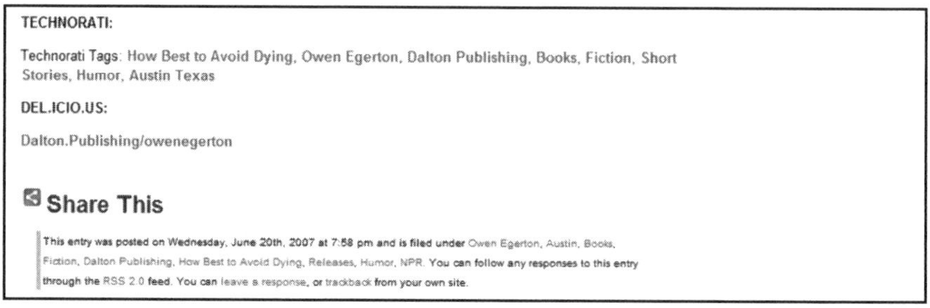

Social Bookmarking Section

In this section, provide links to any relevant Delicious pages. Though not depicted in Figure 10.4, you could also provide links to relevant pages on Digg.com or any other social bookmarking or crowd-sourced news site (see Chapter 7, "Social Bookmarking & Crowd-Sourcing").

Sharing and Commenting

You should also make it easy for the reader to share or bookmark your release in any number of ways. This is accomplished in our example by utilizing the ShareThis widget (see Page 243). Allowing visitors to comment on the release makes it truly interactive.

Social Media Section

If you do not have a social media newsroom to refer readers back to, you should consider adding a section to your release that lists where you are in the Social Web.

This should include links to your profiles or pages on:

- Facebook
- LinkedIn

- Twitter
- Squidoo
- Flickr
- YouTube, etc.

Using a blogging platform such as WordPress to create your releases makes it easy to add these additional social media optimizing features. Commenting is already built in, and there are a number of good plugins for adding Technorati tags to WordPress posts and for social bookmarking (see Chapter 4, "Building a WordPress Powered Website").

If you already have a social media newsroom created in WordPress, you will create each of your social media releases as a post of your newsroom and optimize accordingly (see Figure 10.10 on Page 281).

Social Media Newsroom Examples

The social media newsroom in Figure 10.5 is from social media newsroom pioneer SHIFT Communications and is the template we use in this book. I am always pleased to drop by their newsroom and find that nothing much has changed, save for the content—which is how it should be.

Figure 10.5. SHIFT Communications Newsroom
http://www.shiftcomm.com/newsroom/

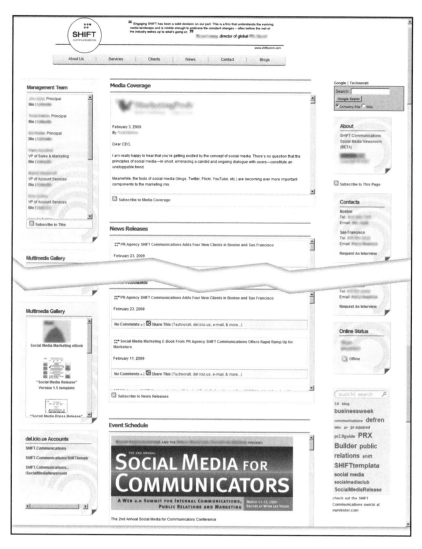

Most of the newsroom sections mentioned above are depicted in the newsroom example in Figure 10.6. I like to point out to clients, especially authors and publishers, that the breakdown of the RSS feeds in a newsroom can be a valuable tool. For instance, the following author features a feed to all of her latest media coverage on her own Website, and the publisher feeds in all of her book reviews onto her media room on their site.

Figure 10.6. Pure Soapbox Social Media Newsroom
http://www.puresoapboxnewsroom.com

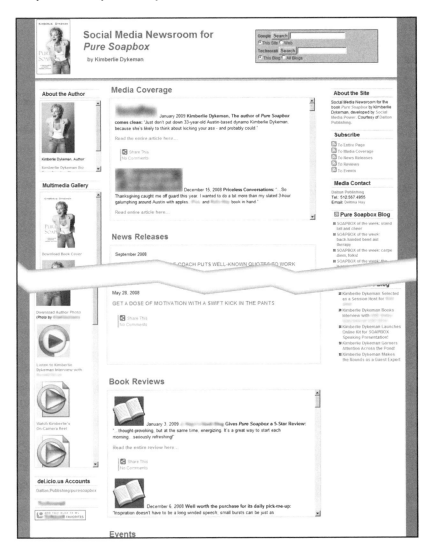

The PR firm in Figure 10.7 uses their newsroom a little differently. They list the media coverage and releases of their clients as opposed to their own. Note that they do have the social media section, but (for obvious reasons) not the book reviews section. They also feature links to their clients' blogs, in addition to their own.

Figure 10.7. Accolades Public Relation's Newsroom
http://www.accoladespr.com/newsroom

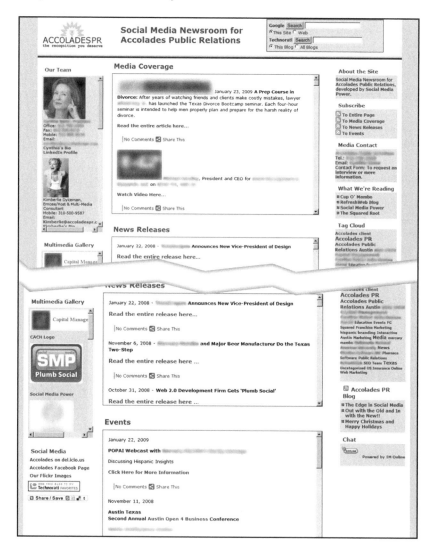

The newsroom in Figure 10.8 is an example of a simple, corporate social media newsroom.

Figure 10.8. Fathom SEO's Social Media Newsroom
http://www.fathomseo.com/pressroom/

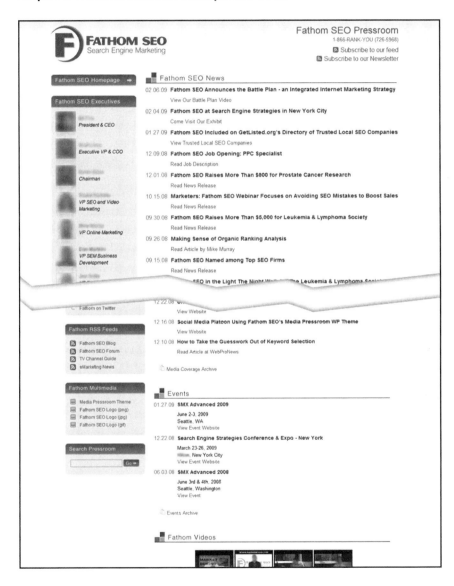

The following performer also includes a section that hosts his latest newsletters, so that he won't have to recreate the information in his newsroom every month.

Figure 10.9. Social Media Newsroom of Les McGehee
http://www.lesmcgehee.com/newsroom

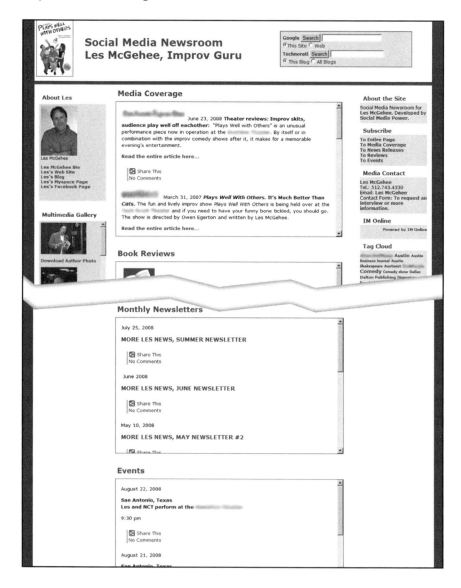

Figure 10.10 shows the top of a social media news release (see Page 271) for this newsroom. This release is created as a post in the WordPress platform that the newsroom was created in. Notice that the release has the same right sidebar as the newsroom, and a link to return to the newsroom on the left. This is the only place where a newsroom should not be "flat" as discussed on Page 262.

Figure 10.10. Social Media News Release

This Chapter On The Resource CD

- Linkable Resources
- Fillable Forms:
  › Social Media Newsroom Prep Sheet

11 More Social Tools

We certainly cannot cover all the tools available on the Social Web in this book, especially since new tools pop up almost daily. However, there are a few more tools we would like to mention in this chapter, ones that can benefit most social media strategies.

Social Calendars

Posting your events in social calendars is a great way to get extra exposure. They offer a convenient way for you to post your events in one place and highlight them in many ways on many different platforms.

Upcoming[1] is a good example. Users can search Upcoming for events in their region, confirm their attendance at events, share events with others, and more. Figure 11.1 shows the main page of Upcoming for Dalton Publishing.

---

[1] http://www.upcoming.org

Figure 11.1. Upcoming.org*

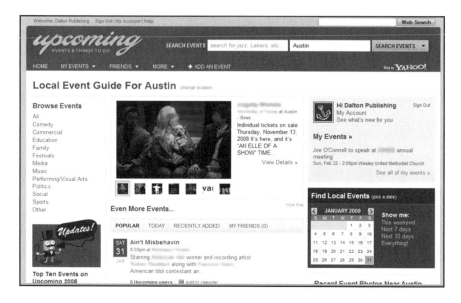

All of Dalton's events are posted to their Upcoming account. They then post an Upcoming badge on their Website (Figure 11.2), their Facebook profile (Figure 11.3), and other places in their Social Web presence

Figure 11.2. Upcoming Badge on a Website

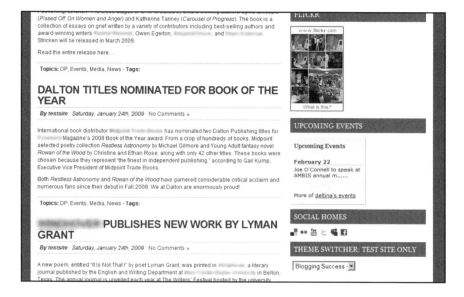

Figure 11.3. Upcoming.org on Facebook

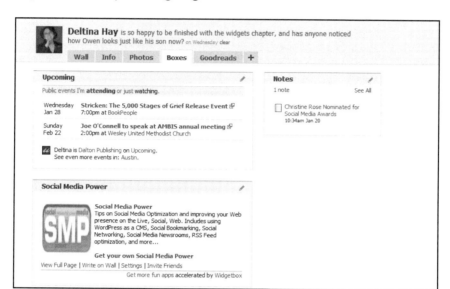

that have applications or plugins that let them import their Upcoming events.

30 boxes[2] is another excellent calendar, to-do list, event organizer, and more that integrates nicely with other social accounts. We talk more about this in Chapter 13, "Looking to the Future," as 30boxes is also what is referred to as a "Lifestreaming" application.

*All Upcoming.org images reproduced with permission of Yahoo! Inc. ©2009 Yahoo! Inc. Upcoming is a registered trademark of Yahoo! Inc.

Social Pages

Social pages are sites where, instead of creating a page about yourself, your book, or your business, you create pages about a particular topic. Visitors can search for pages on particular topics or ones authored by specific people. Pages that do well on such sites are usually instructional pages: "how to" pages and lists like "top 10" pages.

---

[2] http://www.30boxes.com

Squidoo[3] is a good example. "Squidoo is about finding people when you care *what* they know instead of who they know." This is how the Squidoo team describes their service. On Squidoo, a page is called a "lens." Squidoo lenses can be especially successful for consultants or nonfiction authors who have a lot to say about their topics.

You can create as many lenses as you like on Squidoo. A good strategy is to create one for each major topic you write about or type of service you offer. Make each page as rich with helpful information as you can. Don't use your lens only to promote your book or service; use it to demonstrate your expertise in your respective field or book topic.

Figure 11.4 shows one of Social Media Power's lenses. As you can see, there are a lot of ways to integrate your Social Web presence and other social tools into a Squidoo lens, including importing RSS feeds, Delicious. com bookmarks, blogs from Google blog search, Lijit widgets, Amazon products, and more.

Hubpages[4] is another social page site worth checking out.

Wikis

A Wiki ("wiki" is Hawaiian for "fast") is a collaborative Website that allows anyone to update its content. Once established, a Wiki essentially becomes an ever-changing online database of information. Maintaining a Wiki can be a time-consuming process, requiring a lot of moderation, but can be worth it if you have a community of contributors who have a lot to say about your topic. Wikis can also serve as powerful collaboration tools for project management and enterprise teams.

Instead of creating your own Wiki, you may want to contribute to established Wikis in your field. To find these Wikis, search Google using an appropriate search term. "Social media wiki" would work if you happen to be searching for Wikis on social media.

---

[3] http://www.squidoo.com
[4] http://hubpages.com/

Figure 11.4. Social Media Power's Squidoo Lens

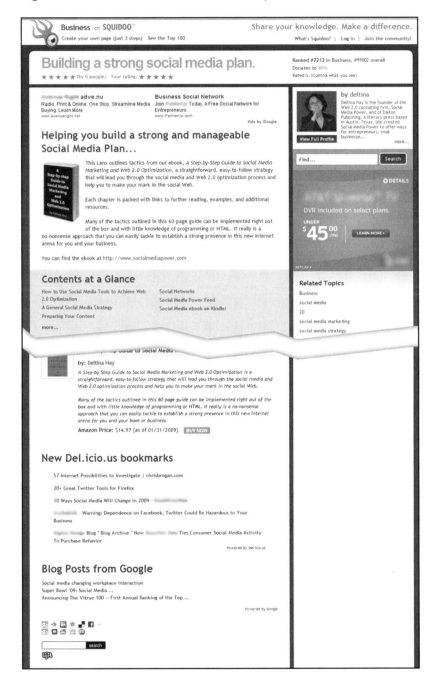

There are a number of platforms available for creating your own Wiki, including MediaWiki,[5] WikiDot,[6] and WikiSpaces.[7]

Social Search Portals

Social search portals offer your visitors a unique search experience right from your Website or blog. You can quickly build a search engine focused on any topic, and over time, this search portal will generate increasingly relevant search results as users vote results up and down for every search query.

Eurekster[8] lets anyone build a social search portal for free. Their product is called a "swicki." Figure 11.5 shows some of the options you have when creating your very own swicki.

Figure 11.6 on Page 290 shows a swicki widget on the site Empowered by WordPress.[9] Their swicki is a search portal called "WordPress CMS" that helps their visitors find more information on the topic of using WordPress as a CMS.

When a term in the Swicki widget is clicked, the visitor is taken to other results that have been tagged with the respective term within this portal and on the Web.

These search portals can prove useful for niche businesses or consulting firms that generate a lot of content on a particular topic, or for authors of nonfiction books. Like Wikis, though, these portals can be time-consuming to maintain, since it is important to keep the information in them fresh and up-to-date.

Read more about search portals in the Semantic Web section in Chapter 13, "Looking to the Future."

---

[5] http://www.mediawiki.org

[6] http://www.wikidot.com

[7] http://www.wikispaces.com

[8] http://www.eurekster.com

[9] http://www.empoweredbywordpress.com

Figure 11.5. Building a Swicki

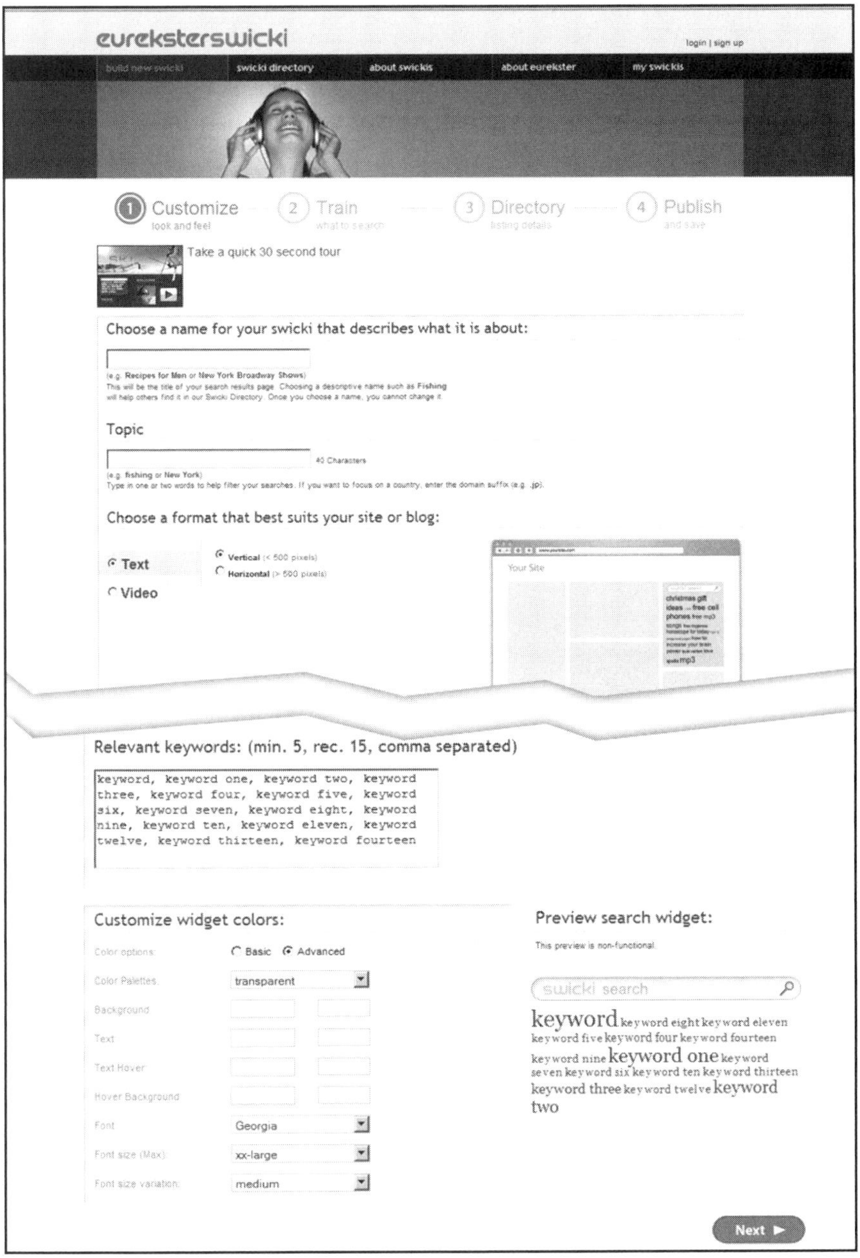

Figure 11.6. Swicki Badge on Website

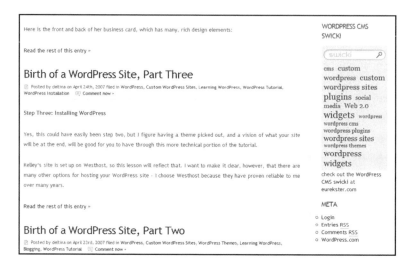

Virtual Worlds

These sites are virtual 3-D worlds created by the participants. This is one social media tool you should experience first-hand before deciding to add it to your strategy. Once you have a feel for a virtual world, you can begin to see possibilities that might apply to you, like building a virtual book club or opening a virtual presentation area for your business. There are also marketing opportunities to be had in these "worlds." For more information, visit Virtual World Reviews.[10]

This Chapter On The Resource CD

- Further Reading
- Linkable Resources

---

[10] http://www.virtualworldsreview.com

12 Pulling It All Together

In this chapter we focus on the big picture: using your social media tools to optimize your existing Website and making them all work together to minimize the efforts of maintaining your presence.

Optimizing Your Website

Remember that social media and Web 2.0 optimization mean optimizing for interactivity, sharing, and collaboration. With that in mind, determine if your existing Website is optimized by asking yourself a few questions about it:

- Can users interact with the content?
- Can visitors share the content easily with others?
- Does the site encourage collaboration?

Social media and Web 2.0 optimized Websites use technologies such as blogs, RSS feeds, widgets, and social bookmarking to allow visitors to interact with and share the site's content, thus creating an environment of collaboration. We have talked at length about these tools and technologies throughout this book, and now is your chance to apply them.

A Website Optimization Plan

Outlined below is a Website optimization plan. Each item listed refers to the chapter or chapters where you can learn about applying a specific tool, if applicable.

Essential Tactics

- Add a blog or RSS feed to your Website and optimize it.
    - › Chapter 3, "RSS Feeds & Blogs"
- Offer several ways for others to subscribe to your RSS feed or blog.
    - › Chapter 3, "RSS Feeds & Blogs"
    - › Chapter 9, "Widgets & Badges"
- If your blog or social media portal is external to your Website, add a prominent link to it on your Website and show the link on every page.
    - › Chapter 9, "Widgets & Badges"
- Add badges or widgets that link to your profiles and pages on social networking sites.
    - › Chapter 6, "Social Networking & Micro-Blogging"
    - › Chapter 9, "Widgets & Badges"
- Use widgets that let visitors share your Website on social bookmarking and crowd-sourcing sites.
    - › Chapter 7, "Social Bookmarking & Crowd-Sourcing"
    - › Chapter 9, "Widgets & Badges"
- Feature your shared images and videos from media communities on your Website using widgets or badges.
    - › Chapter 8, "Media Communities"
    - › Chapter 9, "Widgets & Badges"
- Use widgets or badges to highlight the other tools you utilize on the Social Web, like Upcoming or Squidoo.
    - › Chapter 11, "Other Social Tools"
    - › Chapter 9, "Widgets & Badges"

Additional Tactics

- Add RSS feeds from other sources to your Website.
  - › Chapter 3, "RSS Feeds & Blogs"
- Start a Podcast, Vidcast, or Webcast and feed it from your Website.
  - › Chapter 5, "Podcasting, Vidcasting, & Webcasting"
- Add image and/or video galleries using your media community accounts.
  - › Chapter 8, "Media Communities"
- Start a social media newsroom.
  - › Chapter 10, "Social Media Newsrooms"

Streamlining Your Social Web Presence

With a bit of planning you can streamline the process to keep all of your Social Web accounts fresh and engaging without breaking your back or breaking the bank. The trick is to make your social accounts work together. Most social sites use the concept of open source to make it easy for developers to write applications that enhance the features of the site—we saw this concept in action in many of the previous chapters.

An Integration Plan

Below is an integration plan with examples that you can use to streamline your Social Web presence. Each section refers to the chapter or chapters where you can learn more about implementing the tactic.

Feed Your Feed

Feed your RSS feed or blog into each of your social accounts that have the option or applications available. Figures 12.1, 12.2, and 12.3 shows Dalton Publishing's blog (the first entry of which is "TONIGHT: The World's Most Dangerous Improv") feeding into their Facebook, MySpace, and Ning accounts respectively. Figure 12.4 shows Social Media Power's blog as it is fed into their Squidoo account.

Figure 12.1. Feeding Blogs and Images Into Facebook

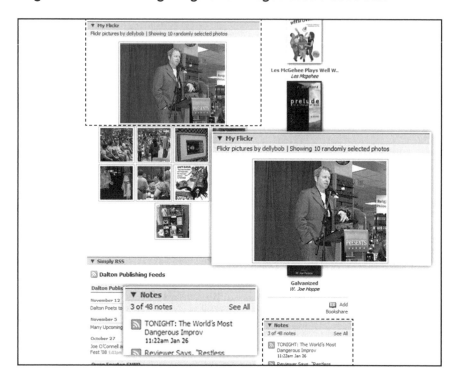

Figure 12.2. Feeding Blogs and Images Into MySpace

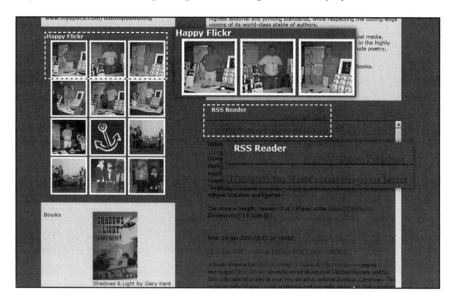

Figure 12.3. Feeding Blogs and Images Into Ning

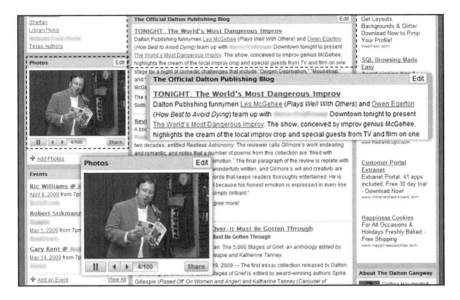

Figure 12.4. Feeding a Blog Into Squidoo

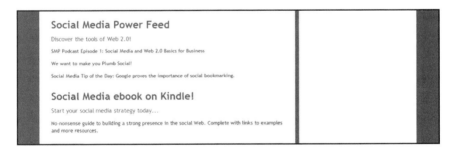

Refer to the following chapters for more information:

- Chapter 6, "Social Networking & Micro-Blogging"
- Chapter 3, "RSS Feeds & Blogs"
- Chapter 11, "More Social Tools"
- Chapter 9, "Widgets & Badges"

Integrate Your Images

Feed your images from Flickr or other image sharing sites into your social accounts that have the option or applications available. Figures

12.1, 12.2, and 12.3 show Dalton Publishing's Flickr images imported onto their Facebook, MySpace, and Ning accounts respectively.

Refer to the following chapters for more information:

- Chapter 8, "Media Communities"
- Chapter 6, "Social Networking & Micro-Blogging"
- Chapter 9, "Widgets & Badges"

Integrate Your Video

Feed your video clips from YouTube or other video sharing sites into your social accounts that have the option available. Figures 12.5 and 12.6 show some of Dalton Publishing's favorite YouTube videos imported into their Facebook and MySpace pages.

Refer to the following chapters for more information:

- Chapter 8, "Media Communities"
- Chapter 6, "Social Networking & Micro-Blogging"
- Chapter 9, "Widgets & Badges"

Figure 12.5. Imported YouTube Videos Into Facebook

Integrating Other Social Tools

The tactics you use here will depend on which social tools and sites are part of your social media strategy. Investigate each of the social tools and sites you use to finds ways to integrate other tools. Listed below are a few

Figure 12.6. Imported YouTube Videos Into MySpace

specific examples to give you a taste of how you might integrate some of your other social tools into your Social Web presence.

Figure 12.7 shows a portion of Social Media Power's Squidoo lens. This lens imports Social Media Power's Delicious.com bookmarks using a Squidoo application. It also features Social Media Power's Lijit search portal widget.

Figure 12.7. Lijit and Delicious Imported Into Squidoo

Figure 12.8 shows an example of importing Upcoming.org events into a Facebook profile. This is accomplished by implementing a Facebook application.

Figure 12.8. Importing Upcoming Events Into Facebook

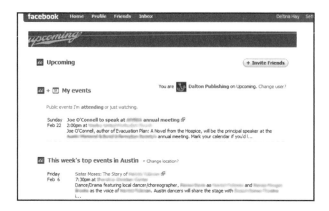

GoodReads[1]is a book sharing and review site with integration features for many social sites including Facebook. Figure 12.9 shows a GoodReads' application on a Facebook profile.

Figure 12.9. GoodReads on Facebook

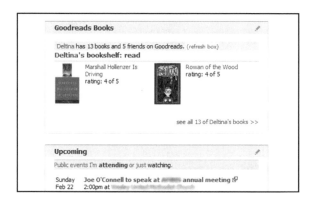

Refer to the following chapters for more information:

- Chapter 7, "Social Bookmarking & Crowd-Sourcing"
- Chapter 11, "More Social Tools"
- Chapter 6, "Social Networking & Micro-Blogging"
- Chapter 9, "Widgets & Badges"

---

[1] http://www.goodreads.com

Using Streamlining Tools

You can add short entries to your mini feeds on Facebook and MySpace, and to your micro-blogging sites like Twitter using Ping.fm,[2] a very handy social tool that will help you to streamline your presence even further. You can add one entry and feed it into many social sites.

Figure 12.10 displays the various social sites you can feed mini entries into using Ping.fm.

Figure 12.10. Ping.fm

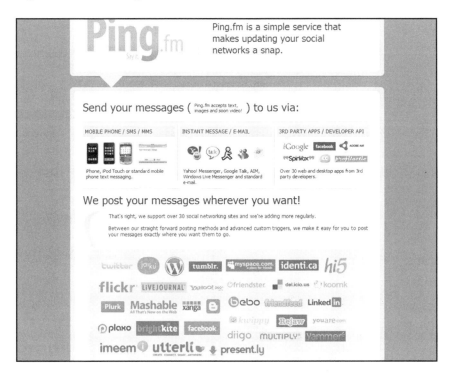

One caveat about using a Ping.fm type service, though, is to refrain from using it to post full-length blog entires. Ping.fm gives you the option to populate your blog as well as your mini feeds, but to get the most from your blog posts they should originate at the source. If you optimize your blog entries (see Chapter 3, "RSS Feeds & Blogs") with SEO plugins and

---

[2] http://ping.fm

proper tagging and categorization, then feeding from a service like this will undercut those efforts. However, there is no harm in using this tool *in addition to* regular, full length, optimized blog posts.

Investigate and Repeat

The very nature of the Social Web is to connect people through social platforms and applications. So, when deciding whether to invest the time and resources into a new social tool or site, you should investigate how well it accommodates other popular social tools.

Ask these questions of each tool or site you consider, where applicable:

- Does it let you feed in and display your own blog posts?
- Does it allow you to pipe in images from your image sharing site?
- Does it allow you to embed your videos from your favorite video sharing tool?
- Has it been added to the repertoire of social sites used by streamlining tools like Ping.fm yet?
- Is the site listed as an option by sharing-widgets like AddtoAny?
- Do your existing social tools or sites have applications that integrate the new tool?
- Do blogging platforms like WordPress have plugins that allow you to integrate the tools into your blog?

For the tools and sites you do decide to use, integrate them as best you can by repeating the applicable steps above.

This Chapter On The Resource CD

- Linkable Resources
- Fillable Forms:
  › Website Optimization Plan
  › Integration Plan

13 Looking to the Future

The new social media will be about aggregated applications that users can define themselves and that allow them to organize their experiences and find relevancy in their networks. These will come in the form of lifestreaming tools, distributed networking, and semantic applications. Moving seamlessly through information will also be important, as mobile technologies gain popularity.

Lifestreaming: The Future of Blogging

A lifestream is similar to a blog in that it is a chronologically ordered collection of information, but its content consists mostly of feeds or "streams" of information from other social sites—like WordPress, Facebook, Flickr, Delicious, Twitter, etc. A lifestream is a running list of your activity within the social sites that you choose to import into it, consisting of anything from imported blog posts to bookmarked Websites, to comments on videos, and so forth.

A lifestream is the ultimate way of pulling all your Social Web accounts together in one place, as we discussed in Chapter 12, "Pulling It All Together," and demonstrates the importance of RSS feed technology.

Each bit of content that is displayed in a lifestream is pulled from another site using an RSS feed. A fantastic resource for learning more about lifestreaming is the Lifestream Blog.[1]

You can use a service to create your lifestream, create your own using plugins for your blog, or build one yourself using software.

Lifestreaming Services

FriendFeed

The lifestreaming service FriendFeed was developed by a couple of ex-Google developers and is probably the most popular lifestreaming service.

To demonstrate FriendFeed, we built an account for Dalton Publishing. Figure 13.1 shows our empty lifestream on FriendFeed.

Figure 13.1. Blank FriendFeed Page

Figures 13.2 and 13.3 show the imported Dalton Publishing blog and Facebook feed.

Figure 13.4 shows the resulting lifestream. Now, whenever Dalton Publishing updates their Facebook account, posts a blog, or uploads an image to Flickr, the entry automatically shows on their FriendFeed lifestream.

---

[1] http://lifestreamblog.com/

Figures 13.2 & 13.3. Populating FriendFeed

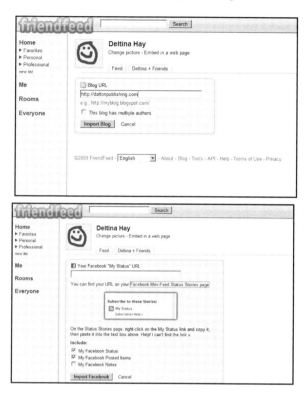

Figure 13.4. A Populated FriendFeed

Figure 13.5 shows the finished stream with all of Dalton's available accounts feeding into their FriendFeed page.

Figure 13.5. Dalton Publishing's FriendFeed

FriendFeed also has what they call "Rooms," which are similar to groups in that they are a place to create streams of information on a particular topic or for a select group of people (see Figure 13.6). Figure 13.7 shows

Figure 13.6. FriendFeed Room

Figure 13.7. FriendFeed Lists

another feature of FriendFeed, which is to group your friends into lists, like professional or personal.

In keeping with what we have learned throughout this book, we made certain that we completed Dalton's profile completely, including uploading their logo (see Figure 13.8).

Figure 13.8. FriendFeed Profile

We also sought out FriendFeed's offerings of badges and widgets on their "Tools" page. We then created the widget we wanted and placed it on Dalton's social media page (Figure 13.9).

Figure 13.9. FriendFeed Badge in Action

Some other lifestreaming services include Tumblr,[2] MyBlogLog,[3] Noovo,[4] and Zannel.[5]

Creating Your Own Lifestream

You can add lifestreaming plugins to your blog to create your own lifestream. Some plugins for WordPress blogs are Simplelife,[6] Lifestream,[7] and Complexlife.[8]

You can also use the FriendFeed embed widget to populate not only a sidebar widget, but an entire page on your blog site. We did this for Dalton by creating the widget with a width of 600 pixels (Figure 13.10) and placed the code in a page on their WordPress site (Figure 13.11).

---

[2] http://www.tumblr.com/

[3] http://www.mybloglog.com/

[4] http://www.noovo.com/

[5] http://www.zannel.com/

[6] http://wordpress.org/extend/plugins/simplelife/

[7] http://wordpress.org/extend/plugins/lifestream/

[8] http://wordpress.org/extend/plugins/complexlife/

Figure 13.10. FriendFeed Embed Widget

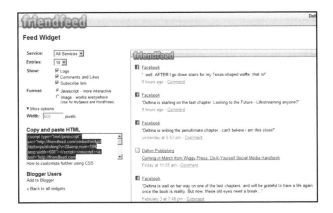

Figure 13.11. Embed Widget on a Webpage

The "Widgetized" Web

Imagine that you built an entire Website (HTML or WordPress/CMS) using only your feeds from other social sites. You could start with an enlarged FriendFeed widget like we did above for the main page, and then add profiles, widgets, and badges from other social sites on your sidebars. That would be all you would need to do to create your own lifestream. Figure 13.12 shows a site[9] that does just that.

---

[9] http://lifestream.plumbsocial.com/

Figure 13.12. Lifestream Using an Embed Widget

The Lifestream Blog[10] lists a number of other ways of creating your own lifestream, including the open source software SweetCron.[11]

This is also referred to as a "widgetized" Website, where the entire site is built from pulling widgets from other sources.

Distributed Social Networking

The concept of distributed social networking is that users can carry their ID and/or their social network around with them on the Web. They would be able to connect their profile, friends, and other content seamlessly across many sites. For instance, if a visitor to a Website has a Google account, and that Website offers Google Friend Connect (see the example below), then the visitor could access the site without having to

---

[10] http://lifestreamblog.com/create/

[11] http://www.sweetcron.com/

create a new account—they could use their Google account to login to the site.

There are many companies vying to become the standard in this arena, but the jury is still out as to who will emerge victorious. Here are some of the contenders:

- OpenSocial[12]
- Facebook Connect[13]
- MySpace Data Availability[14]
- Yahoo! Open Strategy[15]
- Google Friend Connect[16]
- OpenID[17]

Many hope that the winner will be OpenID because it is an open source solution as opposed to a proprietary one, which will make it easier to regulate. This will likely be the case, too, since many of the big companies like Google, Microsoft, Paypal, Yahoo!, and Facebook have joined the board of the OpenID foundation.

You can still take advantage of the current tools available. Google Friend Connect and Facebook Connect are particularly interesting. These tools will not go away even if they do not become the standard. Chances are that they will just change the infrastructure of the applications to adapt to whatever standard is adopted.

Google Friend Connect

The general idea is that you add your site to the Google Friend Connect platform, upload a couple of Google-provided HTML files to your site, then use the platform to create widgets and other applications that you can then place on your site for your visitors to use. Figure 13.13 shows the set-up screen.

---

[12] http://www.opensocial.org/
[13] http://blog.facebook.com/blog.php?post=41735647130
[14] http://developer.myspace.com/community/myspace/dataAvailability.aspx
[15] http://developer.yahoo.net/blog/archives/2008/04/introducing_the_1.html
[16] http://www.google.com/friendconnect/
[17] http://openid.net

Figure 13.13. Google Friend Connect Set-Up

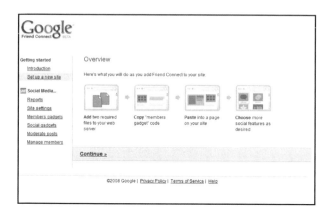

Figure 13.14 shows a Google Friend Connect widget in action on SocialMediaPower.com that allows their visitors to sign on to their site with their Google ID. They can even change their profile settings or share your site with their friends in other networks.

Figure 13.14. Google Friend Connect in Action

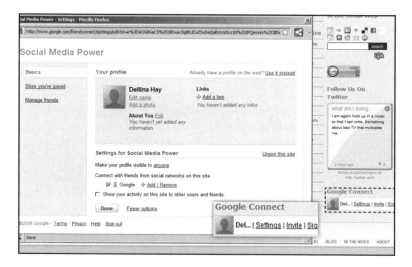

Facebook Connect

Facebook Connect works similarly to its Google counterpart. Figures 13.15 and 13.16 shows a demonstration offered by the Facebook Connect platform.

Figures 13.15 & 13.16. Facebook Connect Demonstration

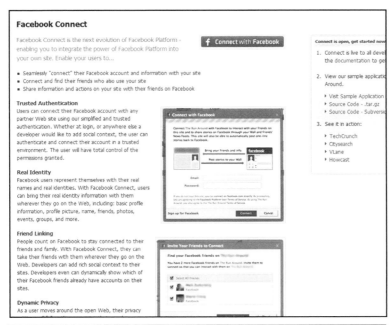

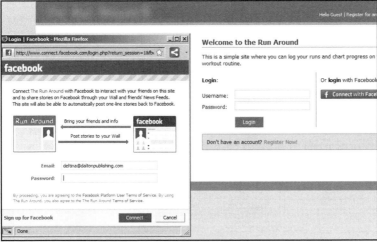

You have probably already seen Facebook Connect on many of the sites you visit—offering ways for you to share reviews, ratings, or other information about sites and products with your Facebook connections.

Social Ranking, Relevancy, And "Defriending"

Facebook will soon launch what is being called "Social Rank" which will be a way for users to see the relevancy of their connections within social networks much the same way users apply Google's "PageRank" feature to Web pages to find relevancy in searches. Twitter is also working on a similar feature.

The implementation of such tools will open up a way for you to "defriend" people in your network. Scaling down and building relevant networks is a trend that will see more weight this year and beyond.

Web 3.0 Or The "Semantic" Web

While Web 2.0 is about interaction between users of the Internet, Web 3.0 will be about interaction between the user and the information itself. What form this will ultimately take is unclear, but many predict it will be based on a semantic model where a Web browser or semantic application will determine the meaning of text and other data, and then create connections for users based on that meaning.

As an example, imagine that you want to take a trip to a particular region on a limited budget. What an ideal semantic application can do for you is help you plan your trip based on what it already knows about you from your browsing or social networking history. Furthermore, you would be able to enter your query as a traditional question, as opposed to using key terms. So, you would enter a search query like: "I want to go to Vegas for 3 days on 500 dollars." And what the semantic application will return for you are flights, hotels, shows, and more based on what it already knows about your likes and dislikes.

Though the example above is a futuristic scenario, early semantic applications are already beginning to emerge. These have become possible because of the ontologies that have developed as a result of the tagging culture of Web 2.0. The PageRank tool discussed in Chapter 14, "Measuring Your Success" is an example of one such application.

Here are a few more worth checking out:

- Yahoo! Search Monkey:[18] an open developer platform for search
- Microsoft's Powerset:[19] a natural language search engine
- Calais:[20] a toolkit of products that enable users to incorporate semantic functionality within their blog, content management system, Website, or application
- Dapper:[21] dynamic display ads that take live content from your Website and beam it into the ad
- Hakia:[22] a search engine focusing on natural language processing methods to try and deliver meaningful search results
- Nuconomy:[23] experiments in creating and delivering highly targeted, dynamic display advertising

All of the major Internet technology players are working toward their own version of semantic applications. Many of these applications will take more of an "open platform" or "mashup" type of approach like Yahoo! Pipes,[24] or a "cloud computing" approach like Amazon EC2.[25]

Mobile Technology

More and more people are turning to their mobile devices to connect to the Internet and to each other. Micro-blogging and many other social applications offer opportunities to connect via a mobile device as easily as they do on a computer.

---

[18] http://developer.yahoo.com/searchmonkey/

[19] http://www.powerset.com/

[20] http://www.opencalais.com/

[21] http://www.dapper.net/ads/

[22] http://www.hakia.com/

[23] http://www.nuconomy.com/

[24] http://pipes.yahoo.com/pipes/

[25] http://aws.amazon.com/ec2/

Creating applications for mobile devices like the iPhone[26] have become much easier for developers since Apple introduced a more open platform. As a result, you can find a mobile application or plugin for just about any social tool you already have in place. Here are some examples:

- Facebook mobile application[27]
- WordPress mobile plugin[28]
- Flickr mobile tool[29]
- YouTube mobile tool[30]
- Mobile RSS feed readers and conversion tools are also emerging:
    › Google Reader for mobile[31]
    › Feed2Mobile, an RSS feed converter[32]

Micro-blogging sites like Twitter have done well in this environment because of their simplicity, but new social networking sites have emerged from this environment that focus more on "where you are" as opposed to "what you are doing." Google's Latitude is one such network.[33] You can research more of these networks at Social Media Trader.[34]

---

[26] http://www.apple.com/iphone/

[27] http://www.facebook.com/apps/application.php?id=2915120374&b

[28] http://wordpressmobile.mobi/

[29] http://www.flickr.com/tools/mobile/

[30] http://www.youtube.com/mobile

[31] http://www.google.com/intl/en_us/mobile/default/reader.html

[32] http://feed2mobile.kaywa.com/

[33] http://www.google.com/latitude/intro.html

[34] http://socialmediatrader.com/38-social-networking-sites-for-your-mobile/

Keeping Your Eye On The Social Media Pie

To keep on top of the latest trends in social media, subscribe to the feeds of some of the leaders in social media news and trends.

These include, but are not limited to:

- ReadWriteWeb[35]
- Mashable[36]
- SocialMedia.biz[37]
- Social Media Trader[38]
- Social News Watch[39]

Staying on top of the latest trends will keep your social media strategy fresh and effective and will clue you in to which tactics are still working and which ones are fading out.

This Chapter On The Resource CD

- Further Reading
- Linkable Resources

---

[35] http://www.readwriteweb.com/
[36] http://mashable.com/
[37] http://www.socialmedia.biz
[38] http://socialmediatrader.com/category/blogging/
[39] http://socialnewswatch.com/

14 Measuring Your Success

Unfortunately, there is no easy, one-click solution to measuring your success in the Social Web. If you are mostly interested in how your efforts have improved your Website rankings or traffic, then you can use traditional Web statistics tools like Google Analytics. There are even ways you can measure how well your efforts have paid off in social bookmarking, crowd-sourcing, and social networking sites. However, measuring the more qualitative elements like conversations, brand awareness, and relationship building can be more of a challenge.

Know Your Goals

Knowing what it is you want your social media strategy to accomplish will help you measure its success. Define your goals clearly as you plan your strategy so you will have a way to measure your return on investment (ROI) easily. Some of these goals may include:

- Increasing Website traffic
- Driving sales or new business
- Monitoring brand awareness
- Improving customer relations

- Managing reputation
- Establishing credibility
- Creating buzz
- Improving public relations

Obviously, each of these goals requires a different measurement approach, but each still falls into one of two classic metric categories: qualitative or quantitative.

A Qualitative Framework

There are many schools of thought on how to establish a framework for *qualitative* measurement of social media. Reproduced here are two that I feel have merit:

Peter Kim of BeingPeterKim.com[1] defines the following framework for measuring social media engagement based on user interactions with different social media channels:

1. **Attention.** The amount of traffic to your content for a given period of time. Similar to the standard Web metrics of site visits and page/video views.

2. **Participation.** The extent to which users engage with your content in a channel. Think blog comments, Facebook wall posts, YouTube ratings, or widget interactions.

3. **Authority.** Ala Technorati, the inbound links to your content—like trackbacks and inbound links to a blog post or sites linking to a YouTube video.

4. **Influence.** The size of the user base subscribed to your content. For blogs, [it is] feed or email subscribers; [it is] followers on Twitter or Friendfeed; or [it is] fans of your Facebook page.

Kim also suggests taking into account an x-factor that he calls sentiment, since "the spirit driving user participation matters."

---

[1] http://www.beingpeterkim.com/2008/09/a-framework-for.html

Aaron Uhrmacher of Mashable.com[2] offers this advice for measuring qualitative social media ROI :

First, determine what you want to measure, whether it's corporate reputation, conversations, or customer relationships. These objectives require a more qualitative measurement approach, so let's start by asking some questions. For example, if the objective is to measure ROI for conversations, we start by benchmarking ourselves with questions like:

- Are we currently part of conversations about our product/industry?
- How are we currently talked about versus our competitors?

Then to measure success, we ask whether we were able to:

- Build better relationships with our key audiences?
- Participate in conversations where we hadn't previously had a voice?
- Move from a running monologue to a meaningful dialogue with customers?

There are companies that offer services to assist with this kind of measurement, which requires a great deal of human analysis on top of the automated results to appropriately assess the tonality and brand positioning across various social media platforms.

A Quantitative Framework

Measuring site traffic, sales, and other more quantitative effects of your social media plan may be an easier task, but you still need to have baseline numbers and specific goals in place to accurately measure your ROI.

A basic framework may start by measuring the following:

- Placement in Website search engines:
  - › Google
  - › Yahoo!
  - › Ask.com

[2] http://mashable.com/2008/07/31/measuring-social-media-roi-for-business/

- Placement in blog search engines:
  - › Google Blog Search
  - › Technorati
- Placement of social networking pages in searches:
  - › Facebook pages
  - › Squidoo pages
- Ranking in social bookmarking sites:
  - › Delicious.com
  - › StumbleUpon
- Popularity in crowd-sourcing sites:
  - › Digg.com
  - › Reddit.com
- Popularity of shared multimedia within media communities:
  - › Flickr.com
  - › YouTube.com

In addition to monitoring your own progress in these channels, you should frequently run searches to see how your competitors are doing.

Tools To Help You Measure

Listed below is a selection of time-honored and new tools that can help you get additional insight into how well your social media plan is contributing to your overall Web presence.

Google Analytics[3]

Google Analytics is a must-have tool to measure and analyze traffic on a Website. Figures 14.1, 14.2, and 14.3 show many of the features of Google Analytics.

---

[3] http://www.google.com/analytics

Figure 14.1. Google Analytics

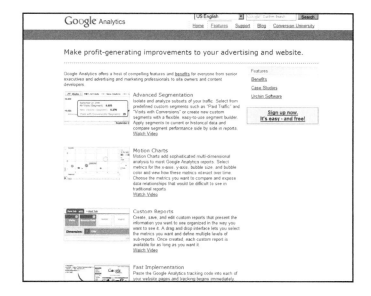

Figure 14.2. Google Analytics

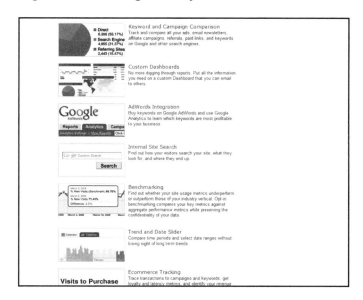

Figure 14.3. Google Analytics

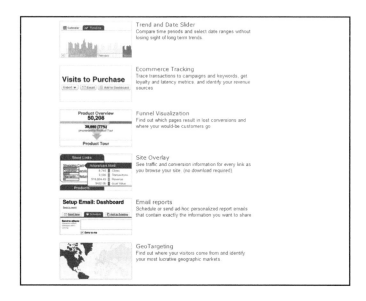

Google Alerts[4]

Google Alerts (see Figure 14.4) are email updates of results based on a specific topic. As an example, you can create a Google Alert for a specific blog post using the title of the post. You can request results from the Web, from blogs, from news stories, or from all of these sources.

Figure 14.4. Google Alerts

---

[4] http://www.google.com/alerts

Google Trends[5]

You can use Google Trends (Figure 14.5) to get an idea of Web search trends around certain key terms or other topics. Google Trends also shows how frequently your topics have appeared in Google News stories, and in which geographic regions people have searched for them the most.

Figure 14.5. Google Trends

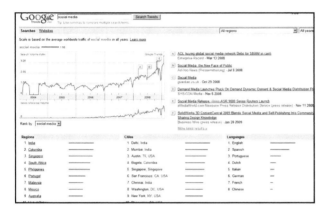

FeedBurner

Take advantage of the analysis tools for your RSS feed or blog offered by FeedBurner. See Chapter 3, "RSS Feeds & Blogs" Page 77 for details.

Blog Statistics Tools

Depending on which blogging platform you use, you have access to a number of plugins that help analyze traffic to your blog. Figure 14.6 shows the WordPress Stats[6] plugin for WordPress.

---

[5] http://www.google.com/trends
[6] http://wordpress.org/extend/plugins/stats/

Figure 14.6. WordPress Stats

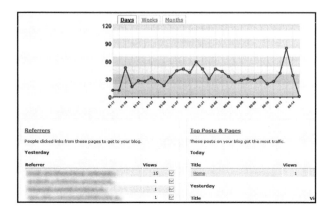

Technorati[7]

In addition to being a blog search engine, Technorati also has some rating features. Technorati Authority is one of those features; it is the number of blogs linking to a Website in the last six months. The higher the number, the more Technorati authority the blog has.

BlogPulse[8]

BlogPulse is also more than just a blog search engine. As shown in Figure 14.7, this site offers many tools to help track blog trends, conversations, statistics, and more.

Twitter Search[9]

Use this tool to track real-time Twitter conversations on a given key term. Figure 14.8 shows a search on the term "social media."

---

[7] http://www.technorati.com

[8] http://www.blogpulse.com

[9] http://search.twitter.com

Figure 14.7. BlogPulse

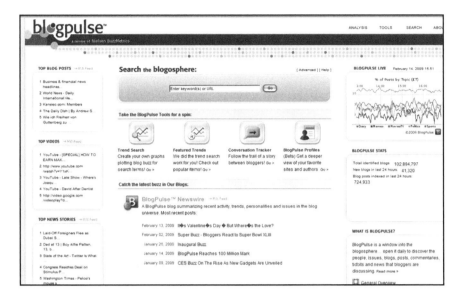

Figure 14.8. Twitter Search

PostRank[10]

PostRank is a scoring system that ranks online content, such as RSS feed items, blog posts, articles, or news stories. According to their site, "PostRank is based on social engagement, which refers to how interesting or relevant people have found an item or category to be. Examples of engagement include writing a blog post in response to someone else, bookmarking an article, leaving a comment on a blog, or clicking a link to read a news item."

The PostRank system uses what it calls the 5 Cs to rank content (see Figure 14.9). This can help you get an idea of what these types of ranking sites look for in what they call "relevant content."

Figure 14.9. PostRank 5 Cs

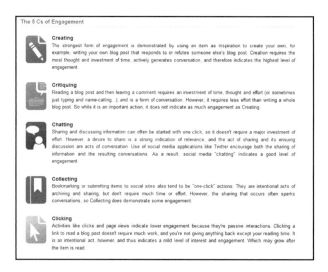

Another nice feature of this site is that it allows you to enter an RSS feed or blog URL and returns statistics about its posts, including which are the most popular, based on how many times they are shared on a variety of Social Websites. Figure 14.10 shows these results for the Social Media Power blog.

[10] http://www.aiderss.com

Figure 14.10. PostRank Stats

Xinu[11]

Xinu is a nice service that shows not only how well your site or blog is doing in traditional search engines, but also in blog search engine, crowd-sourcing, and social bookmarking sites. In addition to page rank, Xinu also shows backlinks, syndication stats, and indexed pages. Figure 14.11 shows this service in action.

Come To Your Own Conclusions

Each person or business has their own definition of what success means for a social media strategy. Be careful not to fall for the advice given by many "analysts" out there. You may read about how your feed should have so many subscriptions, your blog posts so many comments, your social networks so many friends, etc., but these numbers are subjective. Only you know how your reputation or customer relations are improving, how your sales are increasing, how your credibility it is rising, and so forth.

---

[11] http://www.xinureturns.com/

Figure 14.11. XinuReturns.com

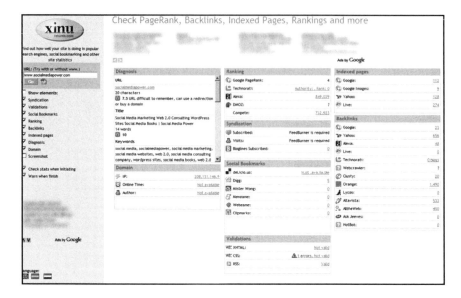

This Chapter On The Resource CD

- Further Reading
- Linkable Resources:

15 Conclusion

A few concluding points...

Marketing In The Social Web

When marketing in the Social Web, many businesses make the mistake of applying old methods to the new tools. The Social Web is not a place for the old hard pitch. People on the Social Web want to be listened to; they want to interact. They do not want to hear praises by the branders; they want to read what others have to say about a product or service. And they do not want to be inundated with offers and event announcements. If they find your message appealing, they will want to learn more about what you have to offer. Reference the resource CD for some recommended books and sites about social media marketing.

Practicing Good "Netiquette"

Before establishing your presence on any social site, read the site's submission guidelines or terms of use. Do not assume that just because others are engaging in questionable behavior that it *is acceptable* behavior.

Refraining from any sort of "spamming" should go without saying, but the types of things that are considered spam in the Social Web might surprise you. For instance, only bookmarking your own posts or pages and only contributing self-promoting items to social networks are typically unacceptable behaviors that can get you blacklisted or just plain ignored.

If you find you are using plugins or applications created by independent developers, consider sending them a donation—even a few dollars can mean a lot to them.

If you use other people's material, always give them credit—even if the information seems generalized. This will accomplish a couple things for you: It will establish you as a courteous user and it will give you links back to more places in the Web.

Be kind and courteous—even when others are not.

Getting Help

Do not forget that there are many good forums and wikis out there to help you. Open source applications and many of the social tools discussed throughout this book were built through collaboration, so it is natural that others are more than willing to share their knowledge with you to help you succeed. And, once you become skilled, you may want to choose a forum in which to share your own knowledge.

Maintaining And Expanding Your Foundation

Remember, you first want to create a foundation in the Social Web that you can build upon and expand using new tools that you have researched for usefulness and their ability to integrate with your existing Social Web presence.

You also want to occasionally evaluate the tools that are working and not working for you, and perhaps weed some out or ramp them up. Just because it seemed like a good idea initially does not mean that a tool will benefit your presence indefinitely.

Finally, you want to keep abreast of each tool's latest features and keep any open source platforms and installed plugins you are using up-to-date with the latest versions.

My Final Word On Key Terms

Imagine for a moment that there were no "traditional" Websites as we know them. That instead, all you had was your presence in social networking, social bookmarking, crowd-sourcing, media communities, and other social sites. Further, imagine that there were tools similar to "traditional" search engines that helped Internet users find other people, products, or services that matched a specific criteria. How do you think such a tool would work?

They would likely accomplish this task by searching profiles, conversations, connections, and other activity in the Social Web for relevancy to the users' search criteria, and return the results accordingly.

Now imagine that you have used and reused, and used and reused again, your best key terms throughout your entire Social Web presence in a natural way. I imagine such consistent use of key terms would yield the kind of great search results that anyone might seek in the Social Web.

So, I finally rest my case on the use of good key terms. And there was much rejoicing!

Here's to your success in the Social Web...

Appendix A: Installing WordPress

Preliminary Tasks

First, you need to install the software that keeps WordPress running properly: specifically, PHP[1], MySQL[2], and phpMyAdmin[3]. PHP is the scripting language WordPress is written in. MySQL is the database WordPress uses to store all of your posts, pages, and most everything else associated with your WordPress site. phpMyAdmin is a convenient interface used to access and manage your MySQL database. Provided you don't run into major problems with WordPress in the future, you will likely only need to access MySQL this one time—just to create your database and your database admin account.

Install the latest versions of these applications that your host has to offer. I use the host Westhost.com, and they have generously offered to let me demonstrate this process using their site manager. So, if you have a hosting account with Westhost, you can follow these instructions

[1] http://www.php.net/
[2] http://www.mysql.com/
[3] http://www.phpmyadmin.net

precisely, otherwise, your chosen host will have similar tools available for you to accomplish the same tasks.

Go to your site manager. This is the URL yoursitename.com/manager (remember that these instructions are for Westhost hosted accounts only). See Figure A.1. Enter the username and password that Westhost emailed to you when you created your account, and click "login." You see a screen similar to Figure A.2. Click on "Install & Manage" under the Site Applications heading in the left sidebar.

Figures A.1 & A.2. Preliminary Tasks to Perform

From this screen (See Figure A.3), click on "PHP 5.2.6" (or whatever is the latest version) under the Development heading. Check the box to agree to the terms on the next screen you see. A screen like Figure A.4 displays. Leave the check boxes as they are and click "Finish."

Figure A.3. Preliminary Tasks

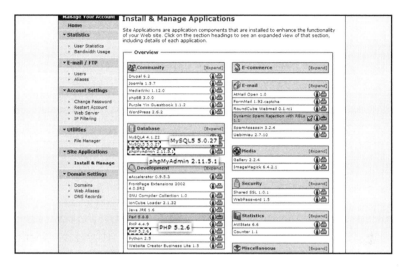

Figure A.4. Preliminary Tasks: Installing PHP

From the main Install & Manage screen again (Figure A.3), click on "MySQL 5.0.27" (or whatever is the latest version). Click on the check box to agree to the terms on the next screen.

The next screen you see is Figure A.5, which asks for a password. For convenience, you may want to make this the same password as you use to access your site manager. Once you enter the password, be sure to make note of it and click "Finish."

Figure A.5. Preliminary Tasks: Installing MySQL

Again, from the main Install & Manage screen (Figure A.3), click on "phpMyAdmin 2.11.5.1 (or whatever is the latest version). Click the agree to terms check box on the next screen. On the next screen (Figure A.6), note that your username and password for phpMyAdmin will be the same as the username and password you use to access your site manager.

Figure A.6. Preliminary Tasks: Installing phpMyAdmin

Important: Before you continue, create a text file (Wordpad or Notepad file) and keep it open on your desktop. You want to save all of the configuration information you create from here on out in this file for future reference.

Now, create the database and database admin user that WordPress needs to run. To access your phpMyAdmin panel, go to the URL http://yoursite. com/pma. (Remember, this applies only to a Westhost hosted account. If you are with another host, you should check with them as to how to access phpMyAdmin.)

Figure A.6 shows the phpMyAdmin panel. Create a database as shown, but for security reasons do not name it "wordpress." I suggest naming it something like "XYZwordpress," where "XYZ" is a three letter code you can easily associate with your site. Enter the database name and click "Create."

Figure A.6. Creating the Database

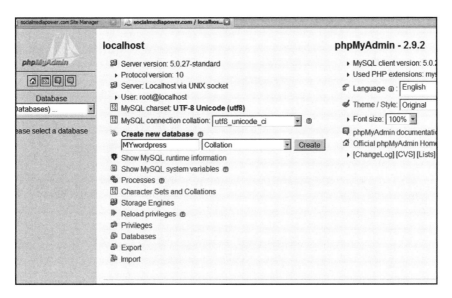

Return to the home panel of phpMyAdmin and click on "Privileges." Choose "Add a new user." Refer to Figure A.7 and do the following:

- Enter the admin username. (Do not make this name obvious.) Use a name like XYZadmin as opposed to just admin. (Again, "XYZ" is a three letter code you can easily associate with your site.)
- Choose "Local" for host. (This may be different for some hosting sites—Godaddy.com, for example.)

- Click the "Generate" key to generate a big, ugly password. (For security reasons, you want a big and ugly password.)
- Click "Copy" to copy the big, ugly password into the password fields.
- Click "Check All" for Global privileges.
- Before you click "go," put the database name, admin user name, and the big, ugly password in your text file so you will not lose it.
- Select "Go" at the bottom of the screen.

You are now armed with the information you need to configure and install WordPress.

Figure A.7. Creating the Database User

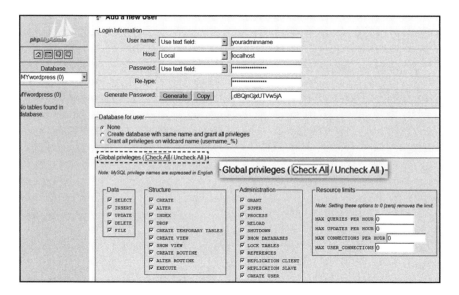

Downloading And Installing WordPress

Follow these steps to download WordPress and prepare the wp-config file:

- Go to WordPress.org and download the latest version of WordPress. Be sure and download the .zip file and not the tar.gz file. Unzip the folder (extract all files) onto your desktop.

- Open the wordpress folder and find the file named "wp-config-sample. php." Right click on the file and rename it "wp-config.php".
- Open wp-config.php in a text editor (use Wordpad or Notepad, NOT Word). The file will look similar to the file depicted in Figure A.8.
- Change the code that is highlighted in Figure A.8 as follows:
    › "XYZwordpress" is the name you gave your database.
    › "XYZadmin" is the database admin user you created.
    › The password is the big, ugly password you generated as your database admin password.
    › Use the URL (http://api.wordpress.org/secret-key/1.1/) as suggested in Figure A.8 to generate your secret keys.
    › Change the table prefix "wp" to any different two letter code.
- Once these changes are made, save your new wp-config.php file.

Figure A.8. WordPress Configuration File

```php
<?php
// ** MySQL settings ** //
define('DB_NAME', 'XYZwordpress');    // The name of the database
define('DB_USER', 'XYZadmin');    // Your MySQL username
define('DB_PASSWORD', ',dBQjnGjxUTw5jA'); // ...and password
define('DB_HOST', 'localhost');    // 99% chance you won't need to change this value
define('DB_CHARSET', 'utf8');
define('DB_COLLATE', '');

// Change each KEY to a different unique phrase.  You won't have to remember the phrases later,
// so make them long and complicated.  You can visit http://api.wordpress.org/secret-key/1.1/
// to get keys generated for you, or just make something up.  Each key should have a different phrase.

define('AUTH_KEY', 'first unique key'); // Change this to a unique phrase.
define('SECURE_AUTH_KEY', 'second unique key'); // Change this to a unique phrase.
define('LOGGED_IN_KEY', 'third unique key'); // Change this to a unique phrase.

// You can have multiple installations in one database if you give each a unique prefix
$table_prefix  = 'wp_';  // Only numbers, letters, and underscores please!

// Change this to localize WordPress.  A corresponding MO file for the
// chosen language must be installed to wp-content/languages.
// For example, install de.mo to wp-content/languages and set WPLANG to 'de'
// to enable German language support.
define ('WPLANG', '');

/* That's all, stop editing! Happy blogging. */

if ( !defined('ABSPATH') )
        define('ABSPATH', dirname(__FILE__) . '/');
require_once(ABSPATH . 'wp-settings.php');
?>
```

Uploading the WordPress Files to Your Hosting Account

Before you proceed, you need to have FTP access. Refer back to the "FTP Access" section on Page 103, and follow the instructions for getting FTP access, if you do not already have it.

Using FTP access, upload all of the WordPress files and folders onto the root directory of your hosting account. **IMPORTANT:** You want to upload the files and folders INSIDE the "wordpress" folder, not just the folder itself—read on for clarification.

The following demonstrates the process using the FTP browser WS-FTP and a Westhost hosted account. Note that the process will be similar using any FTP browser or hosting account.

Figure A.9 shows what you should see when you first connect to your Westhost account via FTP. What this shows are the files on the remote computer (your hosted account) on the right, and the files of the local computer (your computer) on the left. To transfer files, either highlight them and click the appropriate arrow, or drag and drop them.

Figures A.9 & A.10. Uploading WordPress via FTP

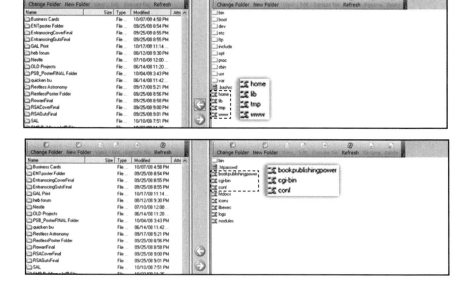

To get to the host's root directory, double-click on "www." (see Figure A.9). Next, double-click on the name of your domain (see Figure A.10). In this example, the domain name is "bookpublishingpower." You will now be in your hosted account's root directory.

Next, in the left, or remote, area of the FTP browser, find the directory on your computer that has the WordPress files you downloaded and unzipped earlier. Figure A.11 shows what you should see now: your wordpress files to the left and your hosted account's root directory on the right. Be careful NOT to upload only the wordpress folder. Instead, you want to open that folder and upload the files and folders that are inside of it.

Now, highlight all of the WordPress files and folders and copy them over to the hosting account. You will also need to change the name of the index.html (or index.htm) file, if one exists. Many hosts place a temporary index file in your root directory that you can replace once the site is developed. In our example, we changed the name of the index. html file to index-old.html.

Figure A.11. Uploading WordPress via FTP

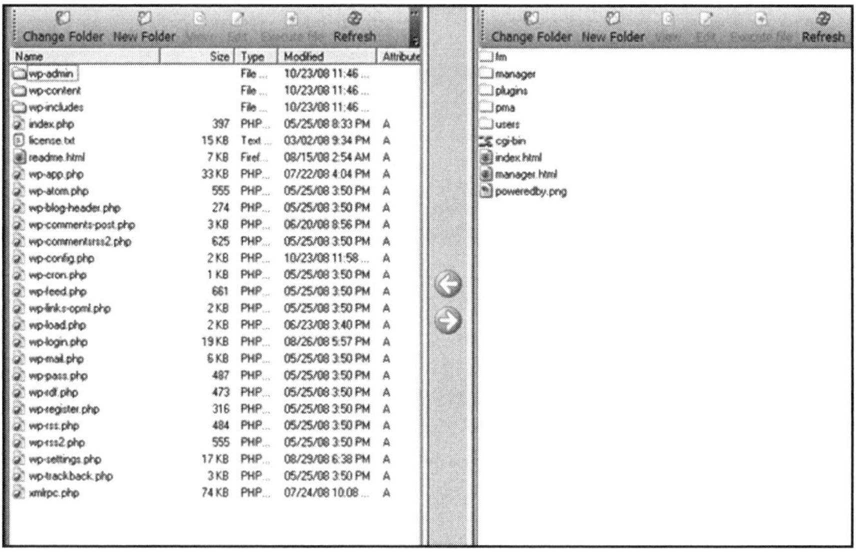

Figure A.12. Uploading WordPress via FTP

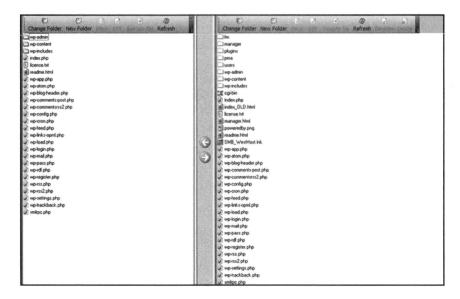

Figure A.12 shows you what the files in your hosting account's root directory should look like once you are finished. Please note that this may vary with different hosts, but the WordPress files and folders will be the same for the most part (they may vary slightly in newer versions).

Installing WordPress

Once all preliminary tasks are complete, the actual installation of WordPress takes around five minutes—see the WordPress famous 5-minute install.[4] To install WordPress, access the WordPress installation script by visiting a specific Web address using a Web browser. Open Firefox or Internet Explorer and visit http://www.YourSite.com/wp-admin/install.php, where "YourSite.com" is your domain name.

Follow the instructions to input a blog name and email address, then click "Install WordPress" (see Figure A.13). As long as there are no database errors on the next screen, you will be finished.

If you do get database errors, check that all of the information in the wp-config.php file is correct, i.e. the database name, the username, the password. If not, correct the config file, re-upload the file using your FTP

---

[4] http://codex.wordpress.org/Installing_WordPress#Famous_5-Minute_Install.

Figure A.13. Installing WordPress

browser, and try the previous step again. If you continue to get errors, visit the WordPress forums for help.[5]

Once WordPress is installed, you will receive an email message with your admin password, and a link to the login area of WordPress so you can get into the back end and start building your site.

You can get more information from the WordPress codex[6] or from the WordPress forums.[7]

[5]http://wordpress.org/support/
[6]http://codex.wordpress.org/Installing_WordPress
[7]http://wordpress.org/support/

Appendix B: Creating Your Own RSS Feed

To create your own RSS feed, follow these general steps:

- Create an XML file that is formatted specifically for RSS readers
- Populate the file with your articles or "items"
- Save the file and upload it to a folder on the Internet
- The link to the feed (or the feed URL) will then be something like:
  - › http://www.yoursite.com/yourRSSfolder/nameoffile.xml

An RSS feed is a way to present information so feed aggregators can read it, the same way HTML is read by Web browsers. This is accomplished using XML.

XML

XML stands for Extended Markup Language. The language is based on the use of tags. Content is presented inside specific tags that are then interpreted by applications written specifically to decipher the content within the tags. For instance, this is a tagged element:

<title>This is the title.</title>

The beginning of the element is the opening tag "<title>," the content is the sentence "This is the title.," and the end of the element is the closing tag "</title>." An application that is written to do so, will know how to pull the content from between the opening title tag and the closing title tag.

XML is different from HTML. HTML is a markup language that *displays* data, where XML is a language designed to store and transport data across many platforms. XML does not have predefined tags like HTML. HTML tags follow a standard that can be read by all Web browsers. XML tags, on the other hand, do not follow any predefined standard; they are created and defined by the author of the XML document. Of course, without an application to make sense of the data, an XML document does the author little good.

Writing an application or "language" to read XML documents is surprisingly easy. That is why XML is becoming a standard in Web data storage and exchange. One such language is RSS. RSS is a language that is written to read and interpret XML data within specific tags. As long as we know what those tags are, we can write an XML file that can be read by a RSS feed aggregator.

In its simplest form, a RSS feed document consists of a declaration line, a <rss> tag, one <channel> tag, and one <item> tag. Below is a stripped-down version of the RSS feed for Social Media Power:[1]

```
<?xml version="1.0" encoding="UTF-8"?>
<rss version="2.0">
<channel>
  <title>Social Media Power</title>
  <link>http://www.socialmediapower.com</link>
  <description>Discover the Tools of Web 2.0!</description>
  <item>
    <title>We want to make you Plumb Social!</title>
    <link>http://www.socialmediapower.com/2008/10/28/we-want-to-make-
      you-plumb-social/</link>
    <description><Introducing www.PlumbSocial.com, our new service for
      streamlining your presence on the Social Web!></description>
  </item>
</channel>
</rss>
```

---

[1] http://www.socialmediapower.com

The first line is the XML declaration. This line defines the XML version and the character encoding. The one used here is pretty standard. For a more in depth explanation of versions and character encoding go to the World Wide Web Consortium (W3C).[2]

The next line is the RSS declaration. It defines the XML document as a RSS document. Some tags or elements have what are called "attributes" that can contain different values. Attributes are used to further define a tag, and are always contained in quotes. The "version" in this line is an example of an attribute. It declares the RSS version as "2.0."

The two main elements of an RSS feed are the <channel> element and the <item> element. The actual RSS feed is defined with the <channel> element. Each individual article or story is defined within an <item> element.

Nested in the <channel> element are its sub-elements: <title>, <link>, and <description>. Sub-elements are used to further expand an RSS tag. Some sub-elements are required, while others are optional. The <item> element has sub-elements as well: <title>, <link>, and <description> in our example.

In XML, every element must have a closing tag, so the last two lines in our example are the closing tags for the <channel> and <rss> elements.

The Elements Of An RSS Feed

The information in this section is an *unadulterated* reproduction from the Berkman Center for Internet & Society at Harvard Law School's Website[3] under the terms of an Attribution/Share Alike Creative Commons license. Dave Winer is the author of the *unedited* document.

---

[2] http://www.w3.org/International/O-charset
[3] http://cyber.law.harvard.edu/rss/rss.html

Required <channel> Elements:

Element	Description	Example
title	The name of the channel. It's how people refer to your service. If you have an HTML website that contains the same information as your RSS file, the title of your channel should be the same as the title of your website.	GoUpstate.com News Headlines
link	The URL to the HTML website corresponding to the channel.	http://www.goupstate.com/
description	Phrase or sentence describing the channel.	The latest news from GoUpstate.com, a Spartanburg Herald-Journal Web site.

Optional <channel> Elements:

Element	Description	Example
language	The language the channel is written in. This allows aggregators to group all Italian language sites, for example, on a single page. For more information go to the W3C (http://www.w3.org/TR/REC-html40/struct/dirlang.html#langcodes).	en-us
copyright	Copyright notice for content in the channel.	Copyright 2002, Spartanburg Herald-Journal
managing Editor	Email address for person responsible for editorial content.	geo@herald.com (George Matesky)
webMaster	Email address for person responsible for technical issues relating to channel.	betty@herald.com (Betty Guernsey)

pubDate	The publication date for the content in the channel. For example, the New York Times publishes on a daily basis, the publication date flips once every 24 hours. That's when the pubDate of the channel changes. All date-times in RSS conform to the Date and Time Specification of RFC 822 (http://asg.web.cmu.edu/rfc/rfc822.html), with the exception that the year may be expressed with two characters or four characters (four preferred).	Sat, 07 Sep 2002 00:00:01 GMT
lastBuildDate	The last time the content of the channel changed.	Sat, 07 Sep 2002 09:42:31 GMT
category	Specify one or more categories that the channel belongs to. Follows the same rules as the <item>-level category element. For more information (http://cyber.law.harvard.edu/rss/rss.html#syndic8).	<category>Newspapers</category>
generator	A string indicating the program used to generate the channel.	MightyInHouse Content System v2.3
docs	A URL that points to the documentation for the format used in the RSS file. It's probably a pointer to this page. It's for people who might stumble across an RSS file on a Web server 25 years from now and wonder what it is.	http://blogs.law.harvard.edu/tech/rss
cloud	Allows processes to register with a cloud to be notified of updates to the channel, implementing a lightweight publish-subscribe protocol for RSS feeds. See below for more information.	<cloud domain="rpc.sys.com" port="80" path="/RPC2" registerProcedure="pingMe" protocol="soap"/>

ttl	ttl stands for time to live. It's a number of minutes that indicates how long a channel can be cached before refreshing from the source. See below for more information.	<ttl>60</ttl>
image	Specifies a GIF, JPEG or PNG image that can be displayed with the channel. See below for more information.	
rating	The PICS (http://www.w3.org/PICS/) rating for the channel.	
textInput	Specifies a text input box that can be displayed with the channel. See below for more information.	
skipHours	A hint for aggregators telling them which hours they can skip. For more information (http://cyber.law.harvard.edu/rss/skipHoursDays.html#skiphours)	
skipDays	A hint for aggregators telling them which days they can skip. For more information (http://cyber.law.harvard.edu/rss/skipHoursDays.html#skipdays)	

<image> sub-element of <channel>

is an optional sub-element of <channel>, which contains three required and three optional sub-elements.

<url> is the URL of a GIF, JPEG or PNG image that represents the channel.

<title> describes the image, it's used in the ALT attribute of the HTML <img> tag when the channel is rendered in HTML.

<link> is the URL of the site, when the channel is rendered, the image is a link to the site. (Note, in practice the image <title> and <link> should have the same value as the channel's <title> and <link>.

Optional elements include <width> and <height>, numbers, indicating the width and height of the image in pixels. <description> contains text that is included in the TITLE attribute of the link formed around the image in the HTML rendering. Maximum value for width is 144, default value is 88. Maximum value for height is 400, default value is 31.

<cloud> sub-element of <channel>

<cloud> is an optional sub-element of <channel>.

It specifies a web service that supports the rssCloud interface which can be implemented in HTTP-POST, XML-RPC or SOAP 1.1.

Its purpose is to allow processes to register with a cloud to be notified of updates to the channel, implementing a lightweight publish-subscribe protocol for RSS feeds.

```
<cloud domain="rpc.sys.com" port="80" path="/RPC2" register
Procedure="myCloud.rssPleaseNotify" protocol="xml-rpc" />
```

In this example, to request notification on the channel it appears in, you would send an XML-RPC message to rpc.sys.com on port 80, with a path of /RPC2. The procedure to call is myCloud.rssPleaseNotify.

A full explanation of this element and the rssCloud interface is here.[4]

<ttl> sub-element of <channel>

<ttl> is an optional sub-element of <channel>.

ttl stands for time to live. It's a number of minutes that indicates how long a channel can be cached before refreshing from the source. This makes it possible for RSS sources to be managed by a file-sharing network such as Gnutella (http://www.gnutellanews.com/).

Example: <ttl>60</ttl>

---

[4] http://cyber.law.harvard.edu/rss/soapMeetsRss.html#rsscloudInterface

<textInput> sub-element of <channel>

A channel may optionally contain a <textInput> sub-element, which contains four required sub-elements.

<title> -- The label of the Submit button in the text input area. <description> -- Explains the text input area.

<name> -- The name of the text object in the text input area.

<link> -- The URL of the CGI script that processes text input requests.

The purpose of the <textInput> element is something of a mystery. You can use it to specify a search engine box. Or to allow a reader to provide feedback. Most aggregators ignore it.

<item> Elements:

A channel may contain any number of <item>s. An item may represent a "story"—much like a story in a newspaper or magazine; if so, its description is a synopsis of the story, and the link points to the full story. An item may also be complete in itself, if so, the description contains the text, and the link and title may be omitted. All elements of an item are optional, however at least one of title or description must be present.

Element	Description	Example
title	The title of the item.	Venice Film Festival Tries to Quit Sinking
link	The URL of the item.	http://nytimes.com/2004/12/07FEST.html
description	The item synopsis.	Some of the most heated chatter at the Venice Film Festival this week was about the way that the arrival of the stars at the Palazzo del Cinema was being staged.
author	authorEmail address of the author of the item. See below for more information.	oprah\@oxygen.net

category	Includes the item in one or more categories. See below for more information.	
comments	URL of a page for comments relating to the item. See below for more information.	http://www.myblog.org/cgi-local/ mt/mt-comments.cgi?entry_id=290
enclosure	Describes a media object that is attached to the item. See below for more information.	
guid	A string that uniquely identifies the item. See below for more information.	http://inessential.com/2002/09/01. php#a2
pubDate	Indicates when the item was published. See below for more information.	Sun, 19 May 2002 15:21:36 GMT
source	The RSS channel that the item came from. See below for more information.	

<source> sub-element of <item>

<source> is an optional sub-element of <item>.

Its value is the name of the RSS channel that the item came from, derived from its <title>. It has one required attribute, url, which links to the XMLization of the source.

```
<source url="http://www.tomalak.org/links2.xml">Tomalak's
Realm</source>
```

The purpose of this element is to propagate credit for links, to publicize the sources of news items. It can be used in the Post command of an aggregator. It should be generated automatically when forwarding an item from an aggregator to a weblog authoring tool.

<enclosure> sub-element of <item>

<enclosure> is an optional sub-element of <item>.

It has three required attributes. url says where the enclosure is located, length says how big it is in bytes, and type says what its type is, a standard MIME type.

The url must be an http url.

```
<enclosure url="http://www.scripting.com/mp3s/
weatherReportSuite.mp3" length="12216320" type="audio/mpeg"
/>
```

A use-case narrative for this element is here.[5]

<category> sub-element of <item>

<category> is an optional sub-element of <item>.

It has one optional attribute, domain, a string that identifies a categorization taxonomy.

The value of the element is a forward-slash-separated string that identifies a hierarchic location in the indicated taxonomy. Processors may establish conventions for the interpretation of categories. Two examples are provided below:

```
<category>Grateful Dead</category>
<category domain="http://www.fool.
com/cusips">MSFT</category>
```

You may include as many category elements as you need to, for different domains, and to have an item cross-referenced in different parts of the same domain.

<pubDate> sub-element of <item>

<pubDate> is an optional sub-element of <item>.

Its value is a date, indicating when the item was published. If it's a date in the future, aggregators may choose to not display the item until that date.

```
<pubDate>Sun, 19 May 2002 15:21:36 GMT</pubDate>
```

<guid> sub-element of <item>

<guid> is an optional sub-element of <item>.

guid stands for globally unique identifier. It's a string that uniquely identifies the item. When present, an aggregator may choose to use this string to determine if an item is new.

---

[5] http://www.thetwowayweb.com/payloadsforrss

```
<guid>http://some.server.com/weblogItem3207</guid>
```

There are no rules for the syntax of a guid. Aggregators must view them as a string. It's up to the source of the feed to establish the uniqueness of the string.

If the guid element has an attribute named "isPermaLink" with a value of true, the reader may assume that it is a permalink to the item, that is, a url that can be opened in a Web browser, that points to the full item described by the <item> element. An example:

```
<guid isPermaLink="true">http://inessential.com/2002/09/01.
php#a2</guid>
```

isPermaLink is optional, its default value is true. If its value is false, the guid may not be assumed to be a url, or a url to anything in particular.

<comments> sub-element of <item>

<comments> is an optional sub-element of <item>.

If present, it is the url of the comments page for the item.

```
<comments>http://ekzemplo.
com/entry/4403/comments</comments>
```

<author> sub-element of <item>

<author> is an optional sub-element of <item>

It's the email address of the author of the item. For newspapers and magazines syndicating via RSS, the author is the person who wrote the article that the <item> describes. For collaborative weblogs, the author of the item might be different from the managing editor or webmaster. For a weblog authored by a single individual it would make sense to omit the <author> element.

```
<author>lawyer@boyer.net (Lawyer Boyer)</author>
```

Another Example

The RSS feed below is the further expanded feed for Social Media Power.[6] You will see many of the sub-elements discussed above in this expanded feed.

```
<?xml version="1.0" encoding="UTF-8"?>
<rss version="2.0">
  <channel>
    <title>Social Media Power</title>
    <link>http://www.socialmediapower.com</link>
    <description>Discover the Tools of Web 2.0!</description>
    <pubDate>Tue, 09 Dec 2008 12:18:38 +0000</pubDate>
    <generator>http://wordpress.org/?v=abc</generator>
    <language>en</language>
    <item>
      <title>A shout for our social media e-book.</title>
      <link>http://www.socialmediapower.com/2008/09/05/a-shout-for-our-social-
      media-e-book/</link>
      <pubDate>Fri, 05 Sep 2008 13:05:14 +0000</pubDate>
      <category>Social Media</category>
      <category>Social Media Books</category>
      <category>Social Media Marketing</category>
      <category>Social Media Tools</category>
      <category>Web 2.0</category>
      <category>WordPress</category>
      <category>social media e-book</category>
      <guid isPermaLink="false">http://www.socialmediapower.com/?p=105</guid>
      <description><JD at Social Media gave our e-book a shout, saying it
      was&#8230;worth the price for anyone looking for a grounding in the nuts and
      bolts of social media. And, that it&#8230;will give you the underpinnings
      for the elements you need to address in your organization&#8217;s social
      media strategy.Thank you, JD!></description>
      <comments>http://www.socialmediapower.com/2008/09/05/a-shout-for-our-social-
      media-e-book/#comments/</comments>
    </item>
    <item>
      <title>The 30 Minute Facebook Application</title>
      <link>http://www.socialmediapower.com/2008/08/28/the-30-minute facebook-
      application/</link>
      <pubDate>Thu, 28 Aug 2008 21:05:25 +0000</pubDate>
      <category>Facebook</category>
      <category>Social Media</category>
      <category>Social Media Marketing</category>
      <category>Social Media Optimization</category>
      <category>Social Media Tools</category>
      <category>Bebo</category>
      <category>blog</category>
      <category>facebook applications</category>
      <category>facebook page</category>
      <category>RSS feed</category>
      <category>social networking</category>
      <category>widgetbox</category>
      <guid isPermaLink="false">http://www.socialmediapower.com/?p=67</guid>
      <description><Continuing our series on tapping the power of Facebook, we
      will demonstrate a way for anyone with an RSS feed to painlessly build a
      Facebook application in only 30 minutes. First, what is a Facebook
      application. If you are familiar with Facebook, you probably have an
      application or two on your page or profile already. If not,
      [...]></description>
      <comments>http://www.socialmediapower.com/2008/08/28/the-30-minute-facebook-
      application/#comments</comments>
    </item>
  </channel>
</rss>
```

---

[6] http://www.socialmediapower.com/feed

Comments in RSS

The format for a comment is:

<!-- This is a comment. -->

Adding More Stories

The example above shows two separate items or stories. To add additional stories to your feed, insert additional items using the <item> tag and sub-elements accordingly, then save and replace the XML file.

Extending RSS

The core functionality of RSS is limited to the elements discussed in the previous sections. Developers extend the functionality of RSS, however, by writing modules or extensions that are defined and accessed using what are called "namespaces." These extensions work just like add-ons to RSS, but are defined in a way that still allow older versions of RSS to work properly.

In the RSS feed example below, there are several namespaces defined within the <rss> element. The namespace is an attribute called "xmlns," and its value is assigned as follows:

xmlns:namespace name="URL of where to find the namespace extensions."

So, in our example, the statement:

```
xmlns:atom="http://www.w3.org/2005/Atom"
```

is telling the RSS reader to go to the URL "http://www.w3.org/2005/Atom" and include the extensions contained there as part of this RSS document, and that each time it encounters the namespace "atom" to go to this URL for more information.

Looking further down the example code will help clarify. The first line that should look unfamiliar is:

```
<atom:link href="http://www.socialmediapower.com/feed"
rel="self" type="application/rss+xml" />
```

This is not a core element, but we are telling the reader that it can find its definition by going to the defined URL in the namespace "atom" that is defined in the <rss> element.

Similarly, you will see many references in this example to elements that are not core elements (<dc:creator> and <wfw:commentRss> for

```xml
<?xml version="1.0" encoding="UTF-8"?>
<?xml version="1.0" encoding="UTF-8"?>

<!-- Here are the defined namespaces, within the rss element -->

<rss version="2.0"
  xmlns:content="http://purl.org/rss/1.0/modules/content/"
  xmlns:wfw="http://wellformedweb.org/CommentAPI/"
  xmlns:dc="http://purl.org/dc/elements/1.1/"
  xmlns:atom="http://www.w3.org/2005/Atom">
  <channel>
    <title>Social Media Power</title>
    <atom:link href="http://www.socialmediapower.com/feed" rel="self"
    type="application/rss+xml" />
    <link>http://www.socialmediapower.com</link>
    <description>Discover the Tools of Web 2.0!</description>
    <pubDate>Tue, 09 Dec 2008 12:18:38 +0000</pubDate>
    <generator>http://wordpress.org/?v=abc</generator>
    <language>en</language>
    <item>
      <title>Social Media Tip of the Day: Build a Solid Social Media
      Strategy</title>
      <link>http://www.socialmediapower.com/2008/08/25/social-media-tip-of-the-
      day-build-a-solid-social-media-strategy/</link>
      <comments>http://www.socialmediapower.com/2008/08/25/social-media-tip-of-
      the-day-build-a-solid-social-media-strategy/#comments</comments>
      <pubDate>Mon, 25 Aug 2008 20:01:01 +0000</pubDate>
      <dc:creator>smpadmin</dc:creator>
      <category><![CDATA[Social Media]]></category>
      <category><![CDATA[Web 2.0]]></category>
      <category><![CDATA[social media strategy]]></category>
      <category><![CDATA[Social Media Tools]]></category>
      <guid isPermaLink="false">http://www.socialmediapower.com/?p=103</guid>
      <description><![CDATA[All of the social media tools and technologies that
      are out there can be overwhelming, no doubt. But, if you focus on the sites
      and tools that truly make sense for your business, you will find that the
      choices narrow down substantially. Take the time to build a solid social
      media strategy before you begin [...]]]></description>
      <content:encoded><![CDATA[<p>All of the social media tools and technologies
      that are out there can be overwhelming, no doubt. But, if you focus on the
      sites and tools that truly make sense for your business, you will find that
      the choices narrow down substantially. Take the time to build a solid
      social media strategy before you begin that includes:</p>
      <ul>
      <li>Gathering and preparing your best content, media, and key terms</li>
      <li>Web 2.0 tools to add to your existing Web site</li>
      <li>How you will enter the blogosphere - if at all</li>
      <li>One or two social networking sites that are good fits for your message
      or business</li>
      <li>Several social bookmarking and crowd-sourcing sites whose content tends
      toward your message</li>
      <li>Media communities to share images, events, video, etc. based on media
      you already have</li>
      <li>Badges, widgets, and feeds to pull all of these tools together</li>
      </ul>
      <p>Thank you for your support!</p>
      <p>The Social Media Power team</p>]]></content:encoded>
      <wfw:commentRss>http://www.socialmediapower.com/2008/08/25/social-media-
      tip-of-the-day-build-a-solid-social-media-strategy/feed/</wfw:commentRss>
    </item>
  </channel></rss>
```

instance). They will, however, be preceded by a namespace name that will define where to find the extensions. You can go directly to any of these URLs to learn more about the extensions they contribute to RSS.

CDATA Sections

One other thing that may look unfamiliar about the RSS feed above is the use of CDATA. A "CDATA section" is a section of content that is marked so that the feed reader interprets the content as character data, not markup data. CDATA is used to ensure that none of the content data is misinterpreted as XML. This is especially useful for tech feeds that may contain coding examples.

Podcasting

A podcast, like a blog, is an RSS feed. When a feed reader is told that a feed is a podcast, it will look for a file within each item that will become the podcast episode. Use the enclosure element to define podcast episode files within each item of a podcast feed.

Here is the syntax of the enclosure element repeated from its definition above:

```
<enclosure url="http://www.scripting.com/mp3s/
weatherReportSuite.mp3" length="12216320" type="audio/mpeg"
/>
```

So, the "url" will be the location of the audio or video file that makes up your podcast episode, the "length" is the size of the file, and the "type" is the type of file.

Here is a stripped down example taken from the XML of the Social Media Power podcast example used in Chapter 5, "Podcasting, Vidcasting, & Webcasting."

```
<item>
    <title>SMP Podcast Episode 1: Social Media and Web 2.0 Basics for
    Business</title>
    <link>http://www.socialmediapower.com/2009/01/06/smp-podcast-episode-1/</link>
    ...
    <enclosure
    url="http://www.socialmediapower.com/podcasts/SocialMediaPowerEpisode1.mp3"
    length="7107653" type="audio/mpeg" />
    ...
</item>
```

You want to optimize a podcast feed specifically for iTunes and Yahoo! Media as well. To do this, add these namespaces:

```
xmlns:media="http://search.yahoo.com/mrss/"
xmlns:itunes="http://www.itunescom/dtds/podcast-1.0.dtd"
```

You can read more about the elements and syntax of the iTunes namespace at FeedForAll.[7] They also discuss the Yahoo! Media namespace[8].

Resources And Further Reading

You can find more RSS modules by Googling "RSS Modules" or "RSS Extensions." But make certain that you include modules only from trusted sources.

The W3C specifies the use and development of namespaces here.[9] Another good source of RSS extensions is RSS-Extensions.[10]

See the resource CD for a fillable XML file you can use as a starting point for creating your own RSS feed.

---

[7] http://www.feedforall.com/itunes.htm

[8] http://www.feedforall.com/mediarss.htm

[9] http://www.w3.org/TR/REC-xml-names/

[10] http://rss-extensions.org

Appendix C: Building Your Own Widget

In Chapter 9, "Widgets & Badges," we talked about creating viral widgets, and even showed you how to create a simple feed widget using your RSS feed or blog on Widgetbox.com. In this appendix we demonstrate a few more sophisticated ways for you to create a widget, even if you do not have coding experience.

Recall that a widget is a snippet of code that you can place on your Website or blog that pulls information from another source. Widgets are typically written using HTML, JavaScript, Flash, or a combination of these. You can create a widget that displays a dynamic Web page, you can write a JavaScript routine that performs a specific task like pulling and displaying content from a data file, or you can create a Flash application that incorporates animation. Regardless of how you create your widget, the basic premise is that you create the code and make it available for others to copy and place on their own site or blog.

The advent of the "open" Web makes creating online applications of any kind much more accessible for novice developers. We demonstrate this concept here by showing you how to use the Google Gadget Editor to create your own widget by copying existing code and altering it to your own specifications.

Specifically, we show you how to:

1. Create a widget using the Google Gadget Editor.
2. Add the widget to the Widgetbox gallery.
3. Add the widget to the Clearspring distribution service.
4. Create a Facebook application from the widget.

Setting Up the Scenario

A client has a divination system called "Nod's Way or Hidden Dragon." It is called "The first ancient oracle of the 21st century," and is similar to an I Ching or Tarot system, consisting of three dice and an oracle that the user consults depending on the roll of the dice.

There are 36 "auspices" in the oracle that take on three possible forms, for a total of 108 possible permutations. These forms are determined by the roll of two eight-sided dice and one four-sided die.

To demonstrate, Figure C.1 shows the first auspice from the oracle book. If a user rolls the dice as in Figure C.2, her reading is everything on page 20 as seen in Figure C.1. Because the square die is blank, her reading does not include anything on page 21. If, however, she rolls the

Figure C.1. Nod's Way or Hidden Dragon

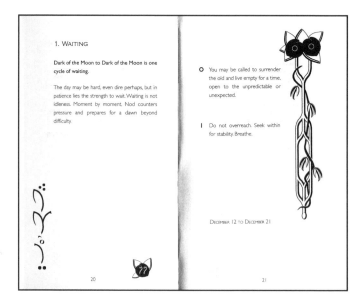

Figure C.2. Nod's Way Dice Roll 1

Figure C.3. Nod's Way Dice Roll 2

Figure C.4. Nod's Way Dice Roll 3

combination in Figure C.3, her reading consists of everything on page 20, in addition to the corresponding entry on page 21 that has a ring to the left of it (because the square die shows a ring). Similarly, if she rolls the combination in Figure C.4, her reading consists of everything on page 20 as well as the "bar" entry on page 21, since the square die shows a bar.

We want to emulate this divination system with a widget on as many different platforms as possible. We start by defining exactly what it is we want our widget to accomplish, and then we come up with a plan to accomplish it.

- What the widget should do:
    › Show images of the three dice as they are "rolled" by the user.
    › Show the resulting reading from the oracle based on the dice roll.
    › Have the widget produce each roll randomly.
- How the widget will do this:
    › Extract the data from an XML file and store it in a list that is indexed from 0 to 107.

> Generate a random number between 0 and 107.
> Pull data from an XML file based on the random number.
> Display the resulting dice images and oracle reading pulled from the XML file.

- The plan of attack:
    > Create and upload the dice image files.
    > Design and upload an XML file that accommodates the oracle data and dice image file names.
    > Use the Google Gadget Editor to create an oracle widget that pulls its content from the XML file.
    > Make the widget available for others to post to an iGoogle page or to a Website.
    > Add the widget to the Widgetbox.com gallery.
    > Add the widget to the Clearspring.com widget distribution site.
    > Use the Clearspring.com platform to create a Facebook application based on the widget.

Creating and Uploading the Dice Images

We create 11 images that represent each side of the eight-sided dice, and three sides of the four-sided die (the square die). Since two sides of the four-sided die are blank, we only need one image for that one. We save the images with the following names:

darkmoon.jpg
fullmoon.jpg
halfmoon.jpg
crescentmoon.jpg
daystar.jpg
myriadstar.jpg
novastar.jpg
void.jpg
barsquare.jpg
ringsquare.jpg
blanksquare.jpg

We then upload the images to a folder on SocialMediaPower.com from where the XML file and widget code can access them.

Creating and Uploading the XML File

Please refer back to Appendix B, "Creating Your Own RSS Feed," to learn about XML files if you do not already know what they are. In a nutshell, XML is a method by which you can define and populate your own data file very easily. You then need to produce code to access the data once it is defined, which is what we demonstrate later.

We define our XML file in the following way. Recall that each "<tag>" and "</end-tag>" is one item or sub-item, and represents a specific portion of the data you are representing, similar to a field in a database, or a column in a spreadsheet. Creating and pulling data from a file like this means that whenever you need to change or add any content used in your widget, you will only need alter and save this file to do so.

```
<nod> (this defines the main element)
   <auspice> (this tag distinguishes each auspice, or permutation)
      <atitle>(the title of the auspice goes here)</atitle>
      <asub> (the description of the auspice goes here) </asub>
      <abody> (the "reading" or main body of the auspice goes
      here) </abody>
      <ititle> (the three possible variations of this auspice: may
      be blank, a ring, or a bar) </ititle>
      <ibody> (the additional insight based on the variation: may
      be blank or based on the ring or bar) </ibody>
      <oneroll> (the image file name representing the first eight-
      sided die) </oneroll>
      <tworoll> (the image file name representing the second eight-
      sided die) </tworoll>
      <threeroll> (the file name representing the square die:
      blank, ring, or bar) </threeroll>
   </auspice>
</nod>
```

The actual file looks like the one below, except with 105 additional entries (since we have 108 total permutations to include).

```
<?xml version="1.0" encoding="UTF-8" ?>
<nod title="ORACLE OF THE DAY">
   <auspice>
      <atitle>Auspice 1: Waiting</atitle>
      <asub>Dark of the Moon to Dark of the Moon is one cycle of
      waiting.</asub>
      <abody>The day may be hard, even dire perhaps, but in
      patience lies the strength to wait. Waiting is not idleness.
      Moment by moment, Nod counters pressure and prepares for a
      dawn beyond difficulty.</abody>
      <ititle> </ititle>
      <ibody> </ibody>
      <oneroll>darkmoon.jpg</oneroll>
```

```
        <tworoll>darkmoon.jpg</tworoll>
        <threeroll>blanksquare.jpg</threeroll>
    </auspice>
    <auspice>
        <atitle>Auspice 1: Waiting</atitle>
        <asub>Dark of the Moon to Dark of the Moon is one cycle of
        waiting.</asub>
        <abody>The day may be hard, even dire perhaps, but in
        patience lies the strength to wait. Waiting is not idleness.
        Moment by moment, Nod counters pressure and prepares for a
        dawn beyond difficulty.</abody>
        <ititle>Variation: Ring</ititle>
        <ibody>You may be called to surrender the old and live empty
        for a time, open to the unpredictable or unexpected.</ibody>
        <oneroll>darkmoon.jpg</oneroll>
        <tworoll>darkmoon.jpg</tworoll>
        <threeroll>ringsquare.jpg</threeroll>
    </auspice>
    <auspice>
        <atitle>Auspice 1: Waiting</atitle>
        <asub>Dark of the Moon to Dark of the Moon is one cycle of
        waiting.</asub>
        <abody>The day may be hard, even dire perhaps, but in
        patience lies the strength to wait. Waiting is not idleness.
        Moment by moment, Nod counters pressure and prepares for a
        dawn beyond difficulty.</abody>
        <ititle>Variation: Bar</ititle>
        <ibody>Do not overreach. Seek within for stability.
        Breathe.</ibody>
        <oneroll>darkmoon.jpg</oneroll>
        <tworoll>darkmoon.jpg</tworoll>
        <threeroll>barsquare.jpg</threeroll>
    </auspice>
</nod>
```

For each auspice there are three possible readings based on how the square die lands. If the die is blank, there is no additional insight, so the <ititle> and <ibody> tags are empty. But if a ring or a bar are rolled, those tags have content accordingly.

Before continuing, refer back to the scenario we established and to the oracle pages depicted in Figure C.1 on Page 362 and make sure you understand how the structure of this file represents the oracle content.

An XML file can be created using a text file with no formatting, or with an XML editor like Dreamweaver. We create our XML file using Dreamweaver and call it oracle-data.xml. We then save it and upload it to SocialMediaPower.com so that the widget code can access it—just as we did the image files.

Creating the Widget Using the Google Gadget Editor

Figure C.5 shows the Google Gadget Editor[1] (GGE). This platform allows you to create, test, and publish your widget (we use the term "gadget" and "widget" interchangeably in this section) all in one place. Even better, Google provides many examples of common uses of widgets that you are welcome to copy and edit for your own use.

Figure C.5. Google Gadget Editor

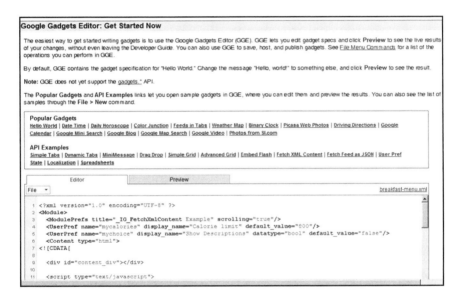

Google gadgets are created as XML files containing JavaScript and HTML. In the following example, JavaScript is used to extract the oracle data from our XML file and to create the HTML that stylizes and displays the oracle content.

Note: Gadgets were formerly called modules, which is why the word "Module" appears throughout the GGE.

Here is the process we use to create our widget using the GGE:

- Select a sample gadget that is similar to what we want
- Save the sample file with another name

---

[1] http://code.google.com/apis/gadgets/docs/legacy/gs.html#GGE

- Alter the code of the file to our specifications
- Tweak and test

We choose the "Fetch XML Content" sample gadget as the basis for our oracle widget since it already has the infrastructure in place for fetching content from an XML file and displaying it in a widget. Figure C.6 shows the code view for the widget in the GGE, and Figure C.7 shows a preview of how the content is displayed as a widget.

Figure C.6. GGE Sample Widget Code View

Figure C.7. GGE Sample Widget Preview

Figure C.8 on Page 386 (at the end of this Appendix) shows the sample widget code in its entirety. The widget displays menu choices based on user-entered calorie restrictions.

We now save the file as "nods-way-widget.xml" (see Figures C.9 and C.10).

Figure C.9. GGE Options

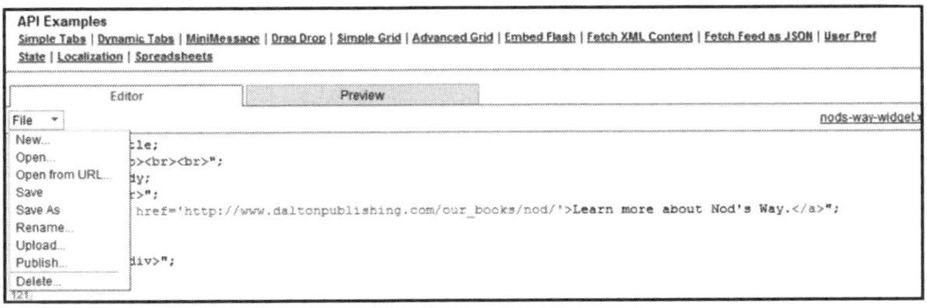

Figure C.10. GGE Saving a File

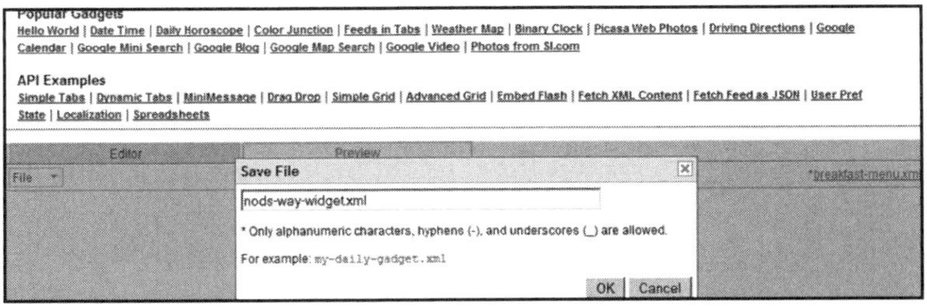

Now we alter the sample code to create our oracle widget code. Generally, here is what the code does:

- Extracts the 108 "auspice" items from the oracle-data.xml file we created using Dreamweaver
- Stores the auspice data in a list that indexes the auspice items from 0 to 107
- Generates a random number between 0 and 107
- Extracts the corresponding auspice from the list (This is what simulates our users "roll" of the dice)
- Extracts the corresponding sub-items for our chosen auspice from the XML file (the auspice title (<atitle>, auspice body <abody>, etc.)
- Stylizes and displays the corresponding oracle reading from the extracted content

The following is the code to create our widget with explanations of the code indicated by //. See Figure C.11 on Page 388 for the unadulterated code. Refer back to the XML file on Page 365 as you review this code.

```
// This first line is to establish the file as an XML file.
<?xml version="1.0" encoding="UTF-8" ?>
// The <Module> tag tells the GGE that this is a Google Gadget.
<Module>
// Module preferences are used to provide Google with information
about your gadget – many of these are required in order to be
included in the gadget directory.
<ModulePrefs title="Nod's Way or Hidden Dragon"
    scrolling="false"
    width="180"
    height="400"
    author="Deltina Hay"
    author_affiliation="Social Media Power"
    author_email="quotes+nodwidget@socialmediapower.com"
    thumbnail="http://www.socialmediapower.com/widgets/nodthumb.
    jpg"
    render_inline="optional"
    description="Daily oracle consultation from the Nod's Way
    divination system.">
</ModulePrefs>
// The content type (html or URL) tells the GGE where the content
resides: either embedded as HTML or on a remote site, respectively
<Content type="html">
// This is the CDATA section, which means it is not part of the
xml portion of the code (see APENDIX#,"Creating Your Own RSS
Feed").
<![CDATA[
<div id="content_div"></div>
// Here is where the JavaScript begins that pulls the oracle data:
<script type="text/javascript">
function displayNod() {
// Here is where the XML data file is defined that we uploaded:
var url = "http://socialmediapower.com/widgets/oracle-data.xml";
// This is a function from the Google Gadget library that fetches
data from the XML file:
  _IG_FetchXmlContent(url, function (response) {
  if (response == null || typeof(response) != "object" ||
  response.firstChild == null) {
  _gel("content_div").innerHTML = "<i>Invalid data.</i>";
  return;
  }
// Here is the beginning of the HTML string, defined as a variable
called "html" – we include all of the stylizing in here, too, just
as if we were creating an HTML page.
  var html = "<div style='padding: 0px;background-color:
  #fff;font-family:Verdana, Arial, Helvetica, sans-serif;" +
  "text-align:left;font-size:80%'>";
// Append the Nod widget header image to the html string:
  html += "<div style='padding:0px;'><img src='http://
  socialmediapower.com/widgets/NODHeader.jpg' /></div>";
```

```
// Set style for the main title:
   html +="<div style='text-align:center; font-size: 110%; color:
   red; " +
   "font-weight: 700;'>";
// Display Nod title. Use getElementsByTagName() to retrieve the
<NOD> element. Since there is only one NOD element in the file, you
can get to it by accessing the item at index "0". You can then
use getAttribute to get the text associated with the Nod "title"
attribute (see the oracle-data.xml file).
   var title = response.getElementsByTagName("nod").item(0).
   getAttribute("title");
// Append the title to the HTML string:
   html += title + "</div><br>";
   html +="<div style='text-align:left; padding-left:5px; font-
   size: 80%; color: black; " +
   "font-weight: 300;'>";
// Generate a random number between 0 and 107, and store it in the
variable "ausday"
   var ausday= Math.floor(Math.random()*108);
// Get the <auspice> item from the XML file
   var itemList = response.getElementsByTagName("auspice");
// Loop through the <auspice> items that we want to grab - for
this widget we only want one, the one indexed under the random
number we generated, so we only loop from the variable ausday to
one plus ausday
   for (var i = ausday; i < (ausday +1) ; i++) {
   // For each <auspice> sub-item, extract sub-item content:
   var nodeList = itemList.item(i).childNodes;
   // Loop through child nodes. Extract data from the nodes that
   are associated with the atitle, asub, abody, ititle, ibody,
   oneroll, tworoll, and threeroll sub-items, and store them in
   respective variables
     for (var j = 0; j < nodeList.length ; j++) {
     var node = nodeList.item(j);
     if (node.nodeName == "atitle") {
     var atitle = node.firstChild.nodeValue;
     }
     if (node.nodeName == "asub") {
     var asub = node.firstChild.nodeValue;
     }
     if (node.nodeName == "abody") {
     var abody = node.firstChild.nodeValue;
     }
     if (node.nodeName == "ititle") {
     var ititle = node.firstChild.nodeValue;
     }
     if (node.nodeName == "ibody") {
     var ibody = node.firstChild.nodeValue;
     }
     if (node.nodeName == "oneroll") {
     var oneroll = node.firstChild.nodeValue;
     }
     if (node.nodeName == "tworoll") {
     var tworoll = node.firstChild.nodeValue;
     }
```

```
    if (node.nodeName == "threeroll") {
    var threeroll = node.firstChild.nodeValue;
    }
}
// Append extracted data to the HTML string. The first three
append the images using the direct URL to where the image files
were uploaded, and the image file variables that were extracted
above. The remaining lines just append the content directly
from the remaining variables.
html += "<img src='http://socialmediapower.com/widgets/";
html += oneroll;
html += "' /> ";
html += "<img src='http://socialmediapower.com/widgets/";
html += tworoll;
html += "' /> ";
html += "<img src='http://socialmediapower.com/widgets/";
html += threeroll;
html += "' />";
html += "<br><br>";
html += atitle;
html += "<br><br><b>";
html += asub;
html += "</b><br><br>";
html += abody;
html += "<br><b>";
html += ititle;
html += "</b><br><br>";
html += ibody;
html += "<br>";
// Add a link to where they can learn more about Nod's
Way:
html += "<a href='http://www.daltonpublishing.com/our_books/
nod/'>Learn more about Nod's Way.</a>";
}
html += "</div>";
// Parse the HTML string using a Google Gadget function:
_gel('content_div').innerHTML = html;
});
}
// A Google Gadget Load Handler function:
    _IG_RegisterOnloadHandler(displayNod);
</script>
]]>
</Content>

</Module>
```

Figure C.12 shows the preview of our gadget after tweaking the existing code to our specifications.

Figure C.8 on Page 386 shows the sample widget code that we altered to create our widget. References to the libraries and most of the structure

Figure C.12. Oracle Widget Preview

of the code was already in place in this sample code, so all we needed to do was change the item names to match our own XML file, change the formatting within the <div> tags to our liking, and remove some of the code we did not need.

We did not need any custom user preferences for our widget, so we removed all references to them. User preferences are settings that users can make, beyond the default size and color settings, when they prepare a widget's code to place on their site.

In addition, the original sample code loops through all of the items in their XML file adding them to the list of content that is displayed, but we only require one item (specifically the one corresponding to the random number we generate). Therefore, we needed to find a JavaScript function that would generate a random number for us to store in our "ausday" variable. We found such a function easily with a quick Google search using the term "generate a random number in javascript."

It is our hope that this demonstration will encourage you to go to the GGE and try your hand at creating your own widget using some of their existing code as a guide. To learn more about Google Gadgets, go to the gadget development page.[2]

---

[2] http://www.google.com/webmasters/gadgets/

Publishing the Widget

Figure C.13 shows the publish menu in the GGE. From here you can add the gadget to your iGoogle page, publish it to a Website, or publish it to the iGoogle directory.

Figure C.14 shows the screen for adding the gadget to an iGoogle page, and Figure C.15 shows what the gadget looks like on an iGoogle page.

Figure C.13. GGE Publishing Options

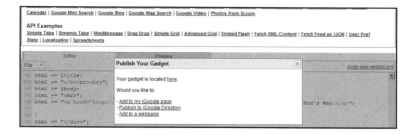

Figure C.14. Add Gadget to iGoogle Page

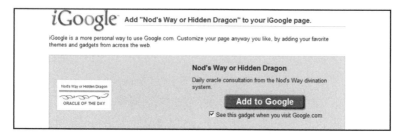

Figure C.15. Oracle Widget on iGoogle Page

Figure C.16 shows the screen for adding the gadget to a Website. As with any widget, copy the code and place it on your site where you want it to appear. Figure C.17 shows how the gadget looks once placed on a Web page.

Figure C.16. Customizing a Gadget for a Webpage

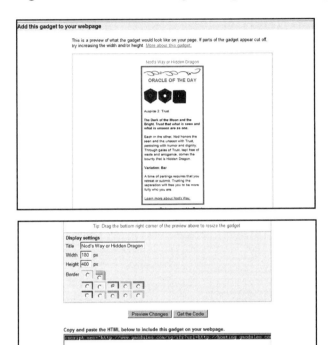

We place this gadget code onto a Web page that we use as a basis for creating a widget in the Widgetbox gallery and Clearspring service discussed later. To gauge how the finished widget compares to our initial plans, refer back to the partial XML file on Page 365 and Figures C.2 and C.3 and C.4 on Page 363 and compare them to the resulting widgets depicted in Figures C.18, C.19, and C.20 on Page 376.

Figure C.17. Oracle Gadget on a Website

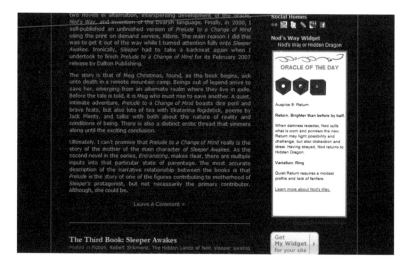

Figures C.18, C.19, & C.20. Oracle Widgets

Adding the Widget to Widgetbox

Widgetbox,[3] as we discussed in Chapter 9, "Widgets and Badges," is a widget gallery and community where you can get extra exposure for your widgets, and take advantage of widget tools and analytics. Our goal is to add our widget to Widgetbox with as little effort as possible.

Figure C.21 shows the main page for creating a widget in Widgetbox. They offer a number of ways to create a widget, and for this demonstration, we choose the "Remote" option.

Figure C.21. Widgetbox.com

To create our Remote widget, we enter the URL of the page we created in the previous section that contains our Google Gadget code (see Figures C.18, C.19, and C.20 on Page 376).

---

[3] http://www.widgetbox.com

The Widgetbox platform has no problem finding our widget and displays it for us to adjust in the next step (Figure C.22). In the following step (Figure C.23) we provide more details about our widget.

Figure C.22. Creating a Widget in Widgetbox

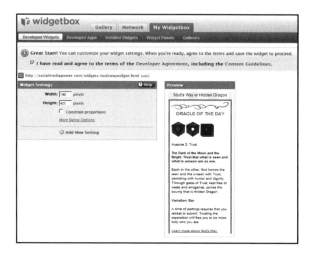

Figure C.23. Creating a Widget in Widgetbox

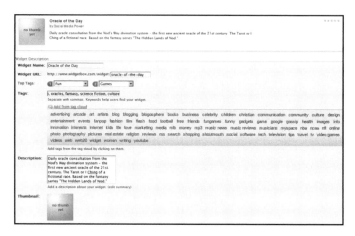

We then run our widget through a series of tests to get it ready to share in the gallery and for launch on other social sites (see Figures C.24, C.25, and C.26).

Figure C.24. Creating a Widget in Widgetbox

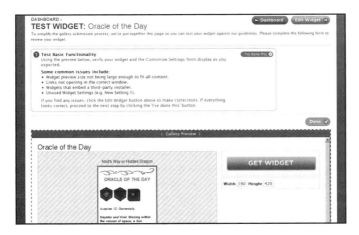

Figure C.25. Creating a Widget in Widgetbox

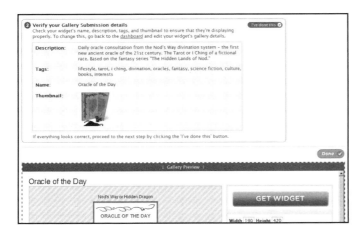

Next, we use the Widgetbox platform to distribute the widget to other social sites. Figure C.27 shows some of the places we can place the widget code to distribute it. We choose to grab the code and place it on the Dalton Publishing Ning network, The Dalton Gangway (see Figure C.28).

Figure C.26. Creating a Widget in Widgetbox

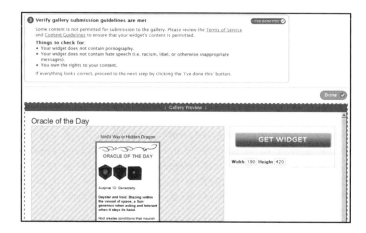

Figure C.27. Distributing a Widget with Widgetbox

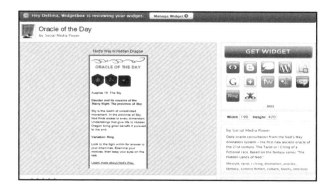

Figure C.28. Widgetbox Widget on Ning

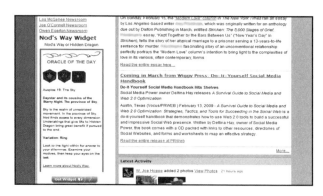

Finally, we want to promote our widget, so we go to the "Promote Your Widget" option from the "My Widgets" menu. There are a number of looks you can give your promo widget, and once we decide on a look, we grab the code and place it on the social media site of *The Hidden Lands of Nod* book series (see Figure C.29).

Figure C.29. Widgetbox Promo Widget

Adding the Widget to Clearspring

The Clearspring[4] platform is so similar to Widgetbox, as far as adding a widget, that we do not demonstrate it here. We do want to point out some additional features of Clearspring that are worth a look.

Figure C.30 shows some of the additional options you have for your widget when you add it to Clearspring.

---

[4] http://www.clearspring.com/

Figure C.30. Clearspring.com Options

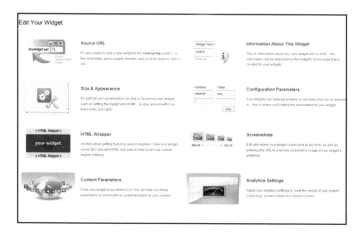

Figure C.31 shows additional ways to publish your widget. We took advantage of the "Publish to Galleries" option (see Figure C.32), and the Facebook publishing option.

Figure C.31. Clearspring.com Options

Figures C.33 and C.34 show a couple of the steps (seven steps in all) in the Clearspring wizard for creating a Facebook application from your widget.

Figure C.32. Clearspring Publish to Gallery

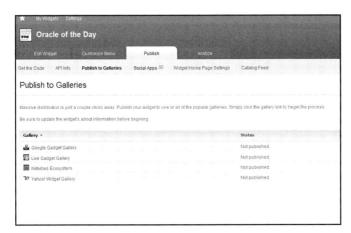

Figure C.33. Creating a Facebook Application

Figure C.34. Creating a Facebook Application

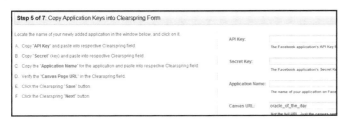

Once your Facebook application is created, be sure to go into Facebook to optimize the application by completing its description and adding thumbnail and icon images (see Figure C.35). Once you add the application to your own profile you can invite all of your friends to add it as well.

Figure C.35. Creating a Facebook Application

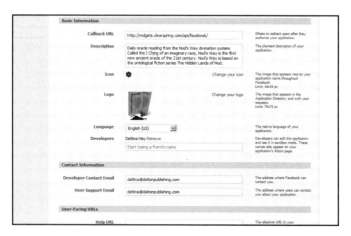

Many Roads to the Same Widget

It is important to understand that the process we used to create and distribute this widget is just one of many ways you can do it. For instance, once the Google Gadget was complete and published, we could have rewritten a bit of the code and turned it into a JavaScript widget and added it to Widgetbox and Clearspring accordingly. Probably the best way to complete a widget is with Flash, because almost all social sites and platforms allow you to place Flash as opposed to JavaScript or HTML onto their sites.

We encourage you to explore the Widgetbox platform for creating your widgets as well. They have a user-friendly platform and good tech and forum support.

Tracking Your Widgets

Both Widgetbox and Clearspring have nice analytics features for your widgets. Figures C.36 and C.37 show samples of widget analytics from Widgetbox and Clearspring, respectively. You can also use Google analytics within your gadgets or on Widget landing pages to track and measure traffic.

Figure C.36. Widgetbox Analytics

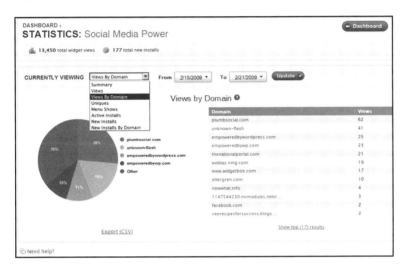

Figure C.37. Clearspring Analytics

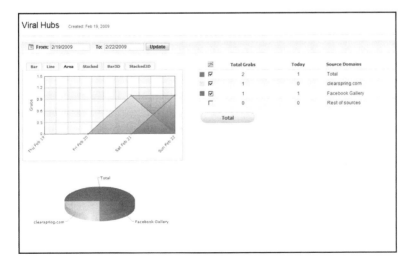

Figure C.8. Sample Widget Code (continued on next page)

```xml
<?xml version="1.0" encoding="UTF-8" ?>
<Module>
  <ModulePrefs title="_IG_FetchXmlContent Example" scrolling="true"/>
  <UserPref name="mycalories" display_name="Calorie limit" default_value="800"/>
  <UserPref name="mychoice" display_name="Show Descriptions" datatype="bool" default_value="false"/>
  <Content type="html">
<![CDATA[

  <div id="content_div"></div>

  <script type="text/javascript">
  function displayMenu() {
      // XML breakfast menu data
        var url = "http://doc.examples.googlepages.com/breakfast-data.xml";

        var prefs = new _IG_Prefs( __MODULE_ID__ );
        // calorie limit set by user
        var calorieLimit = prefs.getString("mycalories");
      var description = prefs.getBool("mychoice");

      _IG_FetchXmlContent(url, function (response) {
        if (response == null || typeof(response) != "object" || response.firstChild == null) {
          _gel("content_div").innerHTML = "<i>Invalid data.</i>";
          return;
        }

            // Start building HTML string that will be displayed in <div>.
      // Set the style for the <div>.
            var html = "<div style='padding: 5px;background-color: #ccf;font-family:Arial,
Helvetica;" +
                "text-align:left;font-size:90%'>";

      // Set style for title.
      html +="<div style='text-align:center; font-size: 120%; color: yellow; " +
            "font-weight: 700;'>";

      // Display menu title. Use getElementsByTagName() to retrieve the <menu> element.
      // Since there is only one menu element in the file,
      // you can get to it by accessing the item at index "0".
      // You can then use getAttribute to get the text associated with the
      // menu "title" attribute.
      var title = response.getElementsByTagName("menu").item(0).getAttribute("title");

      // Alternatively, you could retrieve the title by getting the menu element node
      // and calling the "attributes" function on it. This returns an array
      // of the element node's attributes. In this case, there is only one
      // attribute (title), so you can display the value for the attribute at
      // index 0. For example:
      //
      // var title = response.getElementsByTagName("menu").item(0).attributes.item(0).nodeValue;

          // Append the title to the HTML string.
          //html += title + "</font></h3>";

      // Append the title to the HTML string.
      html += title + "</div><br>";

      // Get a list of the <food> element nodes in the file
      var itemList = response.getElementsByTagName("food");
      // Loop through all <food> nodes
      for (var i = 0; i < itemList.length ; i++) {
            // For each <food> node, get child nodes.
            var nodeList = itemList.item(i).childNodes;
            // Loop through child nodes. Extract data from the text nodes that are
            // the children of the associated name, price, and calories element nodes.
        for (var j = 0; j < nodeList.length ; j++) {
          var node = nodeList.item(j);
                    if (node.nodeName == "name") {
              var name  = node.firstChild.nodeValue;
                    }
          if (node.nodeName == "price") {
              var price  = node.firstChild.nodeValue;
                  }
                if (node.nodeName == "calories")  {
```

```
                    var calories = node.firstChild.nodeValue;
                }
        // If the user chose to display descriptions and
        // the nodeName is "#cdata-section", grab the
        // contents of the description CDATA for display.
        if (node.nodeName == "description" && description==true)
        {
            if (node.firstChild.nodeName == "#cdata-section")
                var data = node.firstChild.nodeValue;
        }
            }

        // Append extracted data to the HTML string.
                html += "<i><b>";
                html += name;
                html += "</b></i><br>";
        html += " ";
        html += price;
        html += " - ";
                // If "calories" is greater than the user-specified calorie limit,
                // display it in red.
                if(calories > calorieLimit) {
            html += "<font color=#ff0000>";
                    html += calories + " calories";
                    html += " </font>";
                }
                else
                    html += calories + " calories";
        html += "<br>";

        // If user has chosen to display descriptions
        if (description==true)
        {
            html += "<i>" + data + "</i><br>";
        }

    }
    html += "</div>";

        // Display HTML string in <div>
        _gel('content_div').innerHTML = html;
    });
}

_IG_RegisterOnloadHandler(displayMenu);
</script>

]]>
</Content>
</Module>
```

Figure C.11. Unadulterated Oracle Code

```
<?xml version="1.0" encoding="UTF-8" ?>
<Module>
<ModulePrefs title="Nod's Way or Hidden Dragon"
  scrolling="false"
  width="180"
  height="400"
  author="Deltina Hay"
  author_affiliation="Social Media Power"
  author_email="quotes+nodwidget@socialmediapower.com"
  thumbnail="http://www.socialmediapower.com/widgets/nodthumb.jpg"
  render_inline="optional"
  description="Daily oracle consultation from the Nod's Way divination system.">
</ModulePrefs>
<Content type="html">
<![CDATA[
<div id="content_div"></div>
<script type="text/javascript">
function displayNod() {
var url = "http://socialmediapower.com/widgets/oracle-data.xml";
_IG_FetchXmlContent(url, function (response) {
if (response == null || typeof(response) != "object" || response.firstChild == null) {
_gel("content_div").innerHTML = "<i>Invalid data.</i>";
return;
}
var html = "<div style='padding: 0px;background-color: #fff;font-family:Verdana, Arial, Helvetica,
sans-serif;" + "text-align:left;font-size:80%'>";
html += "<div style='padding:0px;'><img src='http://socialmediapower.com/widgets/NODHeader.jpg'
/></div>";
html +="<div style='text-align:center; font-size: 110%; color: red; " +
"font-weight: 700;'>";
var title = response.getElementsByTagName("nod").item(0).getAttribute("title");
html += title + "</div><br>";
html +="<div style='text-align:left; padding-left:5px; font-size: 80%; color: black; " +
"font-weight: 300;'>";
var ausday= Math.floor(Math.random()*108);
var itemList = response.getElementsByTagName("auspice");
for (var i = ausday; i < (ausday +1) ; i++) {
  var nodeList = itemList.item(i).childNodes;
  for (var j = 0; j < nodeList.length ; j++) {
    var node = nodeList.item(j);
    if (node.nodeName == "atitle") {
    var atitle = node.firstChild.nodeValue;}
    if (node.nodeName == "asub") {
    var asub = node.firstChild.nodeValue;}
    if (node.nodeName == "abody") {
    var abody = node.firstChild.nodeValue;}
    if (node.nodeName == "ititle") {
    var ititle = node.firstChild.nodeValue;}
    if (node.nodeName == "ibody") {
    var ibody = node.firstChild.nodeValue;}
    if (node.nodeName == "oneroll") {
    var oneroll = node.firstChild.nodeValue;}
    if (node.nodeName == "tworoll") {
    var tworoll = node.firstChild.nodeValue;}
    if (node.nodeName == "threeroll") {
    var threeroll = node.firstChild.nodeValue;}
  }
  html += "<img src='http://socialmediapower.com/widgets/";
  html += oneroll;
  html += "' /> ";
  html += "<img src='http://socialmediapower.com/widgets/";
  html += tworoll;
  html += "' /> ";
  html += "<img src='http://socialmediapower.com/widgets/";
  html += threeroll;
  html += "' />";
  html += "<br><br>";
  html += atitle;
  html += "<br><br><b>";
  html += asub;
  html += "</b><br><br>";
  html += abody;
  html += "<br><b>";
  html += ititle;
  html += "</b><br><br>";
  html += ibody;
  html += "<br>";
  html += "<a href='http://www.daltonpublishing.com/our_books/nod/'>About Nod's Way.</a>";
}
html += "</div>";
_gel('content_div').innerHTML = html;
});
}

  _IG_RegisterOnloadHandler(displayNod);

</script>
]]>
</Content>
</Module>
```

Appendix D: WordPress 2.7

Just as this book was being finalized, the team at WordPress.org released WordPress 2.7. This new version contains a new look and feel as well as some very important new features that the author felt necessary to include in this book before it went to print.

Though many of the screens and menus may look different in WordPress 2.7 than in the examples used throughout this book, the process for performing the tasks discussed remains the same. This also applies to installing WordPress as outlined in Appendix A: Installing WordPress.

In this appendix we highlight significant changes relevant to what we have covered in this book. For a more thorough discussion of the most recent WordPress version, refer to the documentation at WordPress.org.

The Dashboard

Figure D.1 shows the WordPress 2.6 dashboard discussed in Chapter 4. Figure D.2 shows the new WordPress dashboard. One significant difference is that the navigation menu has moved from the top to the side of the dashboard.

Figure D.1. WordPress 2.6 Dashboard

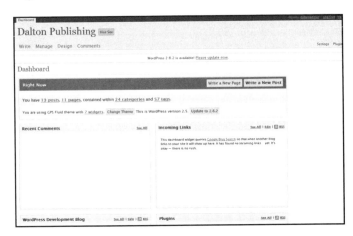

Figure D.2. WordPress 2.7 Dashboard

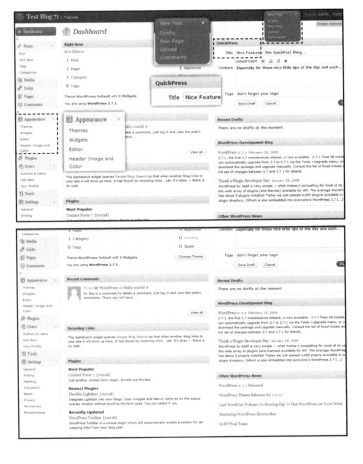

As you can see, the top level navigation items have changed as well, but the sub-menu items remain the same (save for some additional features discussed below).

For instance, in WordPress 2.6 (see Figure D.3), the "Manage" menu ultimately brings you to the "Themes," "Theme Editor," and "Widgets" sub-menu choices, as well as any options available for the existing theme. Similarly, the "Appearance" menu in WordPress 2.7 will take you to those same sub-menus (see Figure D.2 on Page 390).

Figure D.3. WordPress 2.6 Themes Menu

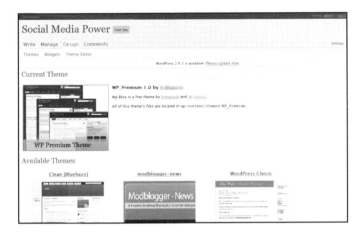

One new feature on the dashboard is QuickPress, where you can publish quick posts on the fly right from the dashboard. You can also add and edit posts and pages quickly from this new dashboard (see the upper right area of Figure D.2 on Page 390).

Posts Menu

Figure D.4 shows the new "Add New Post" screen. The main change to this screen is the more convenient placement of the Tags and Categories options. More interesting is the addition of the "Quick Edit" option. Figure D.5 shows the screen for this new feature. It is a convenient way to make common changes to a post without having to open the entire body of the post.

Figure D.4. Add New Post Screen

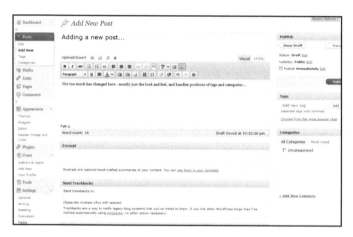

Figure D.5. Quick Edit Feature

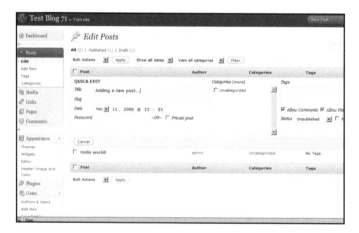

Pages Menu

Figure D.6 shows the new "Edit Page" screen. Again, not a lot has changed save for the more convenient placement of page parent, template, and order options to the left.

Figure D.6. New Edit Page Screen

Plugins

This is where the most exciting changes have taken place in this new version of WordPress. You can now upload and install plugins directly from the WordPress dashboard, as opposed to downloading them and then uploading them to the appropriate folder via FTP as discussed on Page 103.

Figure D.7 shows the "Manage Plugins" screen. This screen has not changed much except that there is now an option to use the "Plugin Browser/Installer" functionality.

Figure D.8 shows this in action. You can browse plugins using search terms or tags, and install them right on the spot. Figure D.9 shows the results when we choose the tag "SEO." And Figure D.10 shows the resulting screen when we choose to install our favorite SEO plugin.

Figure D.7. Manage Plugins Screen

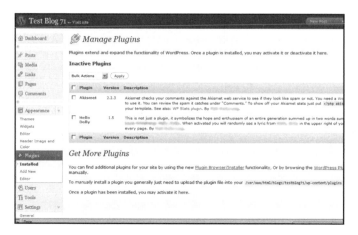

Figure D.8. Plugin Browser/Installer

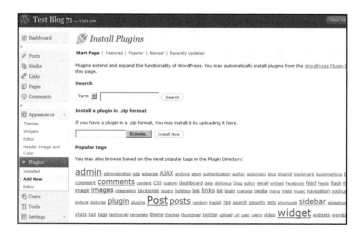

A caveat: With plugins easier to install, you may be inclined to install and play around with many more plugins than you ordinarily would have. It is recommended that you use discretion when doing so. Always research a plugin before installing it by reading other's comments on the plugin as well as visiting the plugin's homepage to get a feel for the reputation of the source.

Figure D.9. Plugin Browser/Installer

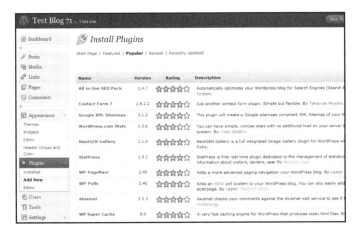

Figure D.10. Plugin Browser/Installer

Upgrading WordPress

As mentioned in previous chapters, it is always recommended that you keep WordPress upgraded to its latest version. There are security patches that come with the latest versions that will keep your WordPress powered site safe.

Index

D

E

F

R

X

About The Author

A veteran Web developer and publisher, Deltina Hay is a pioneer of social media and Web 2.0, especially as it applies to small business and the publishing industry. She is the principal owner of Dalton Publishing and the consulting and Web 2.0 development firm, Social Media Power. She also founded the innovative social media Website service, PlumbSocial.com.

Ms. Hay is noted for her dynamic presentations that focus on do-it-yourself, hands-on tools to truly make the Web a place where all voices can be heard and access is not limited to those with large capital. She has presented on social media and Web 2.0 for IBPA's Publishing University, the Publisher's Association of the South's Winter Conclave, the Writers' League of Texas' Agents and Editors Conference, the Pacific Northwest Bookseller's Association, AuthorSmart.com, and AuthorsAccess.com. She is a regular contributor of social media and Web 2.0 articles to IBPA's *Independent*, *The SPAN Connection*, SiteProNews, SocialMedia.biz, and many online news sites.

Hay has the advantage over many social media consultants in that she is both a developer and a user of social media. As a publisher and small business owner, she knows firsthand how to apply the tools of social media to the industry, and as a developer, she knows how to build them. While she has taught at the university level, Hay's direct working knowledge of social media concepts and how to apply them in the real world make her presentations and writings some of the most exciting and accessible in the industry today. Her graduate education includes applied mathematics, computer science, and psychology.

Though a native Alaskan, Ms. Hay lives in Austin, Texas, with her two cats Wolfgang and Ludwig. She enjoys hiking in the surprisingly diverse Texas State Park system, and *never* complains about the heat, really.